AF647646

STATUS OF RURAL LOCAL BODIES FINANCE IN TAMIL NADU

About the Authors

Prof. G. Palanithurai, Rajiv Gandhi Chair for Panchayati Raj Studies, Gandhigram Rural University, India, is an academic activist. He is specialized in Grassroots Democracy, Decentralized Governance and Development Management. His action research activities are supported by the Ford Foundation, Swiss Development and Cooperation, The Hunger Project, Population Foundation of India, DANIDA, Action Aid International, Ministry of Panchayati Raj, Ministry of Rural Development, Government of India, Toolkit Foundation, Netherlands, UNDP, State Planning Commission and a few other agencies in India and abroad. He has developed a leadership school in Rajiv Gandhi Chair for Panchayati Raj Studies.

He has worked for the preparation of 10th and 11th Five Year Plans for Tamil Nadu through State Planning Commission. He worked for the 1st, 2nd, and 3rd State Finance Commissions and for which he conducted a number of studies related to panchayat finance. He has published 63 books, 139 articles in refereed jounals, 83 monographs, 76 popular articles in his area of specialization in popular dailies. He has availed the fellowship from Shastri Indo-Canadian Institute twice, World Academy of Art and Science, USA, Toolkit Foundation, Netherlands, to conduct studies and write books. He has visited the US, Canada, Singapore, Sri Lanka, Senegal and Malaysia on academic assignments. He has introduced two innovative M.A. Programmes, one in Development Management and another in Governance and Development are supported by University Grants Commission, New Delhi. He has organized 2 International programmes, 15 National programmes and 61 Regional programmes with the financial support of various agencies. He made presentations in 20 international conferences, 145 national programmes and 67 regional seminars and conferences. He prepared two District Human Development Reports for Dindigul and Nagapattinam Districts.

Ms. Kalpana Sathish is an activist working for the promotion and protection of human rights for more than 15 years. Her priority area and expertise is on the field of action research and advocacy for the rights of children and women. She also actively engaged in the networking process with various voluntary organizations, academicians, journalists and lawyers for legal, policy and administrative changes and lobbying with state, media for building a wider public opinion on the rights discourse and local self-governance. Since her entry into the development action, her major focus area is working with the elected women panchayat representatives for ensuring social justice and economic development of grassroots communities. In this process, she also engages in policy and legal analysis about the local self-governance and decentralization process in the country. She has written articles in the leading newspapers on the critiques of present governance system and its inter-connection with societal structure of caste and gender. She also associates with people's organizations representing dalits, adivasis, and coastal communities and engage in advocating their demands.

Recently, Kalpana has been involved in developing a curriculum on child rights, gender rights for school children and post-graduate students. She is also part of the editorial team for a magazine called Children's Parliament, which is reaching the neighbourhood level children's organizations, schools and civil society organizations in the State.

Status of Rural Local Bodies Finance in Tamil Nadu

G. Palanithurai
Kalpana Sathish

CONCEPT PUBLISHING COMPANY PVT. LTD., NEW DELHI-110059

© Prof. G. Palanithurai

All rights reserved. No part of this work may be reproduced, stored, adapted, or transmitted in any form or by any means, electronic, mechanical, photocopying, micro-filming recording or otherwise, or translated in any language, without the prior written permission of the copyright owner and the publisher. The book is sold subject to the condition that it shall not, by way of trade or otherwise, be lent, resold, hired out, or otherwise circulated without the prior publisher's written consent in any form of binding or cover other than that in which it is published.

The views and opinions expressed in this book are author(s) own and the facts reported by him/her have been verified to the extent possible, and the publishers are not in any way liable for the same.

ISBN-13: 978-81-8069-816-3

First Published 2012

Published and Printed by

Concept
Since 1974

Concept Publishing Company Pvt. Ltd.
A/15-16, Commercial Block, Mohan Garden
New Delhi-110059 (India)
T: 25351460, 25351794, *F*: 091-11-25357109
E: publishing@conceptpub.com, W: www.conceptpub.com
Editorial Office: H-13, Bali Nagar, New Delhi-110 015, India.

Cataloging in Publication Data--Courtesy: D.K. Agencies (P) Ltd. <docinfo@dkagencies.com>

Palanithurai, G. (Ganapathy)
Status of rural local bodies finance in Tamil Nadu / G. Palanithurai, Kalpana Sathish.
p. cm.
Includes bibliographical references (p.) and index.
ISBN 9788180698163

1. Local finance—India—Tamil Nadu. 2. Panchayat—India—Tamil Nadu. 3. Rural development projects—India—Tamil Nadu. I. Kalpana Sathish, joint author. II. Title.

DDC 351.54 23

To
The Divine Mother

Preface and Acknowledgements

Tamil Nadu is the state best-suited for its efficient compliance to the direction of the Constitution of India to establish a self-governing institutions at the grassroots as per the 73rd Amendment to the Constitution of India. Enacting a legislation to conform to the constitutional provisions, creating a State Election Commission, constituting a State Finance Commission every five years, constituting a District Planning Committee in every district, conducting an election for the District Planning Committee and constituting high level committees periodically to devolve powers to the local bodies are the compliance activities that the Tamil Nadu state government has performed very well. If anyone asks whether adequate powers are devolved to panchayats, officials used to give the answer that more than seven hundred and thirty-two powers are given to the rural local bodies. Yet, from day one till date panchayat leaders pleaded for powers to take decisions and autonomy for local bodies. People those who are looking at the panchayat from the perspective of Act, Rules, Government Orders, make the observation that Tamil Nadu is one of the best states in creating a stable and vibrant Panchayati Raj system. People who are working with panchayat leaders make the observation that Tamil Nadu state government has created a Panchayati Raj system in form but not in spirit. Academics who are carefully analyzing Tamil Nadu politics will understand the basic argument of the Dravidian political parties on devolution of powers. Their argument is very clear that in the context of centralization of powers, decentralization of powers from the state government to local government by the design of Central Government, no state government will be interested in real devolution of powers and more particularly Tamil Nadu Government is not interested in devolving adequate powers to Local Bodies as there is always demand for state autonomy. There is yet another strange aspect in Tamil Nadu politics in decentralization of powers. The two ethnic political parties (the DMK and the AIADMK) have never concurred on any issue in Tamil Nadu politics but they concurred on one issue that is not to strengthen the Panchayati Raj. It may be due to the ideology that they pursue on state autonomy which was propounded by C.N. Annadurai. States can learn from Tamil Nadu state that how to keep panchayat system functioning without devolving powers. One cannot understand the reality by reading the act, rules, government orders and policies but they have to be corroborated with observations field. Then only one can see the reality. Being an activist academic and an activist, we continuously keep in touch with the field through the Gram Panchayat leaders and the civil society along with officials. For about fifteen years we have been with the stakeholders and constantly we have been working with them as support agency through our organizations. Hence, we have established our grip over the reality. Everywhere we find declining interest on Panchayati Raj system as they are brought under the control of the officials slowly and the state government reduced the autonomy of the panchayats. Resource flow has also been reduced to panchayats. Everywhere panchayat leaders have raised their voice that they are going to resign due to public pressure as they could not meet the demands of the people with the meagre resources given by the state government to the panchayats. Further, there is no autonomy for the panchayats.

At that point of time we got invitation from IRMA Anand to prepare a paper on financial devolution that takes place in Tamil Nadu for a workshop sponsored by the 13th Finance Commission of India. Hence, we have undertaken a study in the field. The paper was circulated in the IRMA workshop and the same study was also shared with civil society and academics. They in fact asked us to publish the articles to make people understand the financial status of the panchayats in Tamil Nadu. The report is only the field reality as such and it is being explained further. We thankfully acknowledge the help rendered by the panchayat leaders and civil society organizations. We have to thank Thiru. M. Vallinayagam, Former Additional Director for Rural Development who constantly helped to clarify some of the official documents. Further the paper presented in the IRMA workshop had been repeatedly referred to and mentioned in the workshop report submitted to 13th Finance Commission, which ultimately made many ask us to publish the documents. There are three articles in this handy volume. First, is the overall position of panchayats in Tamil Nadu done by Prof. G. Palanithurai. Subsequently, the two articles on the field reality of devolution of finance and the autonomy given to panchayats to carry out the schemes are captured by Ms. Kalpana Sathish. All the three articles will reveal the reality of the financial status of the panchayats in Tamil Nadu. We thank everyone who helped us to do a small job with an aim of strengthening the Panchayati Raj system in Tamil Nadu. Our analysis and observations are objective. But we have a strong conviction that panchayats have potentials to empower poor, Dalits and women and hence we have developed a conviction and faith in decentralization and we work for the cause of the Panchayati Raj system.

G. Palanithurai
Kalpana Sathish

Contents

List of Tables

Introduction

Local governments can play an important role in looking after the well-being of the local citizenry. People's basic needs to lead a decent human life will be met by the local governments. Logically speaking local bodies are more participatory in nature and character as local governance was in vogue in the rural areas even before the Nation States came into existence. Hence, they are transparent also. The local governments have to carry out the programmes and schemes of the Central and State Governments towards the well-being of the people apart from the schemes and programmes of the local governments.[1] Since local governments are closer to the people, their felt needs will be met and greater responsiveness will be ensured. As long as local governments are vibrant, sound and strong in terms of resource base and autonomy, pressure on the state and federal government will be minimum for services as the services are delivered only by local bodies. As a result, the State and Central Governments can concentrate on other development issues leaving the basic services to the local bodies. Thus, the total governance in a country can be shared by the three tier governance structure, namely Centre, State and Local. While doing so there will not be any overlapping of functions and there will not be any duplication of works as we see today in our governance. The effectiveness of the functions of local bodies are dependent on the sound financial position and functional autonomy of the local bodies. Local bodies' proximity to the people enhances their potential to address the goals of citizenry.

Local bodies have the potential to draw the public's attention towards their functioning and enabling the citizens to participate in the process of governance and delivery of services. By strengthening the local bodies by the State and Central Governments, the capacity of the local bodies to deepen democracy and to deliver services to the people more effectively, efficiently and professionally will be enhanced. Thus, responsiveness to the people is enhanced. As a result the burden of the Central Government is reduced drastically and in the long run capacity and capability of the citizens will also be improved to address the issues of the people by themselves. Hence, local bodies are considered as local capacity enhancement[2]. The finer aspect of democracy rests on maturity in handling the institutions for the larger benefit of the citizens through consensus and the above can be achieved through a process of participation by the people[3]. Thus, the participatory process ensures local accountability, responsiveness, transparency, public choice, effective innovation, noval experimentations, monitoring of the schemes and programmes of the Central and State Governments and mobilization of the public for collective action. It further enhances the resource mobilization capacity of the local populace. But, generally, the local bodies are not interested in collecting taxes as they will become unpopular among the people. It effectively prepares the people to actively involve themselves in self-governance which requires high level of maturity and understanding. Ideal conditions envisage the smooth functioning of these institutions with the active support of the State and Central Governments. Because the very functioning of the local institutions is very much dependant on the confidence and good-will of both the governments. As long as the local governments are enjoying the confidence of the State and Central Governments, the autonomy of functional and fiscal domain of the local bodies will be intact. In an ideal situation all the above conditions are fulfilled by all the stakeholders. But, in reality it does not happen in many of the countries as the society could not be taken to the zone of maturity. The higher level governments for their survival use the local bodies. Further, in the same activity domain the higher level governments will also be active and as a result one will witness duplication of roles and responsibilities of the local bodies. Further, the technical capacity and professional capacity of the local bodies are always at question and moreover the economy of scale is also another matter in deciding the autonomy of local bodies. Fiscal discipline, allocative efficiency and resource mobilizing capacity of the local bodies are always under severe attack. Yet, decentralization of powers, and strengthening of local bodies have gained currency all over the world in the context of globalization to meet the increased aspirations of the people for more democracy and development. But, the pattern of decentralization of powers and institutionalization of decentralization of powers are largely dependant on the local socio-political conditions. At present, in many countries decentralization is perceived by the policy makers as a good instrument and device to improve the service delivery to the people to the level of their satisfaction by involving the local population in governance and mobilizing the resources locally. Though it is being contested on various reasons[4], the policy makers could not find an alternative to decentralization to meet the local aspiration and easeout frustration. Countries have adopted different models, different strategies in decentralizing powers to local bodies to manage the local conditions[5].

India is a major country which took initiative to decentralize powers to local bodies through the Constitution and by which it is expected that the local bodies have to democratize the society, deepen democracy, and achieve economic development and social justice by evolving a micro plan with the active participation of people. Further it has created an ambitious design to include all the excluded segments of the society in governance and development. As a result, the whole world looks for guidance from India. The need for effective decentralization of powers was deeply felt at different levels and in different periods as India has got 28 states with more than 400 ethnic groups living together as a nation with extreme inequalities and diversities which require a decentralized decision making process to address the local needs and aspirations. It is to be noted and recognized here that over a period of time both the Centre and State Governments have executed more than 2000 schemes and yet the basic needs of the people of all sections could not be met and as a result frustration looms large all over the country. Of course, perspectives vary and the proposal of decentralization was advanced and retreated in India ever since Mahatma Gandhi pronounced his theory on Gram Swaraj[6]. Finally, it was agreed upon to institutionalize the local bodies through the Constitution at the advent of globalization to meet the existing economic and social crises in India in the beginning of 1990s[7]. It was a major breakthrough in terms of its intentions and goals but it is a weak design and hence even after fifteen years of experience the local bodies are struggling to function as institutions of self-governance with minimum of functional autonomy barring a few states. In the fifteen years of experience brought to light a very deceptive way of decentralization of powers engaged by many state governments as they have perfect disagreement with the present decentralization package[8]. It is to be noted here that the decentralization package initiated by Rajiv Gandhi was defeated in the Parliament with the notion that it is a powerful instrument to weaken the state in the context of centralization of powers[9]. It was considered as a design to weaken the state government. Subsequently steps were taken to pass the bills which were initiated during the period of Rajiv Gandhi. The 73rd and 74th Amendments were passed in the Parliament at a critical juncture after removing the contentious clauses in the previous 64th and 65th Amendment Bills through a Parliamentary Committee. But while operationalising the decentralization package, the state governments have realized the tremendous potentials of the package and the states strongly felt that their powers would be taken away by implementing the decentralization package in letter and spirit. Hence, many of the states have started practicing decentralization in form and not in spirit[10]. Tamil Nadu is one such state opposed to decentralization in the present form as it emerges as an institution of self-governance. It consistently opposed the 64th Amendment Bill and the 73rd and the 74th Amendment Bills. It is another paradox that both the political parties, the DMK and the AIADMK have opposed the decentralization package of three-tier governance. Both parties wanted only two-tier local governance down below the district. They do not want an unit of governance at district level. They feel that it is almost a parallel to the state government. It is being looked at from the ideological perspective of their parties. These two parties never concurred on any issue but they have full agreement in opposing decentralization in the present form. Tamil Nadu is known for its efficient bureaucracy and hence it got recognition and appreciation from the centre for its effective implementation of the schemes and programmes. The efficiency of Tamil Nadu is exhibited in evolving a design for implementation of decentralization of powers as per the 73rd Amendment to the Constitution of India. It is a very deceptive design but while looking at the institutions in form one will find every aspect of decentralization is intact, but analyzing the same from the spirit of decentralization, and in functioning, it is dubious. It could be gauged only through the analysis of functioning of the institutions in proper perspective. When questions had been raised about the conditions of decentralization, the reply from the state governments is that it is a state subject hence the state can design decentralization whatever way the state wants. The Central Government has no role in implementation of decentralization of powers.[11] The 73rd Amendment says that powers have to be devolved but it is not a must as it used the word "may by law" and not "shall by law". Further, by conducting the local body election on party basis, the party men and women got elected to local bodies controlled by the political parties. That is why L.M. Singhvi Committee recommended for political local bodies aiming for local bodies without political party affiliation. Had India created such local bodies, by this time local bodies, which are vibrant and would have emerged in such a way. But now, the local bodies are under the control of the political parties. Hence, they are not in a position to raise their voice against the voicelessness of the local bodies. No doubt, functions, functionaries and finances are necessary for the proper and effective functioning of the local bodies. Yet, finance plays a pivotal role. Finance is a major factor by which the panchayat system can be strengthened and at the same time it can be destablished. We have seen in India in the past how panchayat was weakened in the 1970s and 1980s by reducing the flow of resources to Local Bodies. Hence, the Constitutional Amendment made it mandatory that in every five years State Finance Commission has to be constituted to strengthen the base of the panchayats by creating a sound financial system as per the framework of Public Finance.[12] Hence, it is decided to study both the precepts of public finance and the actual reality of the base of the finance of the panchayats. Thus, Tamil Nadu Panchayat Finance was critically analysed. While seeing the process of augmenting resources of panchayats one will come to a conclusion that Tamil Nadu is the best state in operationalizing the 73rd Amendment as the state government follows the logistics. If one visits the field, the reality could be captured. The Central Government has given an award for the Tamil Nadu State Government for its effective implementation of the 73rd Amendment to the Constitution of India by giving more points than even to Kerala. It was severely criticized by the media and the articles written by intellectuals. This mistake was due to the paper work done by the external agencies who evaluated the performance of the state governments in decentralization. To bring out the reality this study was conducted and they are compiled here in this small monograph. This book is the result of a field study conducted with an objective of submitting a small report to 13th Finance Commission. To help the Commission it was conducted and the reports have been submitted. It is a field reality. By going over this monograph one will assess where the Tamil Nadu Panchayats are in terms of its autonomy in decision making, micro planning, and implementation of schemes and programmes of the Centre and State Governments.

Notes and References

1. John L. Mikesell "Fiscal Administration in Local Government: An overview" in *Local Budgeting*, Anwar Shah (ed.), Washington DC: The World Bank, 2007, pp. 15-19.
2. Niraja Gopal Jayal, Amit Prakash and Pradeep K. Sharma (eds.) *Local Governance in India: Decentralization and Beyond*, New Delhi: Oxford University Press, 2006, p. 3.

3. Ranjita Mohanty and Rajesh Tandon (eds.) *Participatory Citizenship: Identity, Exclusion, Inclusion,* New Delhi: Sage Publications, 2006.
4. Remy Prud'homme "The Dangers of Decentralization", *The World Bank Research Observer,* Vol. 10, No. 2, 1995.
5. Anwar Shah (ed.) *Local Governance in Developing Countries,* Washington DC: The World Bank, 2006. Anwar Shah (ed.) *Local Governance in Industrial Countries*, Washington DC: The World Bank, 2006.
6. James Manor, "Local Governance" in *Oxford Companion to Politics in India* (eds.) Niraja Gopal Jayal and Pratap Bhanu Mehta, New Delhi: Oxford University Press, 2010, pp. 61-79.
7. The World Bank, *Fiscal Decentralization to Rural Governments in India*, New Delhi: Oxford University Press, 2004.
8. Government of India, *Second Administrative Reforms Commission Sixth Report: Local Governance: An Inspiring Journey into Future*, New Delhi: Government of India, 2007; Commission on Centre-State Relations, *Local Self-Governments And Decentralized Governance*, Vol. IV, New Delhi: Government of India, 2010.
9. K.C. Sivarama Krishnan, *Power to the People?* New Delhi: Konark Publishers Private Limited, 2000, pp. 40-57.
10. James Manor, *op. cit.*, pp. 68-69.
11. G. Palanithurai, "Local Governance as a Factor in Centre-State Relations in India", *The ICFAI University Journal of Public Administration*, Vol. 5: No. 2 April, 2009, pp. 7-18.
12. Indira Rajaraman, *A Fiscal Domain for Panchayats*, New Delhi: Oxford University Press, 2003.

functionaries from the local bodies and promoting them as government employees. In the same way many of the responsibilities had been taken away and given to independent units created by the government departments. Steps were on to protect the employees working in different departments but there was no sensitivity on the part of the leaders about the service to be delivered by these departments and officials.

As far as powers, functionaries and finances of the local bodies are concerned they are vested with the state governments. In this context, the emergence of local bodies as institutions of self-governance is highly difficult as state governments demand more powers to the states and in the same way state governments demand more resources for development activities. Many of the state governments have to solely rely on the Central Government for the development activities as the state governments finance is always in a weak condition. Fiscal discipline is yet another problem. It is the observation of the Central Government that state governments have no financial discipline. As a result the finance of the state governments is always weak. Hence state governments expect resource flow adequately from the Central Government. In this context, one cannot expect that the state governments would devolve more resources to the local bodies, unless the party in power is totally committed to devolution on an ideological basis.

Against this background, a study has been undertaken in Tamil Nadu as to what extent Panchayati Raj Institutions are independent on resource mobilisaton and resource management. Before moving into the analysis of the financial management system one has to understand the existing perception about the newly created local body system. Normally the popular democratic governments in the world distribute public resources to deliver public goods to the people. Who or which segment of the society gains more in this allocation is a question. Any public authority will decide and distribute. Having said this, from the Centre to local bodies, representatives are in competition in spending the public money in larger quantum. All the three governments are spending public money. But local governments are alone categorized as spending institutions as their revenue domain is limited. To bring efficiency on the part of the institution, may it be Central Government or State Government or Local Government, clarity on responsibilities attached to each tier is needed.

To discharge the responsibilities, powers are required at every level of governance commensurate with the responsibilities. Given the nature and volume of responsibilities volume of resources has to be devolved. In the same logic, to perform the assigned tasks with the devolved resources, functionaries are needed. If all the above aspects are cleared and done with clarity with a sense of commitment, efficiency can be achieved without much difficulty. Further, it is to be noted that over and above the capacity and capability of the staff, the leaders who are in the institutions will determine the level of efficiency in delivering of services and achieving results. In the case of local bodies they have been branded spending institutions as they spend resources not collect the resources. Here it is to be underlined that the institutions which are nearer to the people are always interested in spending and not in collecting resources from the people. In a democracy proximity to the people will prevent collecting resources from the people and encourage them to spend in order to keep their popularity among the people.

It is natural that allocative efficiency is exhibited only in a rational management system. Here the rational management system is one which allocates responsibility of mobilizing resources and spending the same with authority and autonomy by using the law of subsidiarity. The three governance institutions are in proper coordination for the purpose of generating and mobilizing resources and spending the same. A well laid framework of guidelines have to be adopted for resource mobilization and resource allocation and spending. The governing institutions at every level is responsive, responsible and representative. But in India, the vast diversity with wide difference in the living conditions of different social groups made the system act locally and contextually according to the pressure exerted on the system by the individuals or groups or representatives. Thus, in this process some social groups are liable to be excluded, and some regions are liable to be excluded. The issues of the excluded social categories have to be tackled and addressed only at the local level through the local governance. Central Government by its allocation of resources to schemes and programmes expects results from the ground and for which local bodies are essential and so they have to be strengthened.

The state governments have perceived that the local governments by their functions and performance emerge as strong institutions and thereby the leaders of the local bodies will emerge as strong entities at the grassroots which pose a threat to the state government. As a result, the state governments consider the panchayats as subordinate implementing agencies. Only a few state governments want to keep the local bodies as a new partner to share their responsibilities. If panchayats are prepared well and oriented properly panchayats can perform very well in the social development and human development sector. People can be engaged in development and as a result panchayats can emerge as schools of capacity building. It is perceived in the developed countries that by devolving powers, the delivery of services can be achieved through a cost effective way. But in the developing countries devolution of powers is considered as a threat to state government and strengthening the federal government.

There is yet another set of states realistically positioning the local bodies as institutions of self-governance. These states have taken the panchayats from the level of expenditure institutions to institutions of governance with autonomy to mobilize resources and spend the same. It is necessary that the local body institutions have to be seen in the framework of public finance. Further its financial domain has to be made clear. The size, capacity, spatial reach, of the panchayats volume of goods to be delivered, resources available and the population size will decide the allocative efficiency and delivery efficiency of the panchayats. Panchayats have to be seen from the management perspective also. The scale is more important. Otherwise the panchayats will remain as expenditure institutions. Conditions and geographical spread will decide the needs of the panchayats. Thus requirements vary from area to area. There should be a system of financial management at the grassroots in line with state and national financial system. Accounting procedures should also be in the same line.

Basically the fiscal transfer takes place within the framework established for federal countries. It is called Fiscal Federalism. Agencies have been fixed for revenue generation at different levels. The generated resources are distributed on a rationale basis. Still allocation and distributive rationality are being questioned. The expenditure needs and resources availability have to be matched. On most of the occasions they do not match with each other. If a realistic evaluation is made in a particular district on the needs of the people generated through Gram Sabha and the money spent through various schemes and programmes of the various departments, one will find a mismatch. Departments spent a lot but needs are not met because the departments are not meeting the requirements of the community. Arguments are projected that the departments have to work with the local bodies while performing their duties and responsibilities.

When there is a resource gap, normally the gap is filled with transfer of funds. The gap has to be filled by transfer funds from one level of government to another one. It is the responsibility of the Central Government to State Government to provide the needed finance commensurate with the responsibilities assigned to the state. Further, the fund flow is determined on the basis of the real needs of the state. In the same way fund flow from the state government to the local government should be based on the assignments of the responsibilities and the needs. To regulate and rationalise a sound financial management system the Central Finance Commission was constituted. In the same way, State Finance Commissions were constituted. The recommendations of the Central Finance Commission is viewed seriously and put into practice. Barring a few states the State Finance Commissions are not seriously viewed. There are states which never comply with the provisions of the constituting State Finance Commission. There are Finance Commissions constituted but they are not asked to submit reports acted upon. A few states are prompt in constituting State Finance Commission and get periodical reports and decisions are taken. They fully comply with the constitutional provisions. But the panchayat finance is not strengthened. Panchayats are getting funds from the Central Government, through Central Finance Commission awards and the schemes of the Central Governments. Panchayats are getting funds from the state government through the State Finance Commission awards and schemes and programmes of the state government. Apart from the above, the panchayats have to augment resources on their own. How are these resources being spent and on what basis? How is the expenditure accounted for? On what basis is the need assessed? Do we have a scientific system of generating demand and allocating resources and spending procedures? These are matters of controversy. Against the background of Tamil Nadu the panchayat system can be analysed from the perspective of finance.

Emergence of New Panchayati Raj Set-up in Tamil Nadu

In Tamil Nadu, the Tamil Nadu Panchayats Act, 1958 was repealed and re-enacted as the Tamil Nadu Panchayats Act, 1994. The Tamil Nadu Panchayats Act, 1994 retained almost all the sections contained in Tamil Nadu Panchayats Act, 1958 and introduced some new sections to create a three-tier Panchayat structure. District Planning Committee, Gram Sabha, Finance Commission and Election Commission and reservation of seats in the three-tier structure for SC/ST and women were provided for. Excepting the new provisions added as mentioned above, the 1994 Act was a replica of the 1958 Act.

Devolution of Powers

Article 243G of the Constitution of India provides that "the Legislature of a State, may by law endow with the Panchayats such powers as may be necessary to make them function as units of self-government." The Constitutional mandate requires devolving of powers by enacting necessary law whereas Section 257 of Tamil Nadu Panchayats Act, 1994 states, "save as otherwise provided in this Act, government may by notification and subject to such conditions and restrictions as may be prescribed therein, entrust to the Panchayats or any other committees constituted under the Act such powers and responsibilities etc." This is contrary to what is envisaged in the Constitution. But, the powers and responsibilities were not given to the Panchayats even by notification*. Certain powers relating to the 29 subjects mentioned in Schedule IV of the Tamil Nadu Panchayats Act, 1994 (Schedule XI of Constitution of India) were given to the Panchayats by issuing executive orders. The concerned sectoral departments did not act on these orders in the spirit in which they were issued. By issuing executive orders an impression is given to the officials that they need not take them into account seriously. The officials know the difference between notification and executive orders. A notification has to be published for the consumption of the public and it comes out in the Gazette. But executive orders need not be published and they are only meant for officials. Thus the Government of Tamil Nadu made the devolution a non-serious affair. Many of the orders giving powers to the rural local bodies merely state that the Panchayats can assist in identification of beneficiaries, watch and advise the government in implementation of schemes. Real

---

* *Note*: *Notification*: A notification will have more legal force and validity than an executive order issued by government. Section 257 of the Tamil Nadu Panchayats Act requires the powers to be given by notification. The courts have held that a notification issued under the Act will have the same force as the Act. Under Section 262 of the Tamil Nadu Panchayats Act, all notifications issued under this Act have to be published in the Tamil Nadu Government Gazette and should be placed on the table of the Legislative Assembly. Hence the orders issued under this Act other than by way of notification will have no validity. The Supreme Court in ITC Bhadrachalam Paper Board and another *vs.* Mandal Revenue Officer, AP and others [(1996) 6 SCC 634] has held that the statutory requirement of publication of rules/orders in the Official Gazette is mandatory. The object of the publication in the Official Gazette is not merely to give information to the public also but to give final official confirmation to the rules/ orders. The orders issued by the government giving powers to the Panchayats are not published in the Tamil Nadu Government Gazette. Hence the powers given to the Panchayats in Tamil Nadu by executive orders have no legal force.

powers were not given to the Panchayats. Power means authority to decide things. No such decision-making powers are given to Panchayat institutions.

The fate of these Government Orders has been amply brought out by the High Level Committee on Devolution of Powers and Functions to rural Local Bodies constituted under the chairmanship of Thiru M.K. Stalin, Hon'ble Minister for Rural Development and Local Governance in 2007. The Committee has observed in Para 8, Chapter I as follows:

> The committee carefully examined the action taken by the government on recommendations of the first and second high level committees ...... The committee is satisfied with the fact that all departments have issued necessary orders based on the high level committees. However the committee is constrained to point out that many of these orders have remained on paper and not much efforts had been taken in the past to implement the Government orders in letter and spirit....

Article 243G of the Constitution clearly states that the Legislature of the State may, by law, endow the Panchayats with such powers etc. Taking advantage of the word "may" in the said article, the State government considered that giving authority to the Panchayats is purely the discretion of the State government and it is not a Constitutional mandate. In this context it is pertinent to note that the observation of the National Commission to review the working of the Constitution set out in Chapter IX of its report as below, as has been quoted in "Renga Reddy District Sarpanch Association *vs.* Government of Andhra Pradesh, 2004(1) ALT 659 (L.B.) (para 54)".

"The National Commission to review the working of the Constitution, as part of its study, took up an analysis of decentralization and devolution of powers to Panchayats. The Commission's report records that the Union and the State Governments continue to exercise powers in planning and the Panchayats do not enjoy autonomy—financial or administrative—as institutions of local self-government. The

Commission examined whether there has been devolution of powers and responsibility to Panchayats, *inter alia* in functional and financial spheres. The report records that Panchayats, having blossomed into institutions of self-government, have been reduced to an implementing arm of the State Government. On the financial domain the report observes, that to be an institution of self-government, a Panchayat should, as far as possible, be a viable and manageable unit. It should be capable of generating internal resources by using its own fiscal powers that include taxing power commensurate with the functions assigned to it. The Commission felt that major fiscal restructuring and financial resources are necessary to enable the Panchayats to function as viable local self-governing institutions. With regard to personnel of the Panchayati Raj Institutions, the report records that an institution of self-government must have the power to recruit and control the officers and other employees required for managing its functions. The Constitution is totally silent about this viability aspect of institutional autonomy. The failure to address the human resource issues has definitely affected the growth of Panchayats as self-governing institutions. The report also points out that since the task of assigning functions to the Panchayats was given to the State Legislature, State Governments retain the powers of the Panchayats with State Government. The conclusion of the Commission in this area is that the gap between the Constitutional hope and the reality in the area of empowerment of Panchayati Raj Institutions was on account of the inconclusiveness of the text. It recommended amendments to the provisions of Part-IX and Schedule-VII of the Constitution, among other provisions."

The political executive of the State did not have the will to make the Panchayat institutions of self-government. The bureaucracy also did not help in endowing the Panchayats with necessary powers intended to be given by government order. Both have joined together to see that the Local Bodies should not become a vibrant political force to challenge the state government for its omission and commission. From the perception of the political and administrative executives Panchayats are only agents of the State Government.

Even though the Tamil Nadu Panchayats Act, 1994 incorporated certain provisions of the Constitutional Amendment Act, powers, functions, functionaries and finances are not given to Panchayats in the spirit in which the Constitutional Amendment Act was enacted. In fact some of the powers given to the Panchayats that are forward looking have now been taken away. For instance, prior to 1994, Village Panchayats and Panchayat Union Councils were empowered by rules to accord administrative sanction for estimates which have been prepared and approved by competent technical authorities without any financial limit as per the rules issued under the Tamil Nadu Panchayats Act, 1958. Now under the rules relating to execution of works issued in G.O. Ms. No. 286 RD dated 31.12.1998, Village Panchayats can accord administrative sanction only to estimates up to Rs. 1 lakh. Any estimate beyond the above limit has to be sent to the District Collector for administrative sanction. If the estimate is beyond Rs. 3 lakhs it has to be sent to the Director of Rural Development for approval. Similarly, the Panchayat Union Councils can accord administrative sanction for estimates up to Rs. 5 lakhs only.* Beyond that limit, it has to go to the District Collector and the Director of Rural Development for sanction. In the name of giving power to the people through the new dispensation, the State Government has taken away even the existing powers of the Panchayats granted by the Tamil Nadu Panchayats Act. It is nothing but one step forward and two steps backward. Thus, the powers already provided to Panchayats were taken away and the procedure now ordained only results in unnecessary delays and other undesirable consequences. Even simple works like black topping roads up to 1 km will cost more than Rs. 5 lakhs. So practically the functions of the Panchayat are crippled.

* *Note*: The power to accord administrative sanction for estimates has been since increased to Rs. 2 lakhs to village panchayats and Rs. 10 lakhs to Panchayat Union Councils in G.O.Ms. No. 203 R.D and Panchayati Raj district. 20.12.2007. However, the original position has not been restored.

The various rules issued by the State Government are curtailing the powers and authority of the Panchayat. The State Government, in G.O. Ms. 57 RD dated 22.02.2001, allowed the Village Panchayats to run the fair price shops under the Public Distribution System. The Public Distribution System is one of the items to be entrusted to the Panchayats under Schedule IV of the Tamil Nadu Panchayats Act (Schedule XI of Constitution of India). Initially in the above rules it was stated that Village Panchayats which are willing to run the fair price shops under the Public Distribution System located in the Panchayat village shall be identified by the District Collector and the Collector shall grant permission to run the said shop. The word in this rule "shall" was changed to "may" by an amendment made on 14.08.2001 and thus gave discretion to the Collector. The spirit in which the rules were issued was negated by this amendment.

Many rules issued under this Act are not positive towards Panchayats. To cite an instance, the State Government, in G.O. Ms. No. 108, RD dated 28.03.2001, issued the "Tamil Nadu Panchayats (determination of claim to trees growing on public roads and other property vesting in or belonging to Village Panchayats) Rules, 2001", wherein certain provisions of the rules are obnoxious and do not stand to reason. In rule 7 of the above-said rules it has been stated that the Village Panchayats shall have the powers to cut down or sell by auction the live trees on road margins or in water supply sources which are considered dangerous to traffic or dangerous to life or health. But certain conditions have been imposed whereby even in that situation the Panchayats can cut the trees only with the sanction of the Revenue Divisional Officer who shall accord sanction only after getting the report of the Tahsildar. Even if the Revenue Divisional Officer who is superior to the Tahsildar finds that the trees are dangerous to the public he should not give permission without getting the report of the Tahsildar. It is an unnecessary obstruction in the functioning of the Panchayats.

The Inspector of Panchayats/District Collector has been given powers under Section 205 of the Tamil Nadu Panchayats Act to remove the elected President of a Village Panchayat. In the modern democratic set up, the powers of the executive to remove an elected representative is considered undesirable. This power has been often misused. There are many instances to prove this point. In a particular instance one District Collector has threatened a Panchayat President that he will initiate action under Section 205 of the Tamil Nadu Panchayats Act to remove him for the simple reason that he met him with certain public grievances.

Decentralization involves devolution of functions, powers and finance to the local bodies. No real power was given and this has been brought out by the study undertaken by the National Institute of Rural Development (NIRD) as per the direction of the Ministry of Rural Development. It has been pointed out that "the Ministry of Rural Development in its memorandum to the Central Finance Commission states that the requirement of funds by the Panchayats for performing the development functions under various centrally sponsored schemes and state sponsored schemes and regulatory and maintenance needs of the Panchayats should receive special dispensation from the Commission." The Eleventh Finance Commission entrusted the NIRD the task of studying the position of devolution of functions to the rural local bodies, the powers to raise their resources to perform the core services, namely primary education, primary health, rural roads, drinking water supply, sanitation and street lights. The NIRD study reveals that the 73rd Amendment has not significantly altered the functions of the Panchayats at the various tiers. The Centre as well as States have sponsored schemes for rural development without associating the Panchayats in planning and implementation. This has further marginalized them.

The Government of India releases more than Rs. 2000 crores every year to the rural local bodies to provide infrastructure and it is being spent and yet the people's felt needs are not met as there is no micro level planning at the grassroots which results in waste of funds and improper utilization. The Constitutional Amendment Act and the Tamil Nadu Panchayats Act, Section 240, enjoin that the Panchayats should prepare annual plans to achieve economic development and social justice. This is an important function assigned to them so that the felt needs of the people will be met through such planning. So far planning has not been done at the bottom level. Instead it has been imposed from above. The needs of the people have not been reflected in the planning exercise done above the Panchayats and therefore, it was realized at every level as early as 1970 that planning should be done at the grassroots. The District Planning Cell has been created and the District Planning Committee has been constituted and money is being spent for it and yet there is no constant effort to initiate micro planning as per the mandate of the Constitution.

A serious evaluation was done by the Ministry of Panchayati Raj, Government of India and concluded its analysis. "In conclusion it can be stated that the approach to Panchayati Raj as manifested in the Panchayati Raj legislation government orders, policies and schemes seems to be to pay lip service to the concept of decentralisation, while in actuality, run a rigid top-down and inflexible system. Any extent of meticulous drafting and reporting cannot hide the bald fact that what is actually operating is a system of Collector and not Panchayati Raj. The District Panchayat is hardly recognizable as a local self- government. Even the Union Council is nothing more than an implementing agency and it might be only the village panchayat that have some element of discretion in planning and implementation. Controls are applied at all levels by the District Collector who is both the regulator for the panchayat, exercise strict financial control and also compete with the panchayats in their domain through parallel structures and agencies. The above analysis would show that Tamil Nadu has a long way to go before they actually devolve substantive implementation functions to the Panchayats."

FIRST STATE FINANCE COMMISSION'S (SFC) RECOMMENDATIONS

In accordance with Article 243(I) of the Constitution of India, the First SFC in Tamil Nadu was constituted in 1994 to make recommendations on devolution of funds to the Panchayats for five years from 1996-97 to 2001-02. It is to be noted here that the State Finance Commission started its exercise and came to the final stage before it was decided as to what powers and responsibilities have to be given to each and every tier of the three-tier Panchayat system. The First SFC submitted its report before the Committee, which was constituted for making recommendations on entrusting responsibilities to the three-tier Panchayats, submitted its report. The First SFC made 462 recommendations, of which 49 were common to rural and urban local bodies, 107 were related to rural local bodies and 195 were related to taxation and other issues. Of these, only 93 recommendations were accepted in principle and 97 recommendations were not accepted by the government. Even for the 93 accepted recommendations, the government had not issued orders. The details are furnished in Table 1.1.

The First State Finance Commission recommended devolution of State owned tax resources (other than assigned revenues) from 8 per cent to 12 per cent by increasing 1 per cent annually from 1996-97. But the state government decided to freeze it at 8 per cent of its resources for the five years period in spite of the fact that initially in the "Action Taken Report" placed before the Legislature, a commitment was made by the State Government that payment will be made at the rate of 8 per cent, 9 per cent, 10 per cent, 11 per cent and 12 per cent during the period of five years starting from 1996-97. While considering the responsibilities assigned to the Panchayats, the resources devolved to Panchayats are meagre and insufficient. This poor recommendation was due to the fact that the First State Finance Commission considered the responsibilities given to the Panchayats with the 1958 Panchayats Act as a base and on that basis calculated the requirements and made recommendations.

Modifications

In some of the recommendations, the government made modifications which the First SFC had not suggested such as: (i) abolition of house tax matching grant, (ii) abolition of local cess surcharge matching grant, (iii) adoption of population as the only criterion for *inter se* distribution instead of population along with service indicators and per capita income. The modifications

Table 1.1: The Status of First State Finance Commission's Recommendations for PRIs

Sl. No.	*Topics*		*Accepted*	*Accepted in Principle Only*	*Not Accepted*	*Orders not Passed*	*Under Examination*	*Total*
1.	Taxation and other related service		93	—	97	3	2	195
2.	Civic services	Rural	—	—	—	26	—	26
		Urban		106				106
3.	Organizations	Rural	1	—	—	8	—	9
		Urban		5				5
4.	Functions	Rural	1	—	—	—	—	1
		Urban		1				1
5.	Devolution of functions	Rural	1	—	—	—	—	1
		Urban		1				1
6.	Staffing pattern	Rural	2	—	2	1	—	5
		Urban		5				5
7.	Human resources development	Rural	—	9	—	2	—	11
		Urban		11				11
8.	Community participation	Rural	—	—	—	6	—	6
		Urban		6				6
9.	Adequacy of powers	Rural	5	—	—	3	—	8
		Urban		8				8
10.	Control system	Rural	1	—	—	6	—	7
		Urban		7				7
11.	Mechanism for performance	Rural	2	—	—	2	—	4
		Urban		4				4
12.	Database	Rural	4	—	—	2	—	6
		Urban		6				6
13.	Devolution of funds	Rural	22	—	—	—	—	22
14.	Capital fund	Rural	—	—	1	—	—	1
	Total		**132**	169	100	59	2	462

Source: Computed. (Report of the Second SFC).

made by the Government were detrimental to the interests of the Panchayats. The government, in its Action Taken Report placed before the Legislature in April 1997, had accepted the recommendation for direct remittance of the share of minerals and black granite to Village Panchayat account, but, subsequently, the Rural Development Department of the Government have rejected this recommendation. As a result the money goes to the treasury and it does not come to the Panchayats. To get money from the treasury a cumbersome procedure has to be followed for which officials have to take steps from the district administration and they are to be pursued at the secretariat level. At present nobody bothers about it. As a result the Panchayats are not getting their due share.

Unaccepted Recommendations

Some of the major recommendations made by First State Finance Commission which have not been accepted by the government are:

(i) Calculation of local cess and local cess surcharge based on average land revenue.
(ii) Compensation for local bodies towards local cess/local cess surcharge during the period of waiver/remission of land revenue.
(iii) Water tax.

This has also affected the financial resources of the Panchayats.

Utilization of SFC Devolution

The First SFC recommended specifically that the devolution is meant to cover maintenance of assets at the time of the award period as also the assets to be created during the award period and salary and wages of the personnel of the local bodies. This has been visualized with a view to maintaining the assets created and also to avoid delay in payment of salary to the employees of local bodies. In practice, the government have set apart a sizeable sum for capital works with a view to improving basic amenities in both rural and urban areas. Further, the government has deducted the debt payable by local bodies to other institutions from the State Finance Commission's grant. On the other hand, the recommendations relating to remittance of PF dues (contribution) to the respective accounts has not been implemented. Moreover, the entire devolution money has been credited to general fund accounts of the local bodies. When specific orders have been issued for the maintenance of separate cash book for utilization of devolution fund in urban local bodies no specific orders have been issued in respect of rural local bodies. Experience shows that there is need for separate accounts to monitor the utilization of State Finance Commission's devolution (*Source*: Second State Finance Commission Report).

SECOND STATE FINANCE COMMISSION'S RECOMMENDATIONS

The Second State Finance Commission was constituted on 1.12.1999 to make recommendations on the devolution of funds for five years from 2002-03 to 2007-08. The Second State Finance Commission recommended devolution of 8 per cent from State owned tax resources for the first two years and 9 per cent for the next two years and 10 per cent for last one year. But the government issued orders freezing the devolution of funds to 8 per cent for each year. When Finance Commissions are constituted a tradition has been established in Tamil Nadu that IAS officials are to be appointed Chairpersons. No doubt they have the capacity and capability to perform the job but it is a major question whether they have the needed mindset to look properly at the new paradigm. There are other experts in local body finance or public finance and they can also be appointed. With the minimum responsibilities to Panchayats the First Finance Commission recommended 8 per cent to 12 per cent for a period of five years. But in the Second Finance Commission, after fixing enormous responsibilities, the recommendation, instead of starting from 12 per cent, started from the same 8 per cent. It gives the impression that local bodies are not considered institutions of self-governance.

The status of second SFC recommendation as on 31.8.2006 is given below:

Table 1.2: Details of Recommendations

Sl. No.	*Nature*	*No.*
1.	Main Recommendations	132
2.	Sub/recommendations	254
	Total	**386**

Source: Computed.

Table 1.3: Details of Action taken Report

Sl. No.	*Details*	*No.*
1.	Accepted and orders issued	133
2.	Accepted in principle	13
3.	Accepted with modifications	37
4.	Not accepted	38
5.	Pending recommendations	165
	Total	**386**

Source: Computed. (Third SFC report).

Analysis of Implementation of Second State Finance Commission's Recommendations and Observations of Third State Finance Commission

The Third State Finance Commission in its report (Chapter III para 2) has observed as follows:

"Even though most of the recommendations of the second State Finance Commission have been accepted, yet there is laxity in implementing the recommendations by the Administrative Department of the Secretariat. In fact, on the recommendations relating to improving of 'Resource Base', casual approach is noticeable." The Commission has given a detailed list of recommendations accepted by the Government but proper action was not taken for implementation.

One of the major recommendations which will give some relief to rural local bodies is payment of compensation for waiver of local cess and local cess surcharge whenever land revenue is waived due to drought or flood. For Block Panchayats, local cess surcharge is the most important source of income. This recommendation for payment of compensation whenever local cess surcharge is waived was also made by the First SFC. Though the government initially stated in the Action Taken Report that the payment of the compensation will be considered, the government have not taken any decision so far. During 2003-04 the government have waived land revenue, local cess, local cess surcharge throughout Tamil Nadu. But no compensation to local bodies was thought of resulting in huge financial loss to rural local bodies roughly to the tune of Rs. 33.30 crores.

Revenue dues to Panchayats not settled

(i) Local Cess and Local Cess Surcharge

The Second State Finance Commission recommended in para 13.2.4 that local cess/local cess surcharge to the Panchayat/Panchayat Unions due during the period from 1997-98 to 2001-02 should be reworked and adjusted positively within two years, that is, 2002-03 and 2003-04 since local cess/local cess surcharge, which are legitimate dues of Panchayats and Panchayat Unions, are not at all being adjusted properly. This has not been done so far by the government. This results in loss of revenue to the Panchayats.

(ii) Mines and Minerals

The Second State Finance Commission in para 12 pointed out that the dues from mines and minerals have not been adjusted and it recommended that the remaining dues may be cleared by issuing suitable orders. But the government has not acted on this. Thus due share from the mines and minerals have not come to the Panchayats.

(iii) Social Forestry

The Second State Finance Commission in para 8.7 stated that the share of the Village Panchayats from social forestry income from 1995-96 onwards is yet to be settled. The auctioning under social forestry is done by the Forest Department without any role assigned to the Village Panchayats. The Panchayats feel that their auction amount will be more if they are associated. Hence, the Second State Finance Commission recommended that the Village Panchayats' share may be directly credited to their own account after the conduct of auction to avoid delays. It further recommended the constitution of a committee consisting of Secretary to Government, Environment and Forest Department, Chief Conservator of Forests and DRD to monitor timely adjustment. The inaction of the government in taking steps to implement the recommendation to release the backlog dues to the Panchayats in respect of local cess/local cess surcharge, mines, social forestry has not helped the Panchayats to meet the core and basic requirements. A commitment by the government to rectify the above situation is urgently called for.

Release of State Finance Commission's Devolution Fund

The Second State Finance Commission, in para 12 of Chapter XIII, pointed out that the release of SFC Devolution Fund for the first two years 1997-98 and 1998-99 was more or less regular while in subsequent two years there were erratic releases which affected any possible financial planning by the local bodies. It further pointed out that devolution has become discretionary with several local bodies finding it difficult even to pay salary to their employees.

The above instances amply make clear that the amount due to the Panchayats has not been released by the department in time even after a high level body, namely the State Finance Commission, made positive recommendations to the effect that the dues should be paid immediately. As the entitlement due to Panchayats has not been released and hence they are unable to discharge the statutory duties entrusted to them. In order to make the Panchayats functional, the State Government should be made to release the dues in time. The Government is committed to releasing the State Finance Commission's grant every month. But experience shows that the release of the State Finance Commission grant was not made every month. This has seriously affected the functioning of the Panchayats. The State Government should be made to honour its commitment and it should be watched by the Estimates Committee of the Legislature.

Unauthorized Diversion of Statutory SFC Grant due to Local Bodies by Government

The SFC grant is not being regularly released to the Panchayats. In many cases, the grant due to the Panchayats has been unauthorizedly diverted to other purposes and also paid to other departments. In some cases the grant has been adjusted at the state level towards electricity consumption charges (CC) due to the EB without verification and without any intimation to the concerned Panchayats. As this is done at the State level, the release of grant is not reflected in the accounts of the Panchayats. Nay, the Panchayats are not even aware of their entitlement and the release. This further results in the improper maintenance of accounts by the Panchayats. "The grant released through the right hand has been snatched away by the left hand without the knowledge of the body."

The annual entitlement of SFC grant for rural local bodies for the year 2001-02 is Rs. 416 crores, of which the government, in G.O. Ms. 18, RD dated 26.03.2002, restricted the SFC grant to the tune of Rs. 175 crores for rural Panchayats in that year. Obviously, the Panchayats have been deprived of a substantial sum of Rs. 241 crores approximately during the year 2001-02. Even while releasing the above grant of Rs. 175 crores, the government have adjusted the following amounts from Village Panchayats and Panchayat Unions during the year 2001-02 (See Table 1.4).

It is also observed that the entire equalisation and incentive grant from out of State Finance Commission funds for the year 2002-03 due to the three tiers of Panchayats has been diverted for undertaking drought relief works.

Table 1.4: Details of Adjustments of SFC Grant

Sl. No.	Particulars	Amount (Rs. in Crores)
1.	CC Charges (Electricity Charges)	1.78
2.	Payment of pensionary contribution towards Panchayat Union employees	31.85
3.	Contribution for loan amount sanctioned by government to Panchayat Unions for special Self-Sufficiency Programme	7.16
	Total	**40.78**

Source: Computed.

THIRD STATE FINANCE COMMISSION

The Third State Finance Commission submitted its report in September 2006 for the award period 2007-2012. Action taken report was placed before the Assembly in May 2007.

This is what the Commission has to say about the way in which it was treated. "Article 243(1) empowers the State Finance Commission to frame its own procedure for its functioning. But in practice the Government continues to treat the Commission as like any other department forgetting that it is a constitutional body. That is especially visible when it sought the required man-power: out of 44 sanctioned posts only 20 posts could be filled up..." (para 40 Chapter XIV).

As for the monitoring mechanism the Commission observed "The First and Second State Finance Commissions made recommendations of which some of them were partially implemented, some have not been implemented and the remaining were under consideration of the Government. Even though the Second State Finance Commission pointed out the delay on the part of the implementing authority to get its recommendations met with the same fate.... It is a reflection of the general view that the local bodies are still looked upon as the appendage of the State Government and not as a constitutionally recognized bodies. In the above context the Third State Finance Commission analysed the scenario. The Commission recommends that decisions on all recommendations of the Third State Finance Commission shall be taken within 6 months from the date of commencement of the award period. The follow up action on the A.T.R. needs to be monitored on quarterly basis by the High Level Committee constituted for the purpose" (para 30, Chapter XIV).

The details of recommendations made by the Third State Finance Commission, the number of recommendations accepted by the Government and the number of recommendations not accepted etc. are furnished below:

Table 1.5: Details of Recommendations of Third State Finance Commission

Sl. No.	*Details – Recommendations*	*Total*
1.	Recommendations relating to urban local bodies	138
2.	Recommendations relating to rural local bodies	102
3.	Common to urban and rural local bodies	68
	Total	**308**

Source: Computed.

Table 1.6: Details of Common Recommendations

Sl. No.	*Details*	*Total*
1.	Accepted	19
2.	Not accepted	33
3.	Accepted with modifications	10
4.	Accepted in principle	1
5.	Deemed to be accepted	1
6.	No decision	4
	Total	**68**

Source: Computed.

Table 1.7: Recommendations for Rural Local Bodies

Sl. No.	*Details*	*Total No.*
1.	Accepted	30
2.	Not accepted	34
3.	Accepted with modifications	6
4.	Accepted in principle	12
5.	Deemed to be accepted	5
6.	No decision	15
	Total	**102**

Source: Computed.

Not accepted recommendations outnumber the number of accepted recommendations. The Third State Finance Commission recommended financial devolution of 10 per cent to the local bodies for the entire award period. But the Government ordered devolution of funds as indicated in Table 1.8.

Table 1.8: Details of Awards

Sl. No.	*Year*	*Award*
1.	2007 – 08	9%
2.	2008 – 09	9%
3.	2009 – 10	9.5%
4.	2010 – 11	10%
5.	2011 – 12	10%

Source: Computed.

Responsibilities of Three-Tier Panchayats

1. Village Panchayats

Onerous responsibilities are given to the Village Panchayats and they are listed as obligatory and discretionary functions in Sections 110 and 111 of the Tamil Nadu Panchayats Act, 1994. The obligatory functions of Village Panchayats are:

- (i) Construction, repair and maintenance of village roads.
- (ii) Construction, repair and maintenance of water works for supply of water for drinking, washing and bathing purposes.
- (iii) Light of public roads and public places in built up areas.
- (iv) Cleaning of streets and removal of rubbish.
- (v) Construction of disposal of drainage water and its maintenance.
- (vi) Provision of public latrine and arrangements to clean public latrine whether public or private.
- (vii) Opening and maintenance of burial and burning grounds.
- (viii) Opening and maintenance of Public Distribution System.
- (ix) Extension of village sites and regulation of buildings.

Apart from this, the following discretionary functions are given to Village Panchayats:

(i) Planting and preservation of trees in the public roads.
(ii) Lighting in public roads and public places in non-built up areas.
(iii) Opening and maintenance of public market.
(iv) Control of fairs and festivals.
(v) Opening and maintenance of slaughter houses.
(vi) Opening and maintenance of reading rooms.
(vii) Establishment and maintenance of TV sets etc.

2. *Block Panchayats*

The obligatory and discretionary functions of Block Panchayats are listed in Sections 112 to 119 of Tamil Nadu Panchayats Act, 1994. The important obligatory functions are:

(i) Construction, repair and maintenance of Panchayat Union roads.
(ii) Establishment and maintenance of rural dispensaries and payment of subsidies to rural medical practitioner.
(iii) Establishment and maintenance of maternity centres.
(iv) Maintenance and expansion of elementary school buildings.
(v) Remedial measures considered with epidemic diseases.
(vi) Control of fairs and festivals classified as Panchayat Union festivals.
(vii) Veterinary relief.
(viii) Opening and maintenance of Panchayat Union markets.
(ix) Establishment and maintenance of poultries.
(x) Improvement of agriculture.
(xi) Promotion and encouragement to cottage industries.

The discretionary functions given to Block Panchayats are:

(i) Entrustment and execution of NES and CD works.
(ii) Execution of schemes or programme for economic development.

(iii) Provision and maintenance of common, burial and burning ground.

(iv) Lighting of public roads and public places in common areas of Panchayats.

(v) Maintenance of common dispensaries and child welfare centres.

(vi) Any other duty imposed by government.

3. District Panchayat

The functions of the District Panchayat as enumerated in Sections 163 and 164 of the Tamil Nadu Panchayats Act are advisory in nature. They have to advise the government on all matters relating to rural development.

Inadequate Finance and Manpower for Fulfilment of Responsibilities

Village Panchayats are given heavy and innumerable responsibilities which relate to the basic needs of the community. They have to necessarily carry out the functions. For this purpose, they are not equipped with either finance or the required technical or supporting staff. The main income of Village Panchayats is consumed by electricity charges for street lights and water supply and, even in respect of them, they are in huge arrears resulting in unauthorized adjustment at the State level from statutory grants made to them.

In respect of staff, they are provided with one assistant and limited sanitary and water supply staff. More number of hamlets in Village Panchayats, expansion of population and execution of various water supply schemes with government assistance and other infrastructure development executed in the Village Panchayats require maintenance periodically and annually for which the existing staff and the funds now available are quite inadequate. Unless sufficient financial assistance and technical guidance with staff are provided, the various amenities provided at huge government cost will run into disuse and decay.

Block Panchayats were getting substantial assigned revenues during the pre-SFC period, viz. local cess surcharge matching grant, local roads grant, local education grant, minor irrigation grant, land revenue assignment etc., which are no longer in vogue and hence Block Panchayats now find it very difficult to run the administration with only the State Finance Commission grant. Though they are provided with adequate staff to carry out the above functions the increasing salary of staff and expenditure on pensionary commitments etc. have made them financially weak. The Block Panchayats should be provided with adequate financial assistance to attend to the various development schemes entrusted out of centrally sponsored schemes and state sponsored schemes besides the works carried out from their own finance in some Panchayat Unions.

As regards District Panchayats, the District Panchayats are having only an advisory role in the rural local body administration as per Section 163 of the Tamil Nadu Panchayats Act and no asset creation and maintenance are entrusted to them. Therefore, no separate allocation from out of SFC grant is called for after setting apart finance towards requirement of salary for District Panchayats till additional functions are entrusted.

Reduction of Sources of Income

(i) Village Panchayats

The main sources of income of the Village Panchayats are house tax, professional tax and advertisement tax and other non-tax items like building fees, Dangerous and Offensive (D&O) trades etc., and assigned revenues, viz. surcharge on stamp duty, entertainment tax, cable TV, local cess, mines and minerals etc.*

* *Note*: As per the recent orders issued by the Government in G.O.Ms. No. 168 R.D. district. 4.10.2007 the income from assigned revenues will be pooled at the state level and shared between the village panchayats, panchayat unions and district panchayats in the ratio 60:32:8 after earmarking 1/3rd of the total revenue to a special fund. Though this will ensure equitable distribution of revenue between the three tiers, the income to the village panchayat will get reduced.

The vehicle tax originally levied by the Panchayat as per Section 173 of the Tamil Nadu Panchayats Act, 1994 and the house tax matching grant provided as per Section 183 of the Tamil Nadu Panchayats Act were dispensed with. The surcharge on stamp duty which is the main and a substantial source of income to Village Panchayats has been drastically reduced from 5 per cent to 2 per cent and 1 per cent in respect of mortgage of immovable property resulting in more than 60 per cent loss of income to the Panchayats from this source alone. On the introduction of cable TV the income from Entertainment Tax (ET) has been reduced to a considerable extent. Originally the tax on exhibition of cable TV was levied by Village Panchayats but Village Panchayats could not assess the volume of tax properly due to inadequate staff. As a result it was taken over by the government. But the government has not paid any compensation to the local bodies after taking over the levy of tax on cable TV.

Regarding mines and minerals, the government has to apportion the lease amount to Village Panchayats and Panchayat Unions on a 50:50 basis. Now, the government has taken over the mines and the quarrying of sand directly but it has not issued orders for disbursing the dues to the local bodies so far. If the income from mines and minerals are not apportioned to the local bodies they will lose heavily.

In respect of the Block Panchayat, the Act still provides for the payment of land revenue assignment grant as per Section 170 of the Tamil Nadu Panchayat Act. But this has not been paid from 1997-98 onwards. Another important source of income is local cess surcharge matching grant under Section 180 of the Tamil Nadu Panchayats Act and now it has been deleted. Likewise local roads grant paid to Block Panchayats as per Section 182 has also been deleted. Now this is supposed to be merged with State Finance Commission devolution funds except land revenue assignment which is still in the Act but is not paid.

Income and Expenditure of Rural Local Bodies

Though the 73rd Amendments Act provides for more duties and

responsibilities to Village Panchayats and Block Panchayats, mobilization of resources through taxes becomes increasingly difficult due to various factors. The expectations and aspirations of the people for receiving efficient service from the local bodies are more whereas the resources mobilized through taxes and non-taxes cannot meet the demands of the people especially in providing better basic amenities like water supply, maintenance of roads, street lights etc. There is a big gap between the pre-State Finance Commission and the post-State Finance Commission period in receipts. The expenditure has gone up.

An analysis of average revenue and expenditure of Village Panchayats and Block Panchayats during the pre-SFC devolution period and the post-SFC devolution period are given below:

Table 1.9: Village Panchayats—Source of Income for 1996-97 (Pre-SFC Devolution Period)

Sl. No.	*Particulars*	*Average Amount per Panchayat (Rs. in lakhs)*	*Percentage*
1.	Tax and non-tax	0.27	21.8
2.	Assigned revenue	0.75	60.5
3.	Other grants	0.14	11.2
4.	Miscellaneous receipts	0.08	6.5
	Total	**1.24**	

Source: Computed.

Table 1.10: Source of Expenditure details for 1996-97 (Pre-SFC Devolution Period)

Sl. No.	*Particulars*	*Average Amount per Panchayat (Rs. in lakhs)*	*Percentage*
1.	General Administration	0.14	13.6
2.	Maintenance charges	0.69	64.14
3.	Maintenance expenditure	0.12	11.5
4.	Capital expenditure	0.11	10.15
	Total	**1.06**	

Source: Computed.

Table 1.11: Break-up details for Post-SFC Devolution Period (1999-2000)—Source of Income

Sl. No.	Particulars	Average Amount per Panchayat (Rs. in lakhs)	Percentage
1.	Own source including tax and non-tax	0.53	17.51
2.	Assigned revenue	0.82	27.17
3.	Grants	1.48	48.88
4.	Miscellaneous receipts	0.19	6.43
	Total	**3.02**	

Source: Computed.

Table 1.12: Break-up details for Post-SFC Devolution Period (1999-2000)—Expenditure Details

Sl. No.	Particulars	Average Amount per Panchayat (Rs. in lakhs)	Percentage
1.	General administration	0.55	15.14
2.	Maintenance charges	2.08	57.29
3.	Capital expenditure	0.90	24.71
4.	Miscellaneous expenditure	0.10	2.86
	Total	3.64	
	GAP	-0.62	

Source: Computed.

Prior to the SFC devolution, the major source of income derived by Village Panchayats was assigned revenue of surcharge on stamp duty, entertainment tax etc., which constituted 61 per cent of the total income. Though there was not much resource gap between receipt and expenditure, Village Panchayats could not take up capital works (providing better infrastructure) since the major portion of expenditure was consumed on electricity charges and maintenance charges relating to street lights and water supply which constituted 65 per cent of the total expenditure whereas the capital expenditure constituted only 12 per cent.

There is not much improvement at the receipt end even though the SFC devolution passed on income to Village Panchayats at the ratio of 47 per cent of total devolution due to rural local bodies.

Table 1.13: Block Panchayat — Break-up details of average Income for Pre-SFC Devolution Period (1996-1997)

Sl. No.	*Source of Income*	*Average Amount per Block Panchayat (Rs. in Lakhs)*	*Percentage*
1.	Local cess surcharge and non-tax items	24.26	88
2.	Assigned revenue	3.20	12
3.	Miscellaneous receipts	—	—
	Total	27.55	

Source: Computed.

Table 1.14: Break-up Details of Average Expenditure for Pre-Devolution Period (1996-1997)

Sl. No.	*Particulars*	*Average Amount per Block Panchayat (Rs. in Lakhs)*	*Percentage*
1.	General administration	16.84	52
2.	Maintenance expenditure	11.83	36.6
3.	Miscellaneous expenditure	—	—
4.	Capital expenditure	3.61	11.2
	Total	32.35	
	GAP	-4.8	

Source: Computed.

Table 1.15: Break-up Details of Average Income for Post-SFC Devolution Period (1999-2000)

Sl. No.	*Source of Income*	*Average Amount per Block Panchayat (Rs. in Lakhs)*	*Percentage*
1.	Own source including tax and non-tax	6.52	11.99
2.	Assigned revenues	0.08	0.15
3.	Grants	47.76	87.86
4.	Miscellaneous receipts	—	—
	Total	54.36	

Source: Computed.

Table 1.16: Break-up Details of Average Expenditure for Post-SFC Devolution Period (1999-2000)

Sl. No.	*Expenditure Details*	*Average Amount per Block Panchayat (Rs. in Lakhs)*	*Percentage*
1.	General administration	45.05	67.56
2.	Maintenance charges	16.44	24.66
3.	Capital expenditure	5.19	7.78
4.	Miscellaneous expenditure	—	—
	Total	66.68	
	GAP	-12.32	

Source: Computed.

The above figures indicate that out of the total income derived by the Panchayat Union, local cess surcharge, local cess surcharge matching grant, local education grant, local roads grant and land revenue assignment etc., constituted 88 per cent. But in the post-SFC devolution period the financial assistance pattern has been changed and the income from local cess surcharge matching grant, local education grant, local roads grant and other statutory grants were dispensed with and assistance is given in the form of State Finance Commission devolution to Panchayat Unions. Even prior to the SFC devolution period, there was a gap of Rs. 4.80 lakhs between receipt and expenditure. This gap has widened to Rs. 12.32 lakhs per Panchayat Union in the post-devolution scenario owing to the fact that the major portion of expenditure of 52 per cent in the pre-devolution period and 68 per cent in the post-devolution period is incurred for general administration. Under general administration, an expenditure 20 per cent of salary for Panchayat employees is incurred for pensionary contributions.

The above analysis will show that while the income to the Village Panchayats has sharply declined due to reduction in the surcharge on stamp duty which is a major source of income and also due to non-adjustment of receipts legally due to the Panchayats, there has been a steep rise in the expenditure due to street lights and drinking water supply as well as increase in the establishment cost. The electricity board charged at the rate of Rs. 1.60 paise per KWH till 30-11-2001 and it has been increased to Rs. 3.40 from 1-12-2001, which is nearly three times the earlier rate. Due to the three-fold increase, many Panchayats are facing the problem of clearing electricity charges and are now in the doldrums*.

EB charges have increased three-fold for supplying drinking water to the inhabitants as well as water supply for other essential purposes. Water supply and street lighting are obligatory duties cast on the Panchayats and they have to necessarily maintain them. In this connection electricity supply to the agriculturalists is provided free of charges. It is a well known fact that many of the agriculturalists availing of this concession are misusing this concession for pumping water and supplying the same to others and derive substantial income from this source. When such concession is being extended to the agriculturalists who are commercially exploiting it, it is a great injustice to charge heavily the Village Panchayats who are rendering social and public obligations. Now most of the Panchayats are in arrears and whatever little grant is given by government is being adjusted towards EB charges even without the knowledge of the Village Panchayats. It is only proper that the electricity supply to Panchayats for water supply and street lights is charged on par with domestic consumers.

Here it is necessary to look at the financial status of the Gram Panchayats as they attend the important and essential needs of the communities. For distribution of resource population being the main criterion, many of the Gram Panchayats cannot get needed money as the population is small. The following table gives the details of population:

Table 1.17: Classification of Village Panchayats on the Basis of Population 2001 Census

Sl. No.	*Population*	*No. of Gram Panchayats*
1.	Below 500	66
2.	501 – 1000	1177
3.	1001 – 3000	7241
4.	3001 – 5000	2569
5.	5001 – 10,000	1379
6.	Above 10,000	186
	Total	**12618**

Source: TN Govt. website.

* *Note*: From 2007 the charge has been reduced to Rs. 3 per unit and the interest on arrear payment has been reduced from 12 per cent to 6 per cent.

Table 1.18: Income-wise Classification of Village Panchayats

Sl. No.	*Income Range in Rs.*	*No. of Gram Panchayats based on the Average Income of 3 Years from 2003 to 2006*	*No. of Gram Panchayats based on the Income in 2007-08*
1.	5000	10	0
2.	5000–10,000	178	0
3.	10001–50000	7422	1059
4.	50001–100000	3181	7283
5.	100001–2500000	1489	3733
6.	2500001–5000000	252	443
7.	5000001–10000000	60	78
8.	10000001–30000000	24	23
9.	30000001 and above	2	23
	Total	**12618**	**12618**

Source: TN Govt. website.

Note: It is necessary to look at the income of the Gram Panchayats.

After taking some corrective measures in electricity consumption rate and allocation of resources on the basis of not only population but also the fixed cost of the expenditure, to some extent the finance of the Gram Panchayat is stabilized and increased.

Ways and Means to Augment the Resources of Panchayats

The Panchayats face several problems in raising local tax revenue such as narrow tax base, lack of administrative machinery, staff trained in tax collection, lack of guidelines to levy new taxes. Local tax collections can be improved by improving the administrative capacity of the local bodies before levying higher tax. The existing staff at the Village Panchayat level is highly inadequate for this purpose. The staff working in other departments connected with the duty of the Panchayats may be suitably redeployed and placed at the disposal of the Panchayats. The rate of fee levied by the Panchayats for installation of machinery and D&O trades is very low since it was fixed as early as 1960. This needs revision and a higher fee may be fixed by suitable notification by government and thereby income can be raised. Another major source of income is levy and collection of house tax. The present law provides for levy of tax on plinth area basis and it has not been resorted to by many Panchayats. The Panchayats should be made to levy the tax on plinth area basis and they should be suitably guided and motivated to do so through incentives.

At present the implementation of the recommendations made by Finance Commission is left to the discretion of the State Government. This attitude should be changed and the recommendations made by such constitutional bodies have to be accepted in all seriousness and implemented unless it is beyond the resources of the State Government. We find that even accepted recommendations have not been implemented on some pretext or other. This position should be changed by making suitable amendments to the Constitution. Following are deduced from the above:

Proper devolution of function, power and funds should be made available to the Panchayats so that they can effectively discharge their duties and functions as true local self-governing institutions as contemplated in the Constitution.

Recommendations made by the SFC and accepted by the government in principle should be faithfully implemented and arrears due to Panchayats should be paid without delay.

While releasing the SFC grant deductions should not be made at the State level. The funds should be credited to the accounts of local bodies and they should be made to pay the dues so that they can watch the receipt of grants and maintain the accounts properly.

To improve tax collection by Village Panchayats proper staff should be given by suitable redeployment of staff working in government departments and their salary should be continued to be met by the government. The Village Panchayats which come forward to increase the rate and assessment of tax and mobilize more new sources of income may be encouraged by suitable support through incentives.

For maintaining the cleanliness of streets and sanitation of the Panchayats, suitable personnel and recurring grant may be sanctioned to the local bodies.

To improve the functioning of the Panchayat, the functions, staff and finance now provided to departments dealing with the 29 subjects (as per schedule XI of Constitution) may be transferred to the Panchayats by issuing statutory orders.

Maintenance cost on drinking water supply and street lights have sharply increased (to almost 70% of the income). Hence special grants may be sanctioned to Panchayats to make good the deficit.

The Central Finance Commission provides 29 per cent from centrally owned tax resources to State Governments as CFC grant. It is recommended that one-third of the amount from out of the CFC grant released be earmarked for local bodies and directly credited to the local bodies' accounts by the Central Finance Commission itself.

Conclusion

Having established the panchayats as institutions of governance, in order to achieve allocative efficiency, a data generating device has to be established at every Gram panchayat. A Central Planning Commission unit by its computer should be able to get the data of a Gram panchayat from any state in India. This will reduce the wastage of expenditure and will increase allocative efficiency. Data generation, validation, data storage and update of the same are the essential duties to be performed by the panchayats.

Secondly, the financial management system has to be standardized and simplified from the International level to Gram panchayat level. A uniform system has to be followed at all levels. Then only it is possible for even ordinary citizen to understand the financial system of the government.

Thirdly, all the three governments should mobilize resources and for which earmarked responsibilities have to be fixed. In the same way autonomy to spending has to be given to all the three governments. A system has to be evolved and by which the wastage of resources has to be curtailed.

The financial system has been operationalised through the formulations of Finance Commission. Now we have two Finance

Commissions in our country to regulate the finance. Central Finance Commission makes recommendations which are made mandatory. But the recommendations of the State Finance Commissions are not made mandatory. Hence the Central and State Finance Commissions have to be constituted simultaneously. Acceptance of the major recommendations of the commissions have to be made mandatory. The terms of reference should be supervised by the Central Planning Commission.

Incentives have to be given to panchayats for effective mobilization of internal resources and equally prudent ways of managing the panchayat finance. There are variety of ways by which the panchayat finance is managed very effectively. In the same way the panchayats have to augment their resources internally. For all those initiatives and involvements, the government has to provide incentives.

The panchayats have to be evaluated from the perspective of impact making activities. Maximum human development indicators have to be fixed and they are to be evaluated annually and they are to be given incentives based on the performance. This will create a big change in the performance. Planning at the grassroots should be made an integral part of the whole process of preparing five year plans at the state level.

The Central Schemes meant for rural development should have a window for panchayat. The role of panchayats have to be included in the scheme and have to be integrated in the plan document of the village. Village panchayats and Direct Planning Committees can be provided with incentive resource if they prepare a plan and implement the same for human development. There are many acts which work as barriers to augment resources for the panchayats and they should be amended.

Panchayats at three levels should be given resource mobilization responsibility. From the Gram Panchayat to District Panchayat, responsibility of taxation has to be fixed. No institution should be designated as institution of expenditure. A uniform logic has to be evolved to distribute resources among the three-tier panchayats. Of the criteria intensity of poverty should be the major criterion. At the same time incentive has to be made to the panchayats for the success of the panchayats in resource mobilization, and impact making development activities that too on social development activities.

A financial management guideline in the form of manual both administrative and financial has to be prepared. There is no guide book for financial management of panchayats in management of finance barring a few states. Ultimately this creates confusion and leaves the panchayats in the hands of the official. Preparation of a simple manual for finance management is the need of the hour. The existing mindset of people believing in the higher institutions for their efficiency and honesty has to go. Strengthening the grassroots institutions in terms of resource management, and governance is an imperative. The above will solve many of the problems in panchayat management.

Auditing has to be done only by CAG and not by the local officials. Procedures adopted at the grassroots for financial management are *ad hoc* and they are not system based. As long as adhocism prevails, the expenditure goes waste. A financial system alone will bring expected results. Panchayat system has to be seen from the management perspective. Cost benefit analysis has to be made. On that basis, unviable panchayats have to be integrated with other panchayats accordingly delimitation analysis has to be made for the whole system. Cost effectiveness has to be maintained.

References

Amba Agarwal, *Fiscal Decentralisation: Financing of Panchayati Raj Institutions in India,* New Delhi: Serial Publications, 2005.

Anwar Shah (ed.), *Local Governance in Developing Countries,* Washington D.C.: The World Bank, 2006.

Anwar Shah (ed.), *Local Governance in Industrial Countries,* Washington D.C.: The World Bank, 2006.

Anwar Shah, "Fiscal Decentralisation in Developing Countries and Transitive Economies: An Overview" in L.C. Jain (eds.) *Decentralisation and Local Governance,* Hyderabad: Orient Longman Private Limited, 2008.

Bahl Roy, *The Rules of Fiscal Decentralisation in Georgia:* Georgia State University, 1999.

Government of India, *Local Governance: An Inspiring Journey into Future,* New Delhi: Second Administrative Reforms Commission, 2007.

Indira Rajaraman, *A Fiscal Domain for Panchayats*, New Delhi: Oxford University Press, 2003.

Institute of Rural Management, *The State of Panchayats: 2007-08*, Vols. I, II and III, New Delhi: Ministry of Panchayati Raj, Government of India, 2008.

Konrad Adenauer Foundation, *Local Government Finance in India,* New Delhi: Manohar, 1998.

M.A. Ommen, "Rural Fiscal Decentralisation in India: A Brief Survey of Literature" in L.C. Jain (ed.), *Decentralisation and Local Governance,* Hyderabad: Orient Longman Private Limited, 2008.

Ministry of Panchayati Raj, *Devolution of Functions in Tamil Nadu to Panchayats—A Status Report,* New Delhi: N-1011/82005 policy II.

P. Bardhan and D. Mookerjee (eds.), *Decentralisation and Local Governance in Developing Countries: A Comparative Perspective,* New Delhi: Oxford University Press, 2007.

S.K. Singh, *Panchayati Raj Finances in Madhya Pradesh,* New Delhi: Concept Publishing Company Pvt. Ltd., 2004.

The World Bank, *Fiscal Decentralisation to Rural Governments in India,* New Delhi: Oxford University Press, 2004.

II

Resource Base of the Panchayats

Financial Devolution for Rural Local Bodies (Panchayats) in Tamil Nadu

A Report on Status and Critique—May 2009

Constitution of India: 73rd Amendment-1991—Decentralization of Powers

Article 243G. Powers, authority and responsibilities of Panchayats—subject to the provisions of this Constitution the Legislature of a State may by law, endow the Panchayats with such powers and authority and may be necessary to enable them to function as institutions of self-government and such law may contain provisions for the devolution of powers and responsibilities upon Panchayats, at the appropriate level, subject to such conditions as may be specified therein with respect to—

- the preparation of plans for economic development and social justice.
- the implementation of schemes for economic development and social justice as may be enshrined to them including those in relation to the matters listed in the Eleventh Schedule.

Eleventh Schedule

The above Article 243G of the Constitution of India seeks

decentralization of powers vested with the State and Central Governments in respect of "Preparation of plans" and "implementation of Schemes" for economic development and social justice. It is in relation to these specific roles that an indicative list ("including those in relation to the matters listed") is included in the Eleventh Schedule of the Constitution.

However, in the beginning of the article, it makes apparent that subject to the provisions of the Constitution, the powers and authority endowed under this article does not in any way subtract from the executive and legislative powers of the Union and State Governments conferred under Article 246. Hence, the Powers listed in Eleventh Schedule has to be read with Article 246 and its related Schedule (Union List/State List/Concurrent List). In essence, the Central and particularly the State Government continue to hold both legislative and executive powers in respect of the powers to be entrusted to the Local Self-Government. Hence the State Government holds the complete executive powers in these matters and it is left to the State Legislature to decide on further devolution through its legislation and thereby in effect no restriction placed on the powers of the Legislature in this regard.

Further, the provision also dilutes the essence of its power by its own statement saying that "the Legislature of a State, may by law endow with the Panchayats such powers as may be necessary to make them function as units of self-government". Taking advantage of the word "may" in the said article, the state governments consider that devolution of powers and authority is purely the discretion of the State Government and it is not a Constitutional Mandate.

In case of Tamil Nadu, further devolution has been done by the below mentioned provision of Section 257 of the Tamil Nadu Panchayats Act, 1994.

> **"Section 257. Power, authority and responsibilities of Panchayats.**—Save as otherwise provided in this Act, the Government may, *by notification and subject to such conditions and restrictions as may be specified therein*, entrust to a Panchayat or any other Committee

> constituted under this Act with such powers and responsibilities with respect to the preparation of plans for economic development and sociai justice and also with such powers and authority as may be necessary to enable them to carry out the responsibilities conferred upon them including those in relation to the matters listed in Schedule-IV."

The above section says that "*the Government may, by notification and subject to such conditions and restrictions as may be specified therein, entrust to a Panchayat or any other Committee constituted under this Act with such powers and responsibilities...*" and it contradicts what is said in the Constitution.

What is done in Reality in Tamil Nadu?

It is now almost 16 years are over since local governance has come into existence in conformity with 73rd Constitutional Amendment in Tamil Nadu. However, not even Notification (as said in the 1994 TN Panchayats Act) has been issued on the devolution of powers and functions as per the above section. It has been claimed by the State through its Policy not that some powers have been given through executive orders, but these orders have not even been communicated to the three levels of Panchayats and the respective line department of the State properly.

In the year 1997, the State Planning Commission had come up with the recommendations on entrustment of powers, functions and functionaries to three-tier Panchayat System. But no action taken on the said recommendations (where the Planning Commission detailed out various powers and authority to be delegated to three-tier Panchayats) instead a High Power Committee headed by the Minister for Local Administration has been formed to study the recommendations of the State Planning Commission. Following the recommendation of this High Power Committee, the State Government issued a series of executive orders to various departments for taking suggestions and some role of the Panchayats for the implementation of various state schemes and "NOT ENTRUSTED ANY POWER OR AUTHORITY TO THREE-TIER PANCHAYATS". In actual terms no power has been given to Panchayats in Tamil Nadu for management and control of delivery of social services and basic needs and development functions like education, health, PDS, agriculture, land improvement, etc.

Some executive orders have been issued by the Rural Development Department even without notification. The functions delegated through these orders to Panchayats are mostly related to assisting in identification of beneficiaries for the schemes of various departments, and to advise the departments to carry out the schemes and programmes effectively. By not notifying these orders the State has given an impression to the officials of State Government departments that they need not take them into account seriously. The State officials know the difference between notification and executive orders. A notification has to be published for the consumption of the Public through Gazette. But in case of Executive orders it is meant only for officials. Hence, there is no public scrutiny on the implementation of the said orders with the result that no care was given to see that same role was devolved to the Panchayats in the execution of matters related to 29 subjects listed in the Eleventh Schedule of the Constitution of India.

A notification will have more legal force and validity than an executive order issued by government. Section 257 of the Tamil Nadu Panchayats Act requires the powers to be given by notification. The courts have held that a notification issued under the Act will have the same force as the Act. Under Section 262 of the Tamil Nadu Panchayats Act, all notifications issued under this Act have to be published in the Tamil Nadu Government Gazette and should be placed on the table of the Legislative Assembly. Hence the orders issued under this Act other than by way of notification will have no validity. The orders issued by the government giving powers to the Panchayats are not published in the Tamil Nadu Government Gazette. Hence the powers given to the Panchayats in Tamil Nadu by executive orders have no legal force.

The Supreme Court in ITC Bhadrachalam Paper Board and another *vs.* Mandal Revenue Officer, AP and others [(1996) 6 SCC 634] has held that the statutory requirement of publication of rules/orders in the Official Gazette is mandatory. The object of the publication in the Official Gazette is not merely to give information to the public also but to give final official confirmation to the rules/orders.

Existing Responsibilities of Three-Tier Panchayats as per TN Panchayats Act, 1994

Village Panchayats are given onerous responsibilities without adequate human resources and they are listed as obligatory and discretionary functions in Sections 110 and 111 of the Tamil Nadu Panchayats Act, 1994. The obligatory functions of Village Panchayats are:

- Construction, repair and maintenance of village roads.
- Construction, repair and maintenance of water works for supply of water for drinking, washing and bathing purposes.
- Light of public roads and public places in built up areas.
- Cleaning of streets and removal of rubbish.
- Construction of disposal of drainage water and its maintenance.
- Provision of public latrine and arrangements to clean public latrine whether public or private.
- Opening and maintenance of burial and burning grounds.
- Opening and maintenance of Public Distribution System.

Apart from this, the following discretionary functions are given to Village Panchayats:

- Planting and preservation of trees in the public roads.
- Lighting in public roads and public places in non-built up areas.
- Opening and maintenance of public market.
- Control of fairs and festivals.
- Opening and maintenance of slaughter houses.

- Opening and maintenance of reading rooms.
- Establishment and maintenance of TV sets etc.

Block Panchayats

The obligatory and discretionary functions of Block Panchayats are listed in Sections 112 to 119 of Tamil Nadu Panchayats Act, 1994. The important obligatory functions are:

- Construction, repair and maintenance of Panchayat Union roads.
- Establishment and maintenance of rural dispensaries and payment of subsidies to rural medical practitioner.
- Establishment and maintenance of maternity centres.
- Maintenance and expansion of elementary school buildings.
- Remedial measures considered with epidemic diseases.
- Control of fairs and festivals classified as Panchayat Union festivals.
- Veterinary relief.
- The establishment and maintenance of chaultries;
- Opening and maintenance of chaultries.
- The opening and maintenance of public markets which are classified as Panchayat Union markets;
- The maintenance of statistics relating to births and deaths;
- Improvements or agriculture, agricultural stock and the holding of agricultural shows;
- The promotion and encouragement of cottage industries; and
- Such other duties as the Government may, by notification, impose.

District Panchayat

The functions of the District Panchayat as enumerated in Sections 163 and 164 of the Tamil Nadu Panchayats Act are advisory in nature. They can only advise the government on all matters related to rural development.

Legal Provisions (Constitution and the Tamil Nadu Panchayats Act) Related to Financial Devolution for Panchayats Constitution of State Finance Commission (SFC)

Articles 243(I) and 243(Y) of the Constitution of India incorporated by 73rd and 74th Amendment Acts heralded a new era in the history of the Local Bodies by providing for the constitution of a State Finance Commission in all the States within one year from the commencement of the Constitution 73rd Amendment Act, 1992 initially and thereafter at the expiry of every five years to recommend devolution of funds to the Local Bodies.

The Central Government also asked the Central Finance Commission (CFC) to comment, on the quantum of Central Government funds to be devolved to the local bodies from Tenth Central Finance Commission onwards.

In conformity with 73rd Constitutional Amendment, Section 198 of Tamil Nadu Panchayats Act makes the State to constitute a Finance Commission every five years to review the financial position of the panchayats and to make recommendations with the following principles to govern:

(i) the distribution between the State and the Panchayats of the net proceeds of the taxes, duties, tolls and fees leviable by the Government which may be divided between them and allocation among the District Panchayats, Panchayat Union Councils and Village Panchayats of their respective shares of such proceeds;
(ii) the determination of the taxes, duties, tolls and fees which may be assigned to or appropriated by the Panchayats;
(iii) the grants-in-aid to the Panchayats, from the Consolidated Fund of the State:
    (a) the measures needed to improve the financial position of the Panchayats;
    (b) any other matter referred to the Finance Commission by the Governor in the interest of sound finance of the Panchayats.

Provisions Related to Levy and Collection of Tax/Non-Tax

Historically since the Local Boards Act in 1882, the Local Bodies in Tamil Nadu were empowered to levy and collect House Tax, Profession Tax, and Tax on Agricultural Land. Chapter IX—Sections 167 to 197 of the Tamil Nadu Panchayats Act deals with Taxation and Finance.

Resource Base for Panchayats

The resource base of Panchayats has been categorized as follows since its inception:

- Own
- Assigned
- Grants (SFC/CFC)
- State and Centrally Sponsored Schemes

In the categories of resources, Panchayats are legally exercising their decision making powers related to own and assigned revenues. But the grants the Panchayats receive from the State and Central Governments are tied ones with strict procedures and guidelines. Further is the fourth category of state and centrally sponsored schemes, Panchayats are considered as mere agencies to identify the beneficiaries and serves as support structure to the state departments for monitoring schemes at the ground level.

An Overview

The finance of local bodies even prior to the 73rd Constitutional Amendment was largely dependent on assigned revenues and the grants-in-aid from the state. In the new dispensation village Panchayats have some amount of own tax and non-tax revenue to meet their own needs. The Panchayat Unions and District Panchayats are in complete dependence on the state. Table 2.1 shows how the major source of revenue comes from grants and assigned tax revenues like local cess, local cess surcharge, stamp

Table 2.1: Resource Base of Rural Local Bodies—Post-SFC

Sl. No.	Name of Local Body	Grants and Assigned Revenue LC & LCS	Tax Revenue House Tax, Profession Tax, Adv.Tax	Non-Tax Revenue, D&O trade Building Fees, 2.C Patta, Fishery Rent	Remarks
1.	Village Panchayat	84.97%	11.42%	3.79%	Bulk of revenue expenditure is on maintenance of civic amenities and administration 45.10 per cent. In last 5 years Non-Tax Revenue increased from Rs. 32.35 lakhs to Rs. 165.58 lakhs.
2.	Panchayat Union	99.54%	0	0.46%	Administrative and maintenance expenditure—76.82 per cent.
3.	District Panchayat	100%			Advisory and Planning body Grant is the only revenue. SFC grant alone is Rs. 2998 lakhs.

Source: 12th Finance Commission, 2004.

duty surcharge. The village Panchayats which have industries, educational institutions, companies and government offices will get more income from the house tax and profession tax.

The above table indicates that the financial position of Local Bodies are highly dependent on the State in Tamil Nadu as almost all the functions and functionaries related to development and revenue are controlled by the State. Unless and until state devolves powers, functions and functionaries for the subjects listed in 11th Schedule of the Constitution of India, Panchayats cannot flourish as a system of Local Self-Governance.

Devolution of Finance from the State

In terms of devolution of finance from the state it is considered that the assigned revenue (taxes, non-tax levied and collected by the state for Panchayat) and the share from states's own revenue are the two major categories.

All the three State Finance Commissions so far have followed a formula of Pool A and Pool B which comprise assigned revenues and share from the state revenue resources respectively.

Table 2.2 shows that while Pool B (share from state revenue) is substantially increasing, the Pool A (assigned revenue) is unstable and almost not clear, while progressing further. This shows the changes in policy level decisions taken by the State Government in terms of devolving funds for Panchayats. Traditionally assigned revenues are considered as an exclusive source of income for Panchayats and hence they have enjoyed more powers in terms of taking decisions on the works to be undertaken. But gradually in the last 15 years, the state governments started reducing/abolishing/diverting the assigned revenue sources (which are explained in the separate title on assigned revenue below). Though it is said that the state compensates local bodies for the loss of this revenue it does not mean that these resources will be utilized independently by Panchayats as they had under assigned revenue [for instance, the compensation under the exemption of entertainment tax for films in Tamil name has been credited as "8229 00 200 AY 000D (Receipts)"—as per Government Order dated 05.08.2009].

Table 2.2: Devolution of Funds Prior to Devolution by First SFC (Before 1997)

Sl. No.	*Details*	*Grants*	*Assigned Revenue*	*Total*
1.	Rural	105.87	66.99	172.86
2.	Urban	179.51	235.88	415.39
	Total	**285.38**	**302.87**	***588.25**

* This does not include commitment of Government on Local Bodies Pension, which was about Rs. 60 crores for that year.

Table 2.3: Statement Showing Devolution of Funds under Pool A (Assigned Revenue) and Pool B (Sharing from State Revenue—8%)

Sl. No.	*Year*	*Pool A*	*Pool B*	*Total*
1.	1997-98	295.1	612.56	907.66
2.	1998-99	364.91	792.94	1157.9
3.	1999-2000 (Actuals)	391.96	805.19	1197.2
4.	2000-01 (Budget Estimate)	298.09	1036.41	1334.50*
5.	2001-02	453.37	407.60**	860.97
6.	2002-03	535.67***	1331.44	1867.11
7.	2003-04	502.80***	1269.67	1772.47
8.	2004-05	394.19***	1766.73	2160.92
9.	2005-06 (RE)	NA	1715.09	
10.	2006-07 (RBE)	NA	2111.66	

* This include commitment of Government on Local Bodies Pension.
** Owing to resource crunch, a portion of the devolution has been adjusted in 2002-03.
*** Local Cess and Local Cess Surcharge Remission/No adjustment.
Source: State Budget documents/SFC Reports.

Even though the First State Finance Commission has recommended for the increase in devolution percentage at 1 per cent every year from 8 per cent to 12 per cent for the years 1997-98 to 2001-02 respectively, the Government has frozen the percentage at 8 per cent for all the five years owing to resource crunch.

Further, second SFC has recommended only 8 per cent for all 5 years of the term. Only in 2007-08, financial year 1 per cent increase was made in the share of SFC grant as per the recommendation of third SFC.

For 2009-10, the allocation is at 9.5 per cent of the State's own tax revenues to the rural and urban local bodies. It is promised that the percentage of devolution will be progressively increased to 10 per cent within the award period of the third State Finance Commission (2007-08 to 2011-12). The ratio of the shares of rural and urban local bodies will be 58:42 as before. Since Village Panchayats are entrusted with most of the basic functions such as maintenance of village roads and streets, drinking water supply, street lights, sanitation and solid waste management and they are also the largest in number (12,620), the allocation for the rural local bodies is shared in the ratio 60:32:8 among Village Panchayats, Panchayat Union Councils and the District Panchayats from the year 2007-08 onwards.

Excerpts from Third State Finance Commission Report (2006)

State's Own Tax Revenue

(i) The State's Own Tax Revenue shows a trend growth rate ranging from 6 per cent in 2001-02 to 21 per cent in 2004-05. Sales Tax and State Excise accounts for 67 per cent and 13 per cent respectively (2004-05) of Own Tax Revenue. Land Revenue decreased in 2002-03 and 2003-04 owing to the drought and the resultant remission of Land Revenue. Receipts from State Excise show a remarkable growth of 54 per cent in 2004-05 because of the new Excise policy involving TASMAC in the retail selling of liquor. Receipts under Stamps and Registration constitute 8 per cent of State's Own Tax Revenue. Despite the reduction in the rates of Stamp Duty and surcharge with effect from 21-11-2003, Stamp Duty fetched more revenue in 2004-05 owing to the revision of guideline value of properties. Transfer of

Entertainment Tax has been made as 'Deduct Entries' in 2004-05 as recommended by Second State Finance Commission. Agricultural Income Tax has been abolished with effect from 1-4-2004 taking into account the need to revive the plantation industry and also the precarious position in which the cost of collection exceeds the actual collections.

(ii) The State's Own Tax Revenue for the base year 2004-05 accounted for 16.78 per cent of the Total Receipts under Consolidated Fund (Revenue + Capital including loans, Contingency Fund and Public Account) and 68 per cent of Revenue Receipts. State's Own Tax Revenue as a percentage of GSDP for 2002-03 is 9.33 per cent which was acknowledged to be the highest in the Country by the Twelfth Central Finance Commission. The tax-GSDP ratio for 2004-05 is 10.25 per cent. Despite the reduction in the rates of Stamp Duty, abolition of Agricultural Income Tax and changed pattern of Entertainment Tax, the Revised Budget Estimate for 2006-07 shows an increase of 16 per cent over 2005-06 pre-actuals because of the higher level of buoyancy estimated under State's Own Tax Revenue, by the Government. Further, owing to the reduction in the percentage of share in Central taxes from 6.637 to 5.385 by the Eleventh Central Finance Commission, Tamil Nadu is reported to have suffered an overall loss of Rs. 1,293 crores. This major fiscal setback also added for the worrisome Revenue Deficit in the past years since 2000-01. However, this deteriorating Revenue Deficit had been revived to a tolerable level through various fiscal reform measures taken by the State Government. Pre-actuals 2005-06 shows a surplus of Rs. 309 crores under Revenue Account.

From the above analysis, though there is some initial fiscal pressure on the part of the State Government during late 1990s, its revenue account showing positive growth over the last 15 years. Hence, there is no logic in restricting the financial devolution towards Panchayats. Further, throughout the three terms Panchayats are only made to take care of the maintenance of basic amenities and new constructions proposed in the state and centrally sponsored schemes. There is no provision made both financially or legally to implement their own schemes and programmes evolved through gram sabha.

Income and Expenditure of Village Panchayats and Panchayat Unions

Prior to SFC devolution (share from total tax revenue of the State Government), the major source of income derived by Village Panchayats was assigned revenue of surcharge on Stamp Duty, Entertainment Tax, etc. which constitute 61 per cent of the total income. Though there is not much difference between receipt and expenditure, Village Panchayats could not take up capital works (providing better infrastructure) since the major portion of the expenditure is consumed by electricity charges and maintenance charges relating to street lights and water supply which constituted 65 per cent of the total expenditure whereas the capital expenditure is only around 12 per cent.

There is not much improvement even after SFC devolution passed on income as grants to Village Panchayats, as maintenance expenditure has increased three-fold due to increase in electricity charges and water charges due to TNEB and TWAD Board. Further there is deficit of -0.62 per Panchayat.

Table 2.4: Village Panchayats: Source of Income for 1996-97 (Pre-SFC Devolution Period)

Sl. No.	*Particulars*	*Average Amount per Panchayat (Rs. In Lakhs)*	*Percentage*
1.	Tax and ncn-tax	0.27	21.8
2.	Assigned Revenue	0.75	60.5
3.	Other Grants	0.14	11.2
4.	Miscellaneous reciepts	0.08	6.5
	Total	**1.24**	

Source: Computed.

Table 2.5: Source of Expenditure Details for 1996-97 (Pre-SFC Devolution Period)

Sl. No.	*Particulars*	*Average Amount per Panchayat (Rs. in Lakhs)*	*Percentage*
1.	General Administration	0.14	13.6
2.	Maintenance charge	0.69	64.14
3.	Capital expenditure	0.12	11.5
4.	Miscellaneous Expenditure	0.11	10.15
	Total	**1.06**	

Source: Computed.

Table 2.6: Break-up Details for Post-SFC Devolution Period (1999-2000): Source of Income

Sl. No.	*Particulars*	*Average Amount per Panchayat (Rs. In Lakhs)*	*Percentage*
1.	Own source including tax and non-tax	0.55	17.51
2.	Assigned revenue	0.82	27.17
3.	Grants	1.48	48.88
4.	Miscellaneous reciept	0.91	6.43
	Total	**3.02**	

Source: Computed.

Table 2.7: Break-up Details for Post-SFC Devolution Period (1999-2000)

Sl. No.	*Particulars*	*Average amount per Panchayat (Rs. In Lakhs)*	*Percentage*
1.	General Administration	0.55	15.14
2.	Maintenance charge	2.08	57.29
3.	Capital Expenditure	0.9	24.71
4.	Miscellaneous Expenditure	0.1	2.86
	Total	**3.64**	
	Gap	-0.62	

Source: Computed.

Further, Table 2.8 shows that very few Panchayats were able to meet their maintenance expenditure from their own sources. This shows that the own revenue of Panchayats needs to be improved a lot. Until then it has to depend on the state governments.

Table 2.8: Financial Status of Village Panchayats

Sl. No.	*Percentage of Maintenance Expenditure from Own Source*	*No. of Panchayats*
1.	Less than 30%	3910
2.	30-50	3407
3.	51 to 60	2628
4.	61 to 70	1412
5.	71 to 80	959
6.	more than 80	302
	Total	**12618**

Source: Second State Finance Commission Report 2002.

Income and Expenditure Pattern of Panchayat Unions

Further Panchayats don't have expertise or human resource for tax levy and collection. The house tax matching grant provided during initial period was a great boost to Panchayats to achieve the target and demand, but later it was omitted through an amendment of the Tamil Nadu Act 30 of 1999. As a result the state departments and the politicians ruling the state have more control over the functioning of the Panchayat system.

There has been a steep rise in the expenditure over the years since 2001 due to street lights and drinking water supply as well as increase in the establishment cost. The electricity board charged at the rate of Rs. 1.20 paise per KWH till March 2003 has increased the charges to Rs. 3.60 per unit. Later in 2008-09 budget period it has been reduced to Rs. 3 per unit due to the great pressure created by the Elected Representatives of Panchayats to the State Government. This charge of electricity for Panchayats in commercial rate it is a great injustice to the Village Panchayats who are rendering social and public obligations. Whatever minimum grant is given by the state has been adjusted for EB charges and Panchayats are left with meagre sources to meet the basic needs of the people.

Further, orders related to purchase of Street Lights (as and when government issues) and other maintenance equipments, greatly disturb the autonomy of the Panchayats even in deciding the basic resource needs of the people. Any violation on this has been considered as Audit Objection and Panchayat Presidents, who are also termed as Executive Authority of the Village Panchayat (as per TN Panchayats Act, 1994) have to face serious interrogations by the government officials and finally they are being removed from the position at the discretionary power of the District Collector who is the Inspector of Panchayats under Section 205 of the Panchayats Act. Removal of a representative elected by people in the hands of a Government Official is an act of mockery of democracy.

Panchayat Unions

The tables below indicate that out of the total income derived by the Panchayat Union, local cess surcharge, local cess surcharge matching grant, local education grant, local roads grant and land revenue assignment etc., constituted 88 per cent. But in the post-SFC grant devolution period the financial assistance pattern has been changed and the income from all above sources are dispensed with and assistance is given only from State Finance Commission devolution to Panchayat Unions.

Table 2.9: Panchayat Union: Source of Income for 1996-97 (Pre-SFC Devolution Period)

Sl. No.	*Particulars*	*Average amount per Panchayat Union (Rs. in Lakhs)*	*Percentage*
1.	Local cess surcharge and non-tax items	24.26	88
2.	Assigned revenue	3.2	12
3.	Miscellaneous receipt	–	–
	Total	**27.55**	**100**

Source: Computed.

Table 2.10: Source of Expenditure Details for 1996-97 (Pre-SFC Devolution Period)

Sl. No.	Particulars	Average Amount per Panchayat Union (Rs. in Lakhs)	Percentage
1.	General Administration	16.84	52
2.	Maintenance expenditure	11.83	36.6
3.	Miscellaneous expenditure	—	—
4.	Capital Expenditure	3.61	11.2
	Total	**32.28**	
	Gap	–4.8	

Source: Computed.

Table 2.11: Break-up Details for Post-SFC Devolution Period (1999-2000): Source of Income

Sl. No.	Particulars	Average Amount per Panchayat Union (Rs. In Lakhs)	Percentage
1.	Own source including tax and non-tax	6.52	11.99
2.	Assigned revenue	0.08	0.15
3.	Grants	47.76	87.86
4.	Miscellaneous reciept	—	—
	Total	**54.36**	

Source: Computed.

Table 2.12: Break-up Details for Post-SFC Devolution Period (1999-2000)

Sl. No.	Particulars	Average amount per Panchayat Union (Rs. in Lakhs)	Percentage
1.	General Administration	45.05	67.56
2.	Maintenance charge	16.44	24.66
3.	Capital Expenditure	5.19	7.78
4.	Miscellaneous Expenditure	—	—
	Total	**66.68**	
	Gap	–12.32	

Source: Computed.

The above figures indicate that out of the total income derived by the Panchayat Union, local cess surcharge, local cess surcharge matching grant, local education grant, local roads grant and land revenue assignment etc., constituted 88 per cent. But in the post-SFC grant devolution period the financial assistance pattern has been changed and the income from all above sources are dispensed with and assistance is given from State Finance Commission devolution to Panchayat Unions.

Even prior to the SFC devolution period, there was a deficit of Rs. 4.80 lakhs per Panchayat Union. This gap has widened to Rs. 12.32 lakhs per Panchayat Union in the post-SFC devolution scenario owing to the fact that the major portion of expenditure of 52 per cent in the pre-devolution period and 68 per cent of post-devolution period is incurred for General Administration.

The above analysis will show that while the income to the Village Panchayats has sharply declined due to reduction in the surcharge on stamp duty which is a major source of income and also due to non-adjustment of receipts legally due to the Panchayats, there has been a steep rise in the expenditure due to street lights and drinking water supply as well as increase in the establishment cost. The electricity board charged at the rate of Rs. 1.20 paise per KWH till March 2003 has increased the charges to Rs. 3.60 per unit. Later in 2008-09 budget period it has been reduced to Rs.3 per unit due to the great pressure created by the Elected Representatives of Panchayats to the State Government. This charge of Electricity for Panchayats is in Commercial Rate. It is a great injustice to charge commercially to the Village Panchayats who are rendering social and public obligations. Whatever minimum grant is given by the State has been adjusted for EB charges and Panchayats are left with meagre sources to meet the basic needs of the people.

Further, orders related to purchase of Street Lights (as and when government issues) and other maintenance equipments are greatly disturbing the autonomy of the Panchayats even in deciding the basic resource needs of the people. Any violation on this has been considered as Audit Objection and Panchayat Presidents, who are also termed as Executive Authority of the Village Panchayat (as per TN Panchayats Act, 1994) have to face serious interrogations by the government officials and finally they are being removed from the position at the discretionary power of the District Collector who is the Inspector of Panchayat under Section 205 of the Panchayats Act. Removal of a representative elected by people in the hands of a Government Official is an act of mockery of democracy.

Details of Revenue of Panchayats

1. Own Revenue

The major own source of Income of the Village Panchayats are house tax, professional tax and advertisement tax and other non-tax revenues like building fee, fee on dangerous and offensive (D&O) trades, etc. and assigned revenues, viz. surcharge on stamp duty, entertainment tax, cable TV, Local Cess, share from Mines and Minerals, etc.

The vehicle tax originally levied by the Panchayat as per Section 173 of the Tamil Nadu Panchayats Act, 1994 and the Local Roads grant as per Section 182 and house tax matching grant provided as per Section 183 of the Act were dispensed with. Now these incomes are supposed to be merged with State Finance Commission devolution of funds except land revenue assignment which is due to Panchayat Unions. In respect of the Panchayat Unions, the Act still provides for the payment of land revenue assignment grant as per Section 170, but this has not been paid from 1997-98 onwards.

The Third State Finance Commission had recommended that all fee collecting institutions like Nursery, Matriculation Schools, Tutorial Colleges, self-financed Engineering, Medical Colleges/ Dental Colleges, Para Medical institutions, Teacher Training institutions, Coaching centres etc. shall be subjected to House Tax. Further, in its ruling on the applicability of exemptions for the educational institutions from the levy of House Tax, the Hon'ble Madras High Court in Sriram Educational Trust and 45 Others *vs.* State of Tamil Nadu observed that the *"Rule 15(c) is in an unqualified term. There are no words of restriction attached to the portion dealing with educational purposes."*

The Government accepted the recommendation of the Third State Finance Commission that the properties belonging to self-financing unaided educational institutions shall be subjected to levy of House Tax by the local body and suitably amended rule 15 (c) of the Tamil Nadu Panchayats (Assessments and Collection of Taxes) Rules, 1999 *vide* G.O. Ms. No. 38 RD & PR (PR.1) Department, dated 05-03-2008. Hence, the said rule is no longer in an unqualified term and the amended provision enables the Village Panchayats to levy and collect House Tax on the buildings used by self-financing educational institutions and also from the Government-aided institutions which are conducting self-financing unaided courses. However, not all the village panchayats have such institutions.

Hence the own tax income for village Panchayats is only House Tax. As per the analysis of Second State Finance Commission on an average collection of house tax by the village Panchayat between 1996-2000 is about 70 per cent. House Tax collection has considerably increased, however, the withdrawal of house tax matching grant, which was provided by the State Government, has affected the Village Panchayats substantially to carry out their own planned programmes.

2. *Assigned/Shared Revenue*

At present, the following are the Assigned Revenue (Tax) provided for Local Bodies through the effect of Tamil Nadu Panchayats Act, 1994:

1. Local Cess/Local Cess Surcharge
2. Surcharge on Stamp Duty
3. Entertainment Tax

In addition to the above, the following are the Shared Revenue (Non-tax):

1. Mines and Minerals
2. Social Forestry Receipts
3. Fishery Rental
4. 2 C Patta trees

These taxes and levies are usually collected by the Government and assigned to local bodies. The Third State Finance Commission has observed that this assigned revenue is a part of the resource base of the local bodies and needs to be kept intact. But time and again, the resource base has been eroded by Government thereby depriving the local bodies their legitimate dues. The following are some of the instances:

- Reduction in Surcharge on Stamp Duty because of the Memorandum of Understanding signed with Ministry of Urban Development.
- Reduction in Entertainment Tax owing to change from compounding pattern to collection on admission basis.
- Amendment to Section 46 by Tamil Nadu Act of 41, 2008 inserting in Section 46: *"the President shall execute or implement all schemes, programmes or activities as may be entrusted to village Panchayat from time to time."* Thereby making the local government in the lowest tier the agent of the State instead of empowering their own planning and decision making process.
- Amendment made in the Tamil Nadu Panchayats Act for abolishing Local Cess Surcharge matching grant in the year 1999 (Section 180).
- Amendment made to Section 187 for removing 20 per cent allocation of Local Cess for Panchayat Union Education Fund. Instead, the allocation of resources to Panchayat Union Schools has been decided at the State level.
- Non-implementation of increase in Local Cess/Local Cess Surcharge as suggested by Second State Finance Commission and ordered by the Government.

Current Position on Disbursement of Assigned Tax Revenues to Panchayats

Based on the interim discussions of the Third High Level Committee, the Government apportioned the Assigned Revenues by issuing orders in G.O. Ms. No. 168 Rural Development and Panchayat Raj

(C4) Department dated 4.10.07 by which the Assigned Revenues (other than lease amounts and seigniorage fees on mines and minerals and proceeds from social forestry auctions) are pooled at the State level and apportioned to three tiers of rural local bodies. Previously it was collected at the Block level and apportioned to the Village Panchayats in that particular Block.

Accordingly, Government allocated Rs. 270 crores for Pooled Assigned Revenue for the year 2007-08. Out of this amount, Rs. 180 crores was released to all the Village Panchayats, Panchayat Unions and District Panchayats on population basis and Rs. 90 crores released to districts for priority schemes.

There is also provsion for:

> "Purchase of all movable items except equipments for Panchayat Raj Institutions and vehicles for Panchayat Union Chairpersons, Block Development Officers, Executive Engineers (Rural Development), and Assistant Executive Engineers (Rural Development) for supervision and monitoring of works of Panchayati Raj Institutions."

There is a specific amendment made in the Tamil Nadu Panchayats Act, 1994 in Section 169 recently in the year 2008. The below highlighted provisions of the Act, clearly show how the State Government is creating space for diverting the Resources legally to be devolved to the Panchayats for its own Schemes and Grants.

Table 2.13: Amendments in 1994 Act

Old provision in 1994 Tamil Nadu Panchayat Act	*New Amendment: Substituted by Tamil Nadu Act 11 of 2008 w.e.f. 21st February 2008.*
Section 169: Rules regarding collection of Local Cess, Local Cess Surcharge and Surcharge on the Duty on transfers of property. The Government may make rules not inconsistent with this Act,	[169. Orders regarding collection of Local Cess, Local Cess Surcharge and Surcharge on the Duty on transfers of property. The Government may, by notification,

(*Contd.*)

Table 2.13: (*Contd.*)

(a) for regulating the collection of Local Cess under Section 167, Local Cess Surcharge under Section 168 and surcharge on the Duty on transfers of property under Section 175;	(a) regulate the collection of Local Cess under Section 167, Local Cess Surcharge under Section 168 and Surcharge on the Duty on transfers of property under Section 175;
(b) for fixing the proportions in which the proceeds of Local Cess, Local Cess Surcharge and Surcharge on the Duty on transfers of property shall be distributed among Village Panchayats, Panchayat Union Councils and District Panchayats; and	(b) fix the proportions in which the proceeds of Local Cess, Local Cess Surcharge and Surcharge on the Duty on transfers of property shall be distributed among Village Panchayats, Panchayat Union Councils and District Panchayats and grant any amount from the said proceeds for the execution of specific scheme, project, programme or plan in any Village Panchayat, Panchayat Union Council or District Panchayat; and
(c) for deduction of the expenses incurred by the Government in the collection of Local Cess, Local Cess Surcharge and Surcharge on the Duty on transfers of property."	(c) deduct the expenses incurred by the Government in the collection of Local Cess, Local Cess Surcharge and Surcharge on the Duty on transfers of property.]

Table 2.14: Fund Flow: Pool A—Assigned Revenue

(*Rupees in crores*)

Sl. No.	*Year*	*Surcharge on Stamp Duty*	*Entertainment Tax*	*Local Cess*	*Local Cess Surcharge*
1.	2000-01	302.19	67.38	6.21	31.05
2.	2001-02	382.55	34.06	6.2	30.56
3.	2002-03	454.32	81.35	Remission — no adjustment	Remission — no adjustment
4.	2003-04	444.52	58.28	Remission — no adjustment	Remission — no adjustment
5.	2004-05	350.04	44.15	Figures not available	Figures not available

Source: Third SFC Report—September 2006.

(a) Local Cess and Local Cess Surcharge

Revenue Department collects the Local Cess and Local Cess Surcharge along with the Land Revenue under the same head of account, i.e. Land Revenue. Section 167 of the Tamil Nadu Panchayats Act, 1994 provides for the levy of local cess at the rate of Re. 1 on every rupee of land revenue realized in the State. The total amount realized from this source is distributed entirely to Village Panchayats. Similarly, Section 168 of the Act, provides for the levy of local cess surcharge at such rate which may be considered suitable but not less than Rs. 5 on every rupee of land revenue.

The Second State Finance Commission which went into the issue has recommended for enhancement of Local Cess from Rs. 5 to Rs. 7. While amendment to the Tamil Nadu Panchayats Act, 1994 is necessary for Local Cess revision, there is no need for any Act Amendment for revision of Local Cess Surcharge as it empowers levy up to a maximum of Rs. 10. The Government while tabling the Action Taken Report in the Assembly have accepted the recommendation for revision of Local Cess/Local Cess Surcharge and issued orders in G.O. Ms. No. 284, Fin (FCIV) Department, dated 12.08.2002.

No follow-up action was taken by Rural Development and Panchayati Raj Department to give effect to the recommendation.

Instead of adhering to the promise made in the assembly on the action taken report in the recent budget presentation for 2009-10, the Finance Minister announced the abolition of Local Cess and Local Cess Surcharge for the benefit of Farmers. This legal source of income for Panchayats has been abolished by the State Government even without consulting the Elected Local Government Representatives. The ruling party in the State claims this as a major achievement for the welfare of farmers during the Parliamentary Election in May 2009.

Budget 2009-10 Announcement—Abolition of Local Cess and Local Cess Surcharge

Under the existing system of land revenue collection, which has been in vogue for a long period, Local Cess, Local Cess Surcharge and Water Cess are being collected along with the land revenue. As this tax serves as proof of possession of farmers over their land holdings, hereafter only a nominal sum shall be levied as 'Land Revenue'. By simplifying the present cumbersome system, land revenue of Rs. 2 per acre of dry land as against an average levy of Rs. 15 per acre at present and Rs. 5 per acre of wet land as against an average levy of Rs. 50 per acre at present, shall be levied from the coming fasli year. Farmers shall not be burdened with any other levy such as Local Cess and Local Cess Surcharge. About 50 lakh farmers will benefit from this measure.

To implement the above policy decision, Sections 167, 168, 169, 176, 186(b) and 188(d) of Tamil Nadu Panchayats Act, 1994 were amended *vide* Tamil Nadu No. 12 of 2009 and the levy of Local Cess and Local Cess Surcharge was dispensed with no announcement made on the loss of income or compensation to be provided for Panchayats due to this policy pronouncement.

(b) Surcharge on Stamp Duty on Transfer of Property

Under Section 175 of the Act, provision is made for crediting the proceeds under surcharge on Stamp Duty to Village Panchayats. Stamp duty and surcharge on stamp duty on transfer of property is collected by the Registration Department and adjusted directly to the Local Bodies by the District Collectors on quarterly basis. A sum of Rs. 63.87 crores has been adjusted during 2005-06.

An amendment has been made in Tamil Nadu Panchayat Act, to pool the revenue collection under stamp duty surcharge at the State level and share between all three tier Panchayats. Previously the amount was collected in the Panchayat Village in the Panchayat Development Block as surcharge on the Duty on transfers of property pooled every year for the entire block and distributed among all the Village Panchayats in the block in proportion to the land revenue of the Panchayat Village.

The surcharge on stamp duty, which is the main and a substantial source of income to Village Panchayats has been drastically reduced from 5 per cent to 2 per cent in the year 2003 and 1 per cent in respect of mortgage of immovable property resulting in more than 60 per cent loss of income to the Panchayats from this source alone.

The Third State Finance Commission said that the Government should get the concurrence of the local bodies before effecting the reduction in rates of Surcharge on Stamp Duty as the quantum is assumed based on the present rates. If at all reduction is effected, the loss in income should be compensated based on the level of flow of transfer prior to reduction.

But no action has been taken on the above recommendation by the State Government so far.

(c) Entertainment Tax

Ninety per cent of the entertainment tax collected in rural areas is assigned to rural local bodies since 1997. This is shared between the Panchayat Unions and Village Panchayats in the ratio of 30:70. Third State Finance Commission (2006) observed this as the single largest source of assigned revenue for the local bodies. The Commission strongly feels that the local bodies should get their legitimate dues and on time.

Based on the recommendation of the First State Finance Commission, the Government have issued orders for transfer of 90 per cent tax proceeds to Local Bodies, as indicated in the action taken report to the Legislative Assembly in April 1997. But during interaction with officials by the Second State Finance Commission it was revealed that the transfer of 90 per cent of the tax proceeds is not effected as per the Government order but restricted to 65 per cent or in certain cases no adjustment is made by citing the non-amendment of Financial Code rules.

Even after the completion of second SFC period (2006), this amount was not adjusted on orders issued for the same in 2002. Besides dues from 1997-2002, the Third Finance Commission has identified this flaw and condemned the state for non-adjustment. It has also identified the non-adjustment of Rs. 34 crores from the period of 2002-03 to 2004-05.

The State Finance Commission (2006) observed this as the single largest source of assigned revenue for the local bodies.

The Commission strongly feels that the local bodies should get their legitimate dues and on time.

Table 2.15: Details of Non-Adjustment

Sl. No.	Local Body	Tax Entitlement	Tax Proceeds Transferred	Difference
1.	Municipal Corporations	162,12,84,974	162,12,82,974	Nil
2.	Municipalities	116,83,14,882	116,37,41,428	45,73,454
3.	Town Panchayats	45,81,69,762	45,80,07,545	1,62,217
4.	Village Panchayats	22,45,93,870	22,37,38,446	8,55,424
5.	Panchayat Unions	28,18,708	28,18,708	Nil

Source: Commercial Taxes Department.

No action taken by the State Government in this regard till this recent financial year of 2008-09.

Reduction in Entertainment Tax Rates

The Government have switched over from compounding pattern to collection on gross admission with effect from 4.10.2004. This has resulted in substantial fall in income under Entertainment Tax during 2004-05 and 2005-06, as could be seen from the figures furnished below:

- 2004-05—Rs. 54.23 crores
- 2005-06 (RE)—Rs. 38.50 crores
- 2006-07 (RBE)—Rs. 3.82 crores

Meanwhile the below announcement of the State without consulting the Local Bodies resulted in severe impact on the income source of all Local Bodies (both urban and rural). Within three years the income has steeply reduced from Rs. 54.23 crores to Rs. 13.82 crores.

Policy Note—Rural Development Department, 2006-07

With a view to encouraging Film Industry and promotion of Tamil Language full exemption from Entertainment Tax has been given with effect from 22.7.2006 to new films if the title is in Tamil. In this way the due share to local government has been curtailed through the decision of the government to please the film industry.

The Twelfth Central Finance Commission has also suggested that whenever any reduction in assigned revenue is contemplated, the local bodies should be consulted. The suggestion may be considered for adoption by the State Government. In case of decline in revenue to the local bodies due to change in the policy of the Government, local bodies should be compensated.

Also on the introduction of cable TV the income from Entertainment Tax has been reduced to a considerable extent. Originally the tax on exhibition of cable TV was levied by Village Panchayats, but showing the inadequacy in staff at Village Panchayat as a reason, the state government took over the levy and collection of Cable TV charges. But no compensation has been provided by the state government after taking over the levy of tax on cable TV services.

Non-Tax Revenue

(A) Water Charges

In Village Panchayats, water supply is almost all through public taps. Wherever house connections are given, deposit amount of Rs. 1,000 is taken and the user charges (i.e. water charge) at the rate of Rs. 30 p.m. is collected. The above system is based on a G.O. issued in 1999. As the water charge is a fixed sum, the Panchayats could not meet the Operation and Maintenance costs. Under the Combined Water Supply Scheme, Tamil Nadu Water Supply and Drainage Board is charging Rs. 3 per kilo litre for Village Panchayats and most of the consumption is not recovered. In fact, Twelfth Central Finance Commission has recommended at least 50 per cent recovery of the recurring costs in the form of user charges in respect of water supply. The income derived from Non-Tax including Water charges during 2002-03 to 2004-05 are as below:

Year	(Rs. in crores)
2002-03	3.04
2003-04	4.32
2004-05	7.87

This includes other levies like D & O licence, fees, fines, lease rentals etc.

(B) D & O Licence Fees

Section 159 of the Tamil Nadu Panchayats Act, 1994 empowers Village Panchayats to issue licence for D&O trade. The rates under D&O licence fee have not been revised. The First State Finance Commission identified 73 trades and suggested revised fee structure. But this has not been given effect resulting in loss of income.

(C) Fishery Rental

The Second State Finance Commission recommended for constitution of a committee consisting of President of Village Panchayat, Revenue Inspector and Inspector of Fisheries Department for the conduct of lease sale and to curb the practice of forming syndicate to under pitch the auction value. Besides, it has recommended that fishery rental in respect of M.I. tanks of Panchayat Union may be shared on 50:50 basis between Panchayat Unions and Panchayats. It also recommended that the proceeds of Fisheries in PWD Tanks should also be shared between or among all Panchayats covered in the tank area. The Government at the Secretaries' level meeting have accepted the recommendation in respect of Panchayat Union tanks among Panchayat Unions and Village Panchayats and also for 100 per cent utilisation of the proceeds relating to fishery rental relating to Village Panchayats but did not accept the recommendation relating to fishery rental in respect of PWD Tanks. However, no formal orders have been issued.

(D) 2C Patta Trees

The usufructs of avenue trees which are leased to Panchayats by

Highways are availed by Village Panchayats by auctioning them. The Second State Finance Commission which went into the issue of wind fallen trees has recommended for constitution of a committee consisting of Village Panchayat representatives, Panchayat Union Commissioner and Revenue official. Besides, it has recommended for conferring powers to Village Panchayats in respect of removal of dead trees. The Government have also issued orders. But no follow up action has been taken for constituting a committee and for conferring powers to Village Panchayats for removal of trees. Hence, the Third State Finance Commission reiterates the recommendation of Second State Finance Commission that

(i) The Constitution of a committee may be notified by the Inspector of Panchayats for auctioning of wind fallen trees in Village Panchayat area.

(ii) Powers may be conferred on Village Panchayats for removal and auctioning of dead trees for ensuring quick disposal of the trees and also to realize sizeable revenue to Village Panchayats.

(E) Social Forestry Receipts

There was no statutory obligation for sharing the Social Forestry Receipts till 1992 but the 73rd Constitutional Amendment Act, had assigned the Social Forestry and Farm Forestry to Rural local bodies under Schedule XI of the Constitution of India. Even before that the Government have realised that there is need to share the Social Forestry Receipts with the Panchayats on the ground that the trees and plantations are grown in local body land and hence issued orders in G.O. Ms. No. 592, Environment and Forests Department, dated 16.8.1989.

As it is a non-tax revenue, it has not been shared regularly with the Village Panchayats. In the District hearing, officials and elected representatives have pleaded for timely adjustment and also their lawful involvement. In fact the Social Forestry Receipts as on 2005 have been adjusted only up to 1995-96. Towards the end of the year, after the issue was taken by Third State Finance

Commission with the Principal Chief Conservator of Forests, the proceeds from 1997-98 to 1999-2000 have been ordered for transfer. Even while ordering the transfer, the Forest Department has directed to reserve 20 per cent for Forest Development.

The Second State Finance Commission which went into the issue has recommended for formation of a Committee with Village Panchayat President as member for conducting auction, sharing of proceeds after deducting the working expenses at 70:30 for Village Panchayats and Forests Department respectively and for monitoring the adjustment at State level. But the Government while issuing orders on the recommendations in G.O.Ms. No. 158, Rural Development Department, dated 14.10.2004 has not accepted for including Village Panchayat President as member in the auction committee and also for monitoring the transfer of proceeds at State level. However, the Government have accepted and modified the sharing of proceeds at 50:50 on gross basis.

This was contested by Principal Chief Conservator of Forests on the ground that Social Forestry plantations are sold every year on a 10-year rotation and the extent of plantations is gradually coming down. Moreover his department has been incurring Rs. 3.5 crores annually towards payment of wages to Social Forestry workers/plot watchers. He has also expatiated that some of them are being absorbed in the regular vacancies of Forest Department and it may take some more years to re-deploy all of them. Also some of them have got direction for payment of minimum wages and the issue is under Government scrutiny. Hence, the department pleaded for implementation of Second State Finance Commission recommendation on sharing.

In the above background, the Third State Finance Commission recommends the following:

(i) There should be a separate detailed head for apportioning the Social Forestry Receipts to Local Bodies.

(ii) There should be budget provision in each year's budget of the Forest Department for apportionment so that the department may adjust the amount within the financial year itself and any dues in the year which are left out shall be adjusted in the next financial year.

(iii) Social Forestry Receipts from 2000-2006 shall be adjusted in 2007-08 as per the formula recommended by State Finance Commission and ordered by Government in para 53(b) above.

(iv) For the award period of Third State Finance Commission the sharing of Social Forestry Receipts shall be 50:50 on the basis of gross proceeds as already agreed to by the Government. The Social Forestry Receipts from 2007 onwards shall be adjusted within the financial year itself and for any failure the department has to pay interest for the sharable revenue.

(v) As contemplated in the Constitution of India, the functions relating to Social Forestry and Farm Forestry may be transferred to local bodies to involve the elected local representatives in the development of the Social Forestry Scheme.

(F) Income from Mines and Minerals

The Mines and Minerals Act, 1957 is a Central Act and the State Government is framing rules for its enforcement. The quarry lease income from minor minerals derived from the above Act and Rules is shared with the local bodies. Previously it was with Revenue Department but subsequently it was entrusted to a separate department called Geology and Mining. The government also has the mandate to apportion the lease amount on Mines and Minerals to Village Panchayats and Panchayat Unions on 50:50 basis. In the year 1998, the state government had passed a specific government order for control and management of quarrying of minor minerals by Village Panchayats, but later it was withdrawn due to the objection raised at the Industries Department level through a court case. Second State Finance Commission also strongly recommended for implementation of these Government Orders. However, later, the government have taken over the mines and the quarrying of sand directly through the change in Policy decision. But no orders for disbursing the dues to the Local Bodies so far.

The Government in its Action taken report placed before the Legislature in April 1997 had accepted the recommendation for direct remittance to the Village Panchayats account of the local body share on minerals and also share from black granite but subsequently Government in Rural Development Department of the Secretariat have rejected this recommendation.

From 2.10.2003, the PWD is operating the sand quarries and the income has gone to Government Account. However, only the seignorage fees have been apportioned to local bodies. There also huge amount of pending due to the Village Panchayats and Panchayat Unions in settling the income the government raised through mines and minerals for the last more than 20 years. As of May 1997, the pending amount due for Panchayats is Rs. 125 crores for the previous five years. All three Finance Commissions constituted in the last 14 years have condemned this and insisted for disbursement of the pending amount, despite no transparency shown on the part of the government in settling the pending disbursals to Village Panchayats and Panchayat Unions.

Assigned Revenue has become Absorbed Revenue by the State

The assigned revenue is the legitimate share of Local Government Bodies as these revenues have been levied and collected from the common people, who belong to that particular constituency of Local Body. These revenues are from their own agricultural land, income from land purchase and entertainment establishments, etc. Since the state has got both technical and human resources for levy and collection of these incomes along with its own shares it was dealt by the bureaucracy at the District level.

But during the third term period of Local Bodies recently in the name of normalization the State has slowly and steadily absorbed the entire revenue of the Panchayats in its own hand. Further to gain their own political mileage the ruling party announced exemptions of these tax and non-tax revenues of Panchayats. By doing so the ruling government have gained double benefit of on one hand getting the popular support from farmers and film industry on the other hand in the name of compensation it is strengthening the hands of its own Rural Development Department to have more control over the Local Government System. The direct beneficiaries of this process are the ruling party and the bureaucracy, not the people or the elected local governance system.

3. *State Finance Commission Grant*

This is a grant that state government shares from its own tax revenue as per the accepted recommendations of the State Finance Commission. This grant is supposed to be untied grant and Panchayats has their own right to decide on the matters of expenses as per the decisions of their elected body and Gram Sabha.

From Table 2.16 it is clear that over the years, particularly during the Third Finance Commission period, the Government has come up with the more stringent measures by not allowing the Panchayats to utilize their legitimate share of State Revenue as per the decisions of their elected body. Instead, the State Government through its Rural Development Department and the District Collectorate retain the Power of taking decisions regarding expenses on SFC Grant, which is solely the resource of Panchayats.

- During the first SFC (1996-2001) and second SFC (2001-2006) period, the equalization and incentive, Reserve funds of only 15 per cent and 13 per cent respectively out of total 8 per cent share were retained with the State and the decision on utilization of these funds decided at the Rural Development Department level. But in the Third SFC, no such grant was reserved. But instead the whole of the share to the Village Panchayats (60%) have been taken under the control of State in the name of Infrastructure Gap Filling Fund (5%—out of which 50% for Anna Marumalarchi Scheme—State scheme, 50% for the discretion of State DRDA and District Collector),
- Remaining 55 per cent has been ordered to be paid for

Table 2.16: Orders of State Government: Grants from State Tax Revenue Excluding Entertainment Tax—As State Finance Commission (SFC) Grant

First SFC Grant	*Second SFC Grant*	*Third SFC grant*
1997-98 to 2001-2002	*2002-03 to 2006-07*	*2007-08 to 2011-12*
• 8% of the total tax revenue of the State excluding entertainment tax shared with Local bodies. • 15% of the above 8% revenue reserved for Eqaualisation and Incentive grant. The share between rural and urban local bodies is 60:40 • Remaining 85% shared as 55:45 between urban and rural local bodies. • Between three tier panchayats 10:45:45 ratio with District Panchayats, Panchayat Unions and Village Panchayats. • Income from stone quarries will be shared with local bodies. • House tax matching grant provided 3 times for the collected amount for the Village Panchayats. • 90% entertainment tax shared with Local bodies from 1997-98.	• 2002-03 to 2006-07- excluding Entertainment Tax, the share of State Tax revenue to local bodies will be 8%. • 87% of the above share will be divided between urban and rural local bodies on the basis of 58:42 respectively. • Remaining 13% will be equalization and incentive fund as done in First SFC period. • 47:45:8 is the ratio of share between village panchayat, panchayat union and district panchayat respectively. • 20% of SFC grant to be utilized for Capital purpose in all Village Panchayats. • Weightages for Horizontal distribution - Total population: 40% - Total Female Population: 40% - SC/ST population and people living in hutment areas: 20% (as per 2001 census) • Remaining 13% of state tax revenue sharing: 2:6:5 is the ratio of sharing between Reserve, Equalisation fund and Incentive funds. Reserve Fund 2% - Collector development fund (50%) - Rainwater harvesting (50%) (Collector will decide nature of rainwater harvesting work) Equalization Fund (6%) - Village Panchayats - 55 %(to meet debt/non-	The devolution of funds from State's Own Tax Revenue for the year 2007-08 will be at 9%. The devoiution of funds for the remain-ning years of the award period will be issued during the years to follow. The existing vertical sharing ratio of 58:42 between rural and urban local bodies shall be followed during the award period. The 58% share of rural local bodies in the devolution grant shall be distributed to Village Panchayats, Panchayat Unions and District Panchayats in the ratio of 60:32:8 respectively as recommended by the Third State Finance Commission. Village Panchayat's share of 60% of the Devolution grant allocated for payment of electricity charges to TNEB and water charges to TWAD Board. The Government shall reserve 5% from out of 60% share of the Village Panchayats from State Finance Commission devolution towards infrastructure gap filling fund. From out of the infrastructure gap filling fund, 50% shall be allocated towards Anaithu Grama Anna Marumalarchi Thittam and out of the balance 50% of the fund, a part of the amount shall be allocated to the Director of Rural Development for providing

(Contd.)

(*Contd.*)

First SFC Grant	Second SFC Grant	Third SFC grant
1997-98 to 2001-2002	2002-03 to 2006-07	2007-08 to 2011-12
	debt dues including electricity charges- panchayats will be decided by DRDA) - Panchayat Unions—45 % (for general administration and maintenance of roads, bridges, etc. unions will be decided by DRDA at state level) Incentive Funds (5%) - Village Panchayats-5% • Incentive funds will be released as matching grant for house tax on the basis of below formula - Collection 49% and below - 50% matching grant - Collection 50-74% - 75% of matching grant - Collection 75-90% - 100% matching grant. - Collection 91% and above – 125% of matching grant. • Transfer of 90% of Entertainment tax to Local bodies will continue • Stamp duty surcharge sharing formula weightage is based population basis 50% and collection basis 50%. - Collection charges will be retained by government 5% for urban and 3% for rural.	basic amenities in the Districts and the rest shall be allocated to the Districts based on population and the District Collectors shall utilise the funds for the same purpose. A minimum grant of Rs.3 lakhs to each Village Panchayat shall be provided as a measure of equalization, from out of the Village Panchayats' share of 55%. The balance amount shall be distributed based on population. Allocation of 135 crores from the SFC grant share to Panchayat Unions and District Panchayats for Panchayat Union School Renovation Programme. Management and Maintenance of Panchayat Schools are the responsibility of Panchayat Unions. The devolution grant shall be distributed within each tier of rural and urban local bodies based on 2001 population. The Government Orders on the basis to be adopted for distribution of funds among various Local Bodies would be issued separately by the respective departments in consultation with Finance Department. The 5% infrastructure gap filling fund for rural local bodies and 3% infrastructure gap filling fund and 2% Operation and Maintenance gap filling fund for urban local bodies shall be deducted from the devolution share of concerned tier of rural / urban local bodies. The balance devolution grant shall be released

(*Contd.*)

(*Contd.*)

First SFC Grant	*Second SFC Grant*	*Third SFC grant*
1997-98 to 2001-2002	*2002-03 to 2006-07*	*2007-08 to 2011-12*
		in 10 monthly instalments (from April to January) as per the existing procedure based on Budget Estimate provisions and the balance based on Revised Estimate provisions for State's Own Tax Revenue. Necessary funds shall be made available in the Budget of Director of Rural Development/ Commissioner of Municipal Administration/ Director of Town Panchayats. The orders relating to this would be issued by Rural Development and Panchayati Raj Department, Municipal Administration and Water Supply Department in consultation with Finance Department. Based on Accounts, if any adjustments have to be made, the same would be adjusted in the first quarter of the following next year Further, the arrears in devolution due to Urban Local Bodies shall be released in 3 annual instalments and the excess devolution made to Rural Local Bodies shall also be deducted in 3 instalments as on 1-4-2007. The pension commitment of local body pensioners shall be deducted from the devolution meant for the respective local bodies instead of respective tiers.

Source: GO (Ms) 225, Finance (Revenue Resources) Department dated 02.5.1997,
GO (Ms) 284 Finance (Finance Commission/IV) Department dated 12.8.2002,
GO No. 199, Finance (Finance Commission/IV) Department dated 25.5.2007

payment of electricity charges to TNEB and water charges to TWAD Board.

- The pension commitment of local body pensioners shall be deducted from the Devolution meant for the respective local bodies instead of respective tiers. This arrangement is affecting the financial wealth of Village Panchayats as there is no provision of government salaried employee deputed for Village Panchayats.
    - In this way, the State has taken over complete control over the share of resources for Village Panchayats.
    - It is also further ordered allocation of Rs. 135 crores from the SFC grant share to Panchayat Unions and District Panchayats for Panchayat Union School Renovation Programme. Management and Maintenance of Panchayat Schools are the responsibility of Panchayat Unions. But here the State has taken unanimous control over the decision uniformly for using the SFC grant without consulting with the respective Panchayat Union Council.

During the year 2007-08, the Government released an amount of Rs. 950.15 crores to the Village Panchayats, Rs. 506.75 crores to the Panchayat Unions and Rs. 126.69 crores to the District Panchayats, totalling a release of Rs. 1,583.59 crores.

Constitution of Fourth State Finance Commission

The Government have, *vide* G.O. Ms. No. 549, Finance (Finance Commission-IV) Department, dated 1.12.2009, constituted Fourth State Finance Commission to review the financial position of the rural and urban local bodies. In reviewing the financial position of the local bodies, the Commission has been directed to assess the financial position of the local bodies as on 31st March, 2010, and submit its report by 31st May, 2011 covering the period of five years commencing on 1st April, 2012.

Central Finance Commission Grant

CFC Fund Sharing Pattern (2006-07 First Half Year)

- Village Panchayats: 80 per cent
- Panchayat Unions: 20 per cent

All Central Finance Grants are tied. The Panchayats are given with strict instructions on the purpose of the grant, e.g. for capital work or maintenance. On the basis of the recommendations of the Twelfth Finance Commission (TFC), the Government of India allotted a sum of Rs. 870 crores for the period from 2005-06 to 2009-10. The guidelines issued by the Government of India stipulate that the TFC Grant should be used for improving the service delivery in respect of water supply and sanitation. The grant can also be utilized for repairs, rejuvenation and also operation and maintenance costs incurred for water supply and sanitation. The grant was shared between the Village Panchayats and Panchayat Unions in the ratio of 80:20. A sum of Rs. 174 crores was released for the year 2006-07. As the Village Panchayats have the responsibility of maintenance of street lights and sanitation, the Government decided that the entire 12th Finance Commission grants may be given to the Village Panchayats instead of giving to the Village Panchayats and Panchayat Unions.

From second half year of 2006-07, 100 per cent TFC allocation is given to Panchayats in the ratio of 80:20. The allocation to the Village Panchayats will be made on the basis of population. The Twelfth Finance Commission grants given should be utilized by the Village Panchayats entirely for the operation and maintenance costs of water supply, street lights and sanitation. Accordingly Government issued orders in G.O. Ms. No. 19, Rural Development and Panchayat Raj (C2) Department, dated 26.2.07. An amount of Rs. 174 crores was released for the year 2007-08.

Accounting System

(A) Village Panchayats

Initially during the first term in 1996, Village Panchayats were maintaining the following *three* Accounts:

1. Village Panchayat Fund Account
2. Village Panchayat Earmarked Fund Account
3. Village Panchayat Scheme Fund Account.

Later in 1997 as per the orders issued in the Government Order (Ms) No. 260, Rural Development Department, dated 9.12.1998. a fourth account in respect of deposits for water connection charges was ordered to be opened and, as such, fourth account is presently being operated in each Village Panchayat. In districts where the National Rural Employment Guarantee Scheme (NREGS) is in operation, a fifth account for the scheme has been opened in each Village Panchayat.

In the Third term of Panchayat Governance, the State Government has issued an order No. 146, RD (C4) department dated 17.8.2007 towards Rationalization of Village Panchayat accounts and the procedure for operation of the accounts.

As per the above order there shall be the following *three* Accounts in each Village Panchayat:

1. **Village Panchayat Fund Account**: The Village Panchayat Water Supply Account presently maintained as Account No. IV shall be closed and the balance amount available in the account will be taken to Village Panchayat Fund Account.
2. **Village Panchayat Payments to TNEB and/or TWAD Board Account**; (later in 1-12-2008 this account name was changed as Village Panchayat Payments to TNEB and/or TWAD Board Account **and/or District Collector Account,** through an order No. 180 RD (PR. I) Department.
3. **Village Panchayat Scheme Fund Account:** In Village Panchayats where NREGS is being implemented, **a fourth Account, Village Panchayat NREGS Account,** will also be operated.

1. Village Panchayat Fund Account

The receipts, which shall be credited to, the types of expenditure that can be incurred out of and the mode of operation of Village Panchayat Fund Account are described as under:

(A) Receipts

1. Revenue from all the components as mentioned in Section 188(1) of the Tamil Nadu Panchayats Act, 1994 (own tax, non-tax, assigned revenues from the state).
2. State Finance Commission Grant other than the portion released to the Village Panchayat Account No. 2.
3. Deposits received for drinking water supply house service connections.
4. Water charges and any other receipts related to drinking water supply including public contribution.

(B) Expenditure

All the day-to-day as well as urgent operations of the Village Panchayats are to be carried out through the funds taken out of the Village Panchayat Fund Account.

All the administrative expenditure, capital works, maintenance expenditure, other essential items and other duties of Village Panchayats which enable the Village Panchayats to function autonomously are to be carried out of the Village Panchayat Fund Account. Hence, the types of the expenditure that can be incurred out of Village Panchayat Fund Account are as follows:

(a) *Administrative Expenditure*
  - (i) Sitting fee for elected representatives
  - (ii) Travelling allowance for elected representatives of Cus and Audit
  - (iii) Pay and Allowances for Village Panchayat Employees
  - (iv) Pension contribution for Village Panchayat Employees
  - (v) Purchase of Stationery
  - (vi) Purchase of Forms and Registers
  - (vii) Building Rent
  - (viii) Expenditure towards Village Panchayat funds and Festivals
  - (ix) Contingency expenditure

- (x) Interest on Loans
- (xi) Any other Administrative Expenditure allowed from time to time

(b) *Capital Expenditure*
- (i) Construction of Building
- (ii) Formation of Roads
- (iii) Construction of Bridges and Culverts
- (iv) Water Supply and Sanitation Works
- (v) Other Capital Expenditure allowed from time to time

(c) *Maintenance Expenditure*
- (i) Maintenance of street lights
- (ii) Maintenance of hand pumps and power pumps
- (iii) Maintenance of village panchayat roads
- (iv) Maintenance of sports centres
- (v) Maintenance of library
- (vi) Maintenance of burial and burning grounds
- (vii) Sanitation works
- (viii) Any other maintenance expenditure allowed from time to time

(d) *Miscellaneous Expenditure*
- (i) Repayment of loan
- (ii) Refund of deposits
- (iii) Advances repaid
- (iv) Any other expenditure as permitted under Section 191 of the Tamil Nadu Panchayats Act, 1994
- (v) Funeral Grants as permitted by the Government.

Administrative sanction for the items of expenditure of this Account shall be accorded based on the norms and conditions specified in G.O. (Ms.) No. 286, Dated: 31.12.1999.

Audit

(C) Mode of Operation

The Village Panchayat Fund Account shall be jointly operated by the President and the Vice-President. In exceptional cases, where there is adversarial relationship between the President and the Vice-President, the Village Panchayat, may by a resolution authorize any member other than the Vice-President to operate the account along with the President, provided that the prior approval of the Inspector of Village Panchayats (District Collector) will be obtained for this.

2. Village Panchayat Payments to TNEB and/or TWAD Board Account

The existing Village Panchayat "Earmarked Grants Account" shall be renamed as "Village Panchayat Payments to TNEB and/ or TWAD Board Payments Account".

(A) Receipts

The details of receipts to be credited to the Village Panchayat payments to TNEB and/or TWAD Board Payments Account shall be:

1. Central Finance Commission Grants.
2. State Finance Commission minimum grant of Rs. 3 lakhs (or such other amount as may be prescribed by Government from time to time) for each Village Panchayat.
3. A part of State Finance Commission Grant (Other than the minimum grant) that may be released to those Village Panchayats where item Nos. 1 and 2 above are not sufficient to cover the payments to TNEB/TWAD Board.

(B) Expenditure

(i) Payment of electricity charges towards (a) street lights, (b) water supply systems maintained by the Village Panchayats, (c) buildings owned and maintained by the Village Panchayats, and (d) other items of electricity consumption as billed to the Village Panchayats.

(ii) Service charges payable to the TWAD Board for Combined Water Supply Schemes, if any.

(C) Mode of Operation

The account shall have to be operated only for the payment of electricity consumption charges to TNEB or the service charges payable to TWAD Board for the Comprehensive Water Supply Schemes if any (inserted in 2008 *vide* order No. 180: or for payment of surplus amount, if any, to the District Collector for redistribution of this amount to Village Panchayat Fund Account of the Village Panchayat concerned). So all cheques from out of the above account will only be pertaining to payment to TNEB and/or TWAD Board (and/or the District Collector). No self-drawal will be permitted. Collectors should instruct all the concerned bank branches in writing to make suitable ledger/computer entries to ensure that payments only to TNEB/TWAD Board are honoured for cheques pertaining to this account and no self-cheques or drawals based upon withdrawal forms are permitted for this account.

The words "for payments to TNEB and/or TWAD Board (and/or District Collector) only" should be printed/stamped on each cheque leaf of the cheque books issued for this account.

3. Village Panchayat Schemes Fund Account

(A) Receipts

1. Funds received under Centrally Sponsored Schemes (other than the funds received under NREGS).
2. Funds received under State Funded Schemes.
3. Funds received from any other Department/Agency/Board/Corporation for implementation of the schemes as may be prescribed.

(B) Expenditure

The funds credited into the Village Panchayat Schemes Fund Account will be spent for payment of the works pertaining to the Central Schemes/State funded and other schemes as prescribed.

(C) Mode of Operation

The above account shall be operated by the President and Vice-President of the Village Panchayats concerned. However, Collectors should instruct the concerned bank branches in writing to make suitable ledger/computer entries to honour the cheques signed by the President and Vice-President only if they are accompanied by the released orders in the form of proceedings of the B.D.O. (Village Panchayats) for the payment of works from the Village Panchayat Scheme Funds concerned. The cheque leaves should also be stamped with "To be paid only if accompanied by proceedings of the B.D.O. (Village Panchayats)" and no self-cheques or drawals based upon withdrawal forms are to be permitted for this account.

4. Village Panchayat NREGS Account

This account will be operated only in districts implementing NREG Scheme in Tamil Nadu. The receipts which shall be credited to, the types of expenditure that can be incurred out of and the mode of operation of Village Panchayat NREGS Account are described as under:

(A) Receipts

The receipts to be credited to the Village Panchayat NREGS Account shall be the funds received under NREG Scheme.

(B) Expenditure

The funds credited into the Village Panchayat NREGS Account will be spent for payment of the works pertaining to the NREG Scheme as prescribed.

(C) Mode of Operation

The above account shall be operated jointly by the President and Vice-President of the Village Panchayats as is done for the

Village Panchayat Funds Account concerned. However, Collectors should instruct the concerned bank branches in writing to honour the cheques signed by the President and Vice-President of the Village Panchayats only if they are accompanied by the release order in the form of proceedings of the B.D.O. (Village Panchayats) for the payment of works from the Village Panchayat NREGS Account concerned. The cheque leaves should also be stamped with "To be paid only if accompanied by proceedings of the Block Development Officer (Village Panchayats)" and no self-cheques or drawals based upon withdrawal form are to be permitted for this account.

All District Collectors are requested to communicate the changes introduced by this Government Order to all banks/Block Development Officer (Village Panchayats) and Village Panchayats in their District.

(B) Panchayat Unions are maintaining the following Accounts

The Commissioner of Panchayat Union (BDO) is the account holder of all accounts of Panchayat Union.

(1) Local Fund Deposit No. I (General Fund Account)
(2) Local Fund Deposit No. II (Village Panchayat Consolidated Fund Account)
(3) Local Fund Deposit No. III (Education Fund Account)
(4) Local Fund Deposit No. IV (Self-Sufficiency Scheme)
(5) Local Fund Deposit No. V (Nutritious Meal Fund Account)
(6) Local Fund Deposit No. X (NABARD (10%) Account)
    - The Accounts formats now maintained by the Panchayat Unions and the one prescribed by the Comptroller and Auditor General are on cash basis similar to the formats followed by all States uniformly.
    - The Panchayat Unions are run with meagre own resources and the major portion of receipts is by way of grants. The income from own sources in Panchayat Unions (rent, lease, toll collection, hire

charges, income from sandai markets, revenue from rest houses, swimming pools etc.) is less than 10 per cent of the total receipts of the Panchayat Unions.

- The Panchayat Unions are not vested with powers to levy taxes. Most of the Panchayat Union Councils depend on Government grant only.
- The state government *vide* G.O. No. 435, dated 4.11.2003 RD Deptt. decided that the accrual system of accounting need not be introduced till additional functions are entrusted to Panchayat Unions making them asset based institutions of their own. At present the Panchayat Unions do not have adequate assets of their own.

(C) District Panchayats are maintaining General Fund Accounts and Scheme Accounts. Chief Executive Officer of District Panchayats is the Account Holder of All Accounts in District Panchayats

Conclusion

The State Government in Tamil Nadu through its policies (irrespective of which party rules) in the last 14 years have communicated that Panchayats are the implementing bodies of the State Programmes and Plans and not Institutions of Self-Government as per the spirit of Constitution.

The State Government consistently violated and contradicted with the recommendations of all the three State Finance Commissions in terms of devolution of financial resources due to the Panchayats. Further, Panchayats are,facing more and more pressure and burden to meet the basic requirements of the people on the ground. Simultaneously the corruption process unleashed in the State Politics also has major reflection in the Politics of Local Governance.

The Rural Development Department of the State is made as the ultimate authority on the functions of Panchayats (especially Village Panchayats) and the autonomy of Elected Local Body

System has not been provided with any empowering process of decision making. Gram Sabha has become a ritual as most of the Powers related to land, common resources, education, health, PDS, agriculture, irrigation, etc. are vested with the State and whatever grievance raised by the people before the elected representatives, who have no control, authority, or management role in these functions have to petition the concerned line department. Now Gram Sabha had been made as venue for collecting petitions from the people and submit the same to the Department of the State Government. Hence, it is extremely important to engage in Policy level discussion on Devolution of Powers, Functions and the required Financial Devolution from the State and Centre constitutionally.

III

Role of Panchayats in Rural Development Schemes

Planning, Implementation and Financial Management

Introduction

Rural population constitutes 56 per cent of the total population of 62.11 million as per 2001 Census. There are 385 Panchayat Unions and 12,619 Village Panchayats encompassing 77,962 habitations in rural areas. Though the Panchayat Governance came into existence exclusively to look after the Rural Development processes, the State still controls the planning and implementation process of such Rural Development Programmes through its Department. At the District Level District Collector through District Rural Development Agency (DRDA) implements all the state and centrally sponsored schemes. District Panchayats are only the advisory body for such implementation. The State budgetary expenditure for Rural Development for the year 2005-06 constituted Rs. 291990.14 lakhs which accounted for 8.78 per cent of the total budgetary allocation. In addition to this, centrally sponsored schemes also implemented by Central Government through Rural Development Department of the State. As of 2008-09, following schemes are implemented by the State under Rural Development Department, under which Panchayati Raj Institutions are administered in the State.

State Schemes

State Schemes Implemented from the State Finance Commission Grant of Panchayats

1. Anaithu Grama Anna Marumalarchi Thittam (AGAMT)
2. Rural Infrastructure Scheme
3. Panchayat Union School Renovation Programme

State Schemes Implemented through Rural Development Department Directly through the District Administration

The following schemes are directly implemented by the District Administration and Directorate of Rural Development Department. The services of Village Panchayat Presidents have been utilized to identify beneficiaries and their support gained for implementation on the ground. No financial allocation made to Village Panchayats or Panchayat Unions or District Panchayats in this regard.

4. Member of Legislative Assembly Constituency Development Scheme (MLACDS)
5. Namakku Naame Thittam
6. Periyar Ninaivu Samathuvapuram

Apart from above Schemes the below mentioned Schemes are implemented through Rural Development Department in which Panchayats and its representatives have no major Role.

7. Mahalir Thittam by the Tamil Nadu Corporation for Development of Women Ltd. (TNCDW)
8. Rural Roads under NABARD-RIDF
9. Twelfth Finance Commission Road Works
10. Programme for Comprehensive Development of Dharmapuri and Krishnagiri districts

Centrally Sponsored Schemes

In the below mentioned Schemes, except MPLADS, PMGSY,

National Project on Biogas Development, RGRP, State Government also shares the revenue expenditure of all other Schemes.

- Indira Awaas Yojana (IAY)
- Sampoorna Grameen Rozgar Yojana (SGRY)
- National Rural Employment Guarantee Scheme—Tamil Nadu
- Swarnajayanti Gram Swarozgar Yojana (SGSY)
- Total Sanitation Campaign (TSC)
- Member of Parliament Local Area Development Scheme (MPLADS)
- Pradhan Mantri Gram Sadak Yojana (PMGSY)
- National Project on Biogas Development
- Rajiv Gandhi Rehabilitation Package (RGRP) funded by Government of India (for Tsunami Rehabilitation in Tamil Nadu).

Role cf Panchayat Governance in Implementation of State and Centrally Sponsored Schemes

Village Panchayats play the role of selection of beneficiaries and identification of places under the State and Centrally sponsored Schemes. Majority of these schemes are implemented directly by the Rural Development Department with the support of Panchayats. For all the 10 state schemes, the State Government through its Rural Development Department has the complete control over the Planning and deciding authority under these schemes instead of Panchayats. Village Panchayats are maintaining a separate bank account called Scheme Fund Account, which has been maintained at Village Panchayat level. The above account shall be operated by the President and Vice President of the Village Panchayats concerned. However, Collectors should instruct the concerned bank branches in writing to make suitable ledger/computer entries to honour the cheques signed by the President and Vice-President only if they are accompanied by the released orders in the form of proceedings of the B.D.O. (Village Panchayats) for the payment of works from the Village Panchayat Scheme Funds concerned. The cheque leaves should also be stamped with "To be paid only if accompanied by proceedings of the B.D.O. (Village Panchayats)" and no self-cheques or drawals based upon withdrawal forms are to be permitted for this account. However, the recent creation of Post BDO (Village Panchayats) and empowerment of those officers to have separate Bank Account is another violation of State Government on the power of Village Panchayats.

Out of 10 state schemes, Village Panchayats are directly involved in the implementation only under the following schemes as the funds allocated for the schemes are diverted from the State Finance Commission grant, which is solely the legitimate grants of Panchayats.

1. Anaithu Grama Anna Marumalachi Thittam (AGAMT)
2. Rural Infrastructure Scheme.

Utilisation of Panchayat Funds for State Schemes

For the implementation of AGAMT and Rural Infrastructure Scheme evolved by the State Government, the SFC grant, meant for the devolution to Panchayats has been utilized since 2006-07.

Prior to the release of legitimate share of SFC grants to Panchayats, the Government shall reserve 5 per cent from out of 60 per cent share of the Village Panchayats from State Finance Commission devolution towards infrastructure gap filling fund. From out of the infrastructure gap filling fund, 50 per cent shall be allocated towards Anaithu Grama Anna Marumalarchi Thittam and out of the balance 50 per cent of the fund, a part of the amount shall be allocated to the Director of Rural Development for providing basic amenities in the Districts and the rest shall be allocated to the Districts based on population and the District Collectors shall utilise the funds for the same purpose.

A minimum grant of Rs. 3 lakhs to each Village Panchayat shall be provided as a measure of equalization, from out of the Village Panchayats' share of 55 per cent. The balance amount shall be distributed based on population. Allocation of Rs. 135 crores has been made from the SFC grant share to Panchayat

Unions and District Panchayats for Panchayat Union School Renovation Programme. Management and Maintenance of Panchayat Schools are the responsibility of Panchayat Unions.

All the grants are tied grants and the District Collector and the Director Rural Development Department has been given the power of authority under this Scheme.

State Schemes in Detail (Guidelines are given as Annexure-I)

1. Anaithu Grama Anna Marumalarchi Thittam (AGAMT) (see Annexure IA for Detailed Guidelines of the State Government)

The Government launched the Anaithu Grama Anna Marumalarchi Thittam (AGAMT) from the year 2006-07 onwards. The scheme is meant for improving rural infrastructure. Every year one-fifth of the Village Panchayats will be allocated with financial assistance of Rs. 20 lakh and all Panchayats planned to be covered over a span of five years. Priority for selection of Village Panchayats is on the basis of low per capita income. The list of the Village Panchayats is prepared at the Block Development Office level and there is no compulsion to consult the Village Panchayat Council for such selection. Committee for selection and finalisation of the location of works has comprised of (a) Village Panchayat President concerned, (b) Block Development Officer (Village Panchayats), (c) Assistant Engineer (RD)/Block Engineer of the concerned Block, (d) Village Administrative Officer concerned.

As per the Government order this list is inviolable and cannot be modified under any circumstances.

The works taken up under AGAMT scheme funds can be broadly grouped into two categories, namely:

A. Compulsory works
B. Optional works.

One pond/oorani/tank per village, sports centre, library, burial ground/cremation ground, water supply are under compulsory work.

Cement concrete pavements, installations of street lights, fishpond, shandy are under optional works. The administrative sanction of the works has been accorded by the District Collector. The proposals for administrative sanction have to be signed jointly by the concerned Village Panchayat President, BDO (VP), Assistant Engineer (RD)/Block Engineer.

The District Collector and the Block Development Officer (Village Panchyats) maintain separate bank accounts for AGAMT at the District level and Block level respectively. The Block Development Officer (Village Panchayats) is directed to maintain a ledger with separate page(s) for each Village Panchayat to indicate the receipts and expenditure pertaining to the scheme.

Out of the Rs. 20 lakhs allocated for each Panchayat, Rs. 15 lakhs are for the tied component and Rs. 5 lakhs are for the untied component. However, this ceiling can be exceeded by drawing on a part of the untied component. The works not permitted under MLACDS will not be permitted under this scheme also. The Block Development Officer (Village Panchayat) is the Tender inviting officer. The Project Officer, (DRDA) is the tender inviting authority for the purchase of sports materials and furniture for libraries under this Scheme.

As per provisions of G.O. Ms. No. 186 R.D. & P.R. (SGS-2) Deptt. dt. 16.11.2007, in respect of works, the estimate of which is Rs. 5 lakhs and below, if there is no response for three consecutive calls or if the rate quoted by the contractors is exorbitant or unacceptable or if the works are abandoned midway by the contractor concerned, these may be entrusted by the District Collector to the Village Panchayat concerned for departmental execution. In respect of works, the estimate of which is more than Rs. 5 lakhs, if there is no response for three consecutive calls or if the rate quoted by the contractors is exorbitant or unacceptable or if the works are abandoned midway by the contractor concerned, these may be entrusted by the District Collector to the Village Panchayat concerned for execution by inviting open tenders.

Issues Concerned to Panchayats as Local Self-Governance

- AGAMT is a State Government Scheme and all the procedures and authority of sanction has been accorded with the District Administration and Rural Development Department. But the funds for the Scheme have been utilized from the State Finance Commission Grant for which the Panchayats holds the legitimate authority.
- Though Village Panchayats are maintaining separate bank account for Schemes, this Scheme empowers the BDO (VP) and District Collector to have separate bank accounts for administering the Funds.
- The Tendering process for the Works under the Scheme has been done at the Block Development Office level instead of Village Panchayat level. As a result transparency to the Village Panchayat Council and Gram Sabha on the tendering process denied.
- District Collector holds the authority of Administrative sanction and not the elected body. Top down approach has been adopted in implementing this scheme.
- If the rates quoted by contractors are exorbitant as per the government norm and if the work is abandoned midway by contractors then the work has been entrusted to Village Panchayats. This approach of the State Government is entirely demeaning the spirit and status of Local Governance in the State and paves way to corruption and misappropriation of funds.
- This scheme is entirely a duplicate of MLA area development scheme and there is no scope for Panchayats to evolve their own plan as per the need of the people.

2. *Rural Infrastructure Scheme (Detailed Guidelines in Annexure IB)*

A new scheme called 'Rural Infrastructure Scheme' has been introduced during 2008-09 *vide* G.O. Ms. No. 111 Rural Development and Panchayat Raj (SGS.1) Department dated 27-6-2008 to create basic infrastructure facilities like Cement

Concrete Roads and Buildings and to stabilize the assets created under National Rural Employment Guarantee Scheme.

Rs. 161493.46 lakhs has been allocated under State Finance Commission devolution for the year 2008-09. The ratio of allocation among Village Panchayat, Panchayat Union and District Panchayat are 60:32:8. Hence Rs. 96896.08 lakhs for VPs, Rs. 51677.91 lakhs for Panchayat Unions and Rs. 12919.47 lakhs for District Panchayats allocated. Rs. 350 crores has been allocated from this SFC devolution for this scheme from three-tier Panchayats. The allocation of funds to Village Panchayats, Panchayat Unions and District Panchayats are Rs. 200 crores, Rs. 100 crores and Rs. 50 crores respectively.

A minimum grant of Rs. 1 lakh is evenly distributed to all Village Panchayats and remaining are released based on their population. Similarly, for Panchayat Unions Rs. 20 lakhs and District Panchayats Rs. 50 lakhs has been allocated evenly. And the remaining funds in the respective tiers distributed according to the population.

The funds are credited to Village Panchayat Grant Account and Village Panchayats are allowed administering the same. However, detailed guidelines for the work to be taken and not to be taken are given through a G.O. Ms. No. 111 Rural Development and Panchayat Raj (SGS.1) Department dated 27-6-2008 and letter of Commissioner of Rural Development and Panchayat Raj and Panchayat Raj D.O.Lr No.331133/08 dt. 21-02-2009.

Issues Concerned to Panchayats as Local Self-Governance

- Village Panchayats are not allowed to plan their own scheme under this Fund, which is derived from State Finance Commission Grant (share of State revenue).
- As the estimate for taking up the works is very low as per the norms of the State Government, the elected representatives themselves are taking up the contract. As a result Panchayat leaders are becoming contractors rather than looking at resolving the issues and complaints of the people.

- All the funds allocated to the village Panchayats are tied funds and no flexibility for the Panchayat Council to take up their own priority work as per the need of the people.
- The accounting system and procedure for compliance of government orders are so complicated as every year the schemes and guidelines are changing in nature that an elected representative without any remuneration is unable to perform.
- Panchayat Presidents, who are elected representatives, are facing threat from the authorities for any minor non-compliance of the government order resulting in removal from the post of President by the District Collector.

Member of Legislative Assembly Constituency Development Scheme (MLACDS)

Member of Legislative Assembly Constituency Development Scheme is fully funded by the State Government. The main objective of the scheme is to take up works to bridge the critical infrastructural gaps in the Assembly Constituencies. Under this scheme, each MLA proposes the works that should be executed in his constituency. The District Collector gives administrative sanction for the works. This scheme was introduced in 1997-98 *vide* G.O. Ms. No. 84, Planning & Development (SG-2) Department, dated 14.07.1997. The allocation per constituency has been increased progressively. Lastly, it was increased from Rs. 1.2 crores to Rs. 1.50 crores *vide* G.O. Ms. No. 107, RD & PR (SGS.I) Department, dated 23.6.2008. Fifty per cent of the allocation (Rs. 75 lakhs) is earmarked for priority works specified by Government. Out of the remaining fifty per cent, MLAs can choose works of their choice not falling within the list of prohibited works which contains 14 types of works. The total allocation for MLACDS for 2008-09 is Rs. 352.50 crores.

During 2008-09, *vide* G.O. Ms. No. 107, RD & PR (SGS-1) Department, dt. 23.6.2008, the following items of works were held as priority under the earmarked component of Rs. 75 lakhs:

Works to be Taken up under the Tied Component of Rs. 75 lakhs

Since a large number of Anganwadi Buildings, Noon Meal Centres, Noon Meal kitchen sheds, especially, in urban areas and to a lesser extent in rural areas are functioning in dilapidated buildings, a phased programme of construction of new buildings for such cases have to be taken up. Hence each MLA should allot Rs. 10 lakhs for construction of Anganwadi Buildings, Noon Meal Centres, Noon Meal kitchen sheds from MLACDS in rural and urban areas and thus a total amount of Rs. 23.50 crores shall be made available for such works in the State. From the remaining amount of Rs. 65 lakhs of the Tied Component, the MLA can choose one or more of the following works for any amount according to his choice, subject to the overall ceiling of Rs. 65 lakhs. Upgradation of gravel/WBM Roads to BT standard.

- Renewal of badly worn out BT Roads (laying of BT layer only with filling up of potholes, if necessary).
- Laying of Cement Concrete Roads.
- Provision of buildings and/or compound walls for Government and Local Body hospitals, Primary Health Centre, Government Veterinary Hospitals and also for Government Schools, Adidravida schools, Kallar reclamation schools, Government colleges and Hostels.
- Provision of infrastructural facilities to Government special schools for the disabled and Government orphanages.
- Provision of additional burial grounds/cremation grounds as per AGAMT pattern in uncovered habitation in AGAMT Village Panchayats of 2006-07, 2007-08 and 2008-09.
- Construction of new houses and upgradation of kutcha houses as per IAY norms.
- Formation of new Public Parks.
- Construction of Public Toilets.

Works to be Taken Up under the Untied Component of Rs. 75 lakhs

Under the untied funds, that is, from the balance untied component of Rs. 75 lakhs, any work not falling within the 'prohibited works' can be taken up under MLACDS.

Negative List/Prohibited Works

The works which are (prohibited works) under the 'negative list' as per G.O. Ms. No. 107, RD & PR (SGS.I) Department, dated 23.6.2008 cannot be taken up under MLACDS unless specifically included under the exceptions.

Table 3.1: Member of Legislative Assembly Constituency Development Scheme (MLACDS)

Sl. No.	Year	Financial Allocation (Rs. in Crores)
1.	2000-01	180.95
2.	2001-02	192.70
3.	2002-03	192.70
4.	2003-04	192.70
5.	2004-05	192.70
6.	2005-06	235.00
7.	2006-07	282.00
8.	2007-08	282.00
9.	2008-09	352.50

The total allocation for MLACDS for 2008-09 is Rs. 352.50 crores.

4. Panchayat Union School Renovation Programme

There are around 22,000 Panchayat Union Primary Schools and 4,500 Panchayat Union Middle Schools which are being maintained by Block Panchayats. As per Tamil Nadu Panchayats Act, 1994, Section 112.e., the opening and maintenance and expansion or improvement of elementary schools, including the payment of grants to private managements in respect of elementary schools is the duty of Panchayat Union Council.

As per Section 187, a separate Panchayat Union Education Fund which has been created in which following receipts have to be credited:

- the land revenue assignment paid by the Government under Section 170;
- the Local Education Grant paid by the Government;
- such contribution from the Panchayat Union (General) Fund as the Government may decide to be necessary in any year in order to balance the budget of the Fund for that year;
- all fines and penalties levied within the jurisdiction of the Panchayat Union Council under the provisions of the Tamil Nadu Elementary Education Act, 1920 (Tamil Nadu Act VIII of 1920);
- all income derived from any endowments or other property owned or managed by the Panchayat Union Council for the benefit of elementary education;
- all other sums which may be contributed or received by the Panchayat Union Council for the purposes of elementary education.

Amendment made to Section 187 through Tamil Nadu Act 30 of 1999 for removing 20 per cent allocation of Local cess for Panchayat Union Education Fund. Instead, the allocation of resources to Panchayat Union Schools has been decided at the State level. This amendment has been made after the policy decision of the government to pool the assigned revenues of the Panchayats at the State level instead of Block level. The repair and renovation of school buildings were taken up under this new scheme which was sanctioned *vide* G.O. Ms. No. 94, Rural Development and Panchayati Raj (SGS4) Department, dt. 12.06.2007.

In 2007-08, an allocation of Rs. 135 crores from the SFC grant share made to Panchayat Unions and District Panchayats for Panchayat Union School Renovation Programme. However, the actual allocation made was Rs. 104.25 crores. Remaining Rs. 30.75 crores was allocated along with the Rs. 60 crores allocation, which was announced by the State through Education Department Policy Note for the year 2008-09.

5. Namakku Naame Thittam (Detailed Guidelines in Annexure IC)

This scheme announced by the State Government in the year 1997-98 (DMK was the ruling party during this regime). As per the announcement made in 1997, 25 per cent of the funds needed for this scheme have been borne by the people as in cash or kind or labour. Initially Rs. 10 crores was allocated by the State in the year 1998-99.

The public contribution should be remitted by means of demand draft to the Collector in the name of "Namakku Naame Thittam". The contribution from Local Bodies, Universities or Public Sector Undertakings will not be accepted under this Scheme.

The guidelines issued under this scheme stated that any development work—construction, irrigation works, street lights, maintenance of all community assets, works related to departments like Adidravida, Tribal Welfare, Backward classes, Electricity, Highways, Health, Sports, Public works, etc. (which has to get the approval of concerned state department), Purchase of Furniture, Computers and accessories for Government and Panchayat Union Schools, Libraries and buildings for the use of the public can be taken. Separate Bank Account has been created at the District level and the District Collector is the holder of this Account. Panchayats are only involved in monitoring the implementation of the Schemes.

A District Level Committee comprised the following persons has been empowered to monitor and evaluate the scheme apart from village panchayats initiating discussion on the plan, implementation and evolution in the 3 Gram Sabha meetings.

- District Collector, who will be the chairperson of the Committee
- Project Officer—DRDA
- All MPs
- All MLAs

- Chief Officers in the District
- District Panchayat Chairperson
- Asstt. Director (Town Panchayat)
- Chairpersons of Municipalities, where Namakku Naame Scheme is being implemented
- Commissioners of Municipalities, where Namakku Naame Scheme is being implemented
- Chairpersons of Panchayat Unions
- NGOs involved in the implementation of the Scheme

In the year 2000-01, the State Government has increased the allocation of grant as Rs. 30 crores. During this period, the State also invited Non-Resident Indians living abroad to contribute to the Scheme.

In the year 2001-02, the scheme has been renamed as Village Self-Sufficiency Scheme and implemented till 2006 (AIADMK was the ruling party during this regime) and priority works taken up were:

- Rural Integrated Sanitary Complex for Women
- Establishment of Street Lights
- Construction of Buildings for Village Administrative Officers

Again in 2007-08, the name of the Scheme revived as "Namakku Naame" and fresh guidelines were issued with the allocation of Rs. 50 crores for the Scheme (though the demand was for Rs. 100 crores as per the estimate of Director, Rural Development Department).

6. Periyar Ninaivu Samathuvapuram (Detailed Guidelines in Annexure ID)

This Scheme has been introduced in the year 1997-98. Under the scheme, model habitations called 'Samathuvapuram' are established in rural areas in which all the communities expected to live with unity and brotherhood and share all basic infrastructure and amenities without discrimination. Government constructs houses and also provides other civic infrastructure in the habitation and the houses are allotted among the beneficiaries belonging to different communities at random. Initially, it was proposed that out of 100 houses allotted (each house of 5 cents of land area) were distributed between SC: 40, BC: 25, MBC:25, and OC: 10. if there is no availability of people as per this ratio in the vicinity of Samathuvapuram Village, the Director of Rural Development and Panchayati Raj, based on the recommendation of District Collector, is authorised to modify this ratio suitably without detriment to the spirit of Samathuvapuram. 40 per cent funds for the land acquisition has been allocated from Adi-dravidar/Tribal Welfare Department and 60 per cent from Backward and most Backward Classes Department.

The following persons shall comprise the Committee for selection of beneficiaries for Samathuvapuram:

1. Project Officer, DRDA, who will be the Chairperson of the Committee
2. Block Development Officer (Panchayat Union)
3. Tahsildar of the Taluk
4. President of the Village Panchayat where Samathuvapuram is located
5. Concerned VAO(s)
6. One member of Panchayat Level Federation of Women Self-Help Groups from the Samathuvapuram village

Each beneficiary under this scheme has been given Rs. 35,000 as grant for construction of houses.

In 1999, the State Government through its Public (Special A) Department order No. 4782 dated 6.12.1999 transferred "Periyar Ninaivu Samathuvapuram Scheme" from the Adi- dravidar and Tribal Welfare Department to the Rural Development Department. The Rural Development Department is responsible for monitoring all the works of Samathuvapuram. The public properties like Roads, Water Supply etc., of the Samathuvapuram Villages also are under the control of the Rural Development Department and the Department is responsible for their proper maintenance. (Detailed Guidelines in Annexure-ID).

Centrally Sponsored Schemes in Detail (Guidelines are given in Separate Annexure-II)

All the Centrally Sponsored Schemes are administered by the District Rural Development Agency (DRDA) in which no elected Panchayat Institutions have any control or role in Tamil Nadu. The funds for Indira Awaas Yojana, SGRY, SGSY, TSC and PMGRY are credited to Village Panchayats Scheme Fund Account. Panchayats cannot deviate from the stipulated guidelines provided by the Centre and State as these funds are tied grants. Only selection of the beneficiary and the area has been suggested by the concerned Village Panchayat through Gram Sabha.

The aggregate expenditure on major poverty alleviation programmes like SGRY, IAY and SGSY stood at Rs. 569.03 crores in 2005-06 as against Rs. 520.65 crores in 2004-05 with an incremental annual growth of 9.29 per cent. In the total expenditure of Rs. 569.03 crores incurred during 2005-06, SGRY accounted for 57.7 per cent followed by IAY (30.5%) and SGSY (11.9%). In 2005-06, Government of India shared 60.82 per cent of the total expenditure incurred on poverty alleviation programmes.

(A) Indira Awaas Yojana (IAY)

The Indira Awaas Yojana was launched as separate housing scheme from 1997-98 onwards. The basic objective of the scheme is to help construction of new dwelling units as well as conversion of unserviceable kutcha houses into pacca/semi-pacca houses to the marginalised sections of the society, especially houses to members of the Scheduled Castes/Scheduled Tribes, freed bonded labourers in rural areas and also to non-SC/ST Rural poor people who are living below the poverty line by extending them grants-in-aid. Selection of individual beneficiaries is left in the hands of Village Panchayats. District Administration decides the quantum of houses and the village panchayats. Government of India has also asked the States to earmark 15 per cent of the beneficiaries from amongst the minorities. New houses as well as upgradation of kutcha houses are being taken up under the scheme. It is funded by the Centre and the State in the ratio of 75:25. During 2005-06, 42,195 new houses were constructed with an allocation of Rs. 145.78 crores. Apart from this, 21,449 kutcha houses were upgraded with Central-State assistance of Rs. 27.57 crores.

From 1.4.2005 onwards, the unit cost of a new house has been fixed at Rs. 25,000 for ordinary soil and Rs. 27,500 for difficult soil. Based on the budget announcement of the Union Finance Minister in February 2008, this amount is likely to be increased by Rs. 10,000 and the unit cost raised to Rs. 35,000 for ordinary soil and Rs. 37,500 for difficult soil. Moreover, the State Government provides an additional amount for RCC roofing cost in addition to its matching share. With effect from 2006-07, the above RCC roofing cost has been raised from Rs. 9,000 to Rs. 12,000 per house. The minimum plinth area of a house should be 20 square metres. All new houses are provided with the toilets and smokeless chulhas. Beneficiaries undertake the construction with locally available materials employing low cost technologies. As the cost of construction of new houses has increased substantially, it has been decided to raise the RCC roofing cost from the existing Rs. 12,000 to Rs. 20,000 per house.

This, along with the increase in unit cost as announced by the Central Government will raise the total cost of an IAY house from existing Rs. 37,000 and Rs. 39,500 to Rs. 55,000 and Rs. 57,500 for ordinary soil and difficult soil respectively. A further subsidy of Rs. 1,200 out of Total Sanitation Funds is dovetailed to enable each beneficiary to construct a toilet in the IAY house.

Upgradation of Kutcha Houses

This can be taken up to a maximum of 20 per cent of IAY allocation. The unit cost is Rs. 12,500. During 2008-09, 69,239 new houses are likely to be constructed and 15,386 kutcha houses upgraded at a financial outlay of Rs. 400 crores, inclusive of the State Government's additionality of Rs. 138.48 crores towards the RCC roofing cost.

(B) Sampoorna Grameen Rozgar Yojana (SGRY)—Now Merged with NREGS (National Rural Employment Guarantee Scheme)

The primary objective of the scheme is to provide supplementary wage employment to rural labour for ensuring food security and improving the nutritional levels in rural areas. The secondary objective is creation of durable community assets and development of rural infrastructure. The State Government had fixed the minimum wage at Rs. 80 per day to the labourers engaged in works under this scheme. A sum of Rs. 251.33 crores was allocated for this scheme during 2005-06.

The district allocation is apportioned in the ratio 20:30:50 among the District Panchayat, Panchayat Unions and Village Panchayats. During 2007-08, this scheme has been implemented in 19 Districts only as it had already been merged with the National Rural Employment Guarantee Scheme (NREGS). This scheme came to an end on 31.3.2008 and the scheme is replaced by National Rural Employment Guarantee Scheme with effect from 1.4.2008.

(C) National Rural Employment Guarantee Scheme

The National Rural Employment Guarantee Act was enacted in September 2005. The National Rural Employment Guarantee Scheme was launched on 2.2.2006 and was initially implemented in six districts, viz. Cuddalore, Dindigul, Nagapattinam, Sivagangai, Tiruvannamalai and Villupuram from 2.2.2006 onwards and in four more districts, viz. Thanjavur, Tiruvarur, Tirunelveli and Karur from 1.4.2007 onwards. From 1.4.2008 onwards, the scheme was extended to the remaining twenty districts of the State.

The National Rural Employment Guarantee Act, 2005 (NREGA) guarantees 100 days of employment in a financial year to any rural household whose adult members are willing to do unskilled manual work. This Act is an important step towards the realization of the right to work. It is also expected to enhance people's livelihoods on a sustained basis, by developing the economic and social infrastructure in rural areas. The Village Panchayat will issue job cards to every registered individual. Payment of the statutory minimum wage and equal wages for men and women are the notable features of the scheme.

National Rural Employment Guarantee Scheme—TN under National Rural Employment Guarantee Act was formulated in G.O. M.S. No. 89, RD & PR (CGS1) dt. 2.8.2006 and published in Tamil Nadu Government Gazette Extraordinary No. 181 dt. 2.8.2006.

The cost of the scheme is shared between the Centre and the State in the ratio of 90:10. The Central Government will bear the following costs:

(a) The entire cost of wages for unskilled manual workers.
(b) 75 per cent of the cost of material and wages for skilled and semi-skilled workers.
(c) Administrative expenses, which will include, *inter alia*, the salary and allowances of Programme Officers and their support staff and work site facilities.
(d) Administrative expenses of the Central Employment Guarantee Council.

The State Government will bear the Following Costs

(a) 25 per cent of the cost of material and wages for skilled and semi-skilled workers.
(b) Unemployment allowance payable in case the State Government cannot provide wage employment within 15 days of application.
(c) Administrative expenses of the State Employment Guarantee Council.

Priority of Works

Taking into account the field conditions in Tamil Nadu, the works are being taken up in Tamil Nadu in the following priority:

(a) Formation of new ponds.

(b) Renovation of existing Ponds, Kuttais, Kulams, Ooranies, Temple tanks etc.
(c) Desilting of channels.
(d) Desilting and strengthening of bunds of irrigation tanks.
(e) Formation of new roads.
(f) Other water conservation/soil conservation measures/ flood protection measures.

Special Steps Taken to Ensure Successful Implementation of NREGS

On assumption of office in the month of May 2006, this Government noticed that the scheme had not taken off properly. This was evident from the fact that the expenditure made up to 31.3.2006 was only Rs. 3 crores and that works had been taken up only in 924 Village Panchayats out of a total of 3,830 Village Panchayats in the six Districts.

This Government was quick to identify the issues and bottlenecks that were responsible for the poor progress in the implementation of the programme and came out with a series of initiatives to address those issues and to remove the implementation bottlenecks.

As a result of the concerted efforts taken by this Government, a sum of Rs. 1,677.991 crores has been utilized and over 1,994 lakh mandays of employment generated up to 31.3.2009. About 82 per cent of the workforce comprises women and 59 per cent are Scheduled Castes.

Issues Concerned to Panchayats as Local Self-Governance in Implementing NREGS

Though the Centre's guidelines under the scheme provides several enabling provisions to Panchayats to ensure employment guarantee to the rural labour and engage in sustainable land use management through several works, the control and intervention of rural development authorities making the scheme as mere technical exercise. There is no input for developing a plan through participation of Panchayat Council and Gram Sabha for effective resource management of the Village and ensuring employment for all needy labourers.

The local guidelines and instructions proposed by the authorities for fixing up of wages and priority works are hindering the self-autonomy of Village Panchayats. As a result most of the Panchayats are not able to utilize the budget estimated to their Panchayats.

Most of the Panchayats in Tamil Nadu complain that the minimum wages fixed by the State (Rs. 80) has not been approved by the authorities stating the reason the duration of time.

Most of the common lands and water bodies are encroached by the dominant persons of the village, and in Tamil Nadu Panchayats have no legal support from police or revenue authorities to remove such encroachments. As a result they are not in a position to evolve plans for productive use of those land and water resources like production of food crops, fruit bearing trees, etc. Panchayats should be strengthened to remove encroachments from the common property resources like Poramboke lands, water bodies, etc. and preserve it for production of food crops, fruit bearing trees, and appoint local workers for maintenance of the same. This would add income generation for the Panchayat and ensure employment and food security for the local people.

(D) Swarnajayanti Gram Swarozgar Yojana (SGSY)

SGSY is the largest ongoing anti-poverty programme since 1999. The programme envisages organisation of the rural poor into Self-Help Groups for building their capacities, to manage their own resources and then to go for bank credit. Once the group attains the required maturity of handling larger resources, bank credit follows with subsidy. Initially, an amount of Rs. 25,000 is sanctioned to a group with a subsidy of Rs. 10,000 as Revolving Fund to augment the resources of the Group for undertaking micro credit activities. During 2005-06, Revolving Fund was released to 28,153 SHGs and Economic Activity Assistance was extended to 2,547 SHGs in the State. Another 1,421 individual beneficiaries had received Economic Activity Assistance. Further, a total of 96,591 SHG members were trained during the period 2005-06.

In order to ensure that there is a convergence of activities taken up under SGSY scheme, Mahalir Thittam (SHG project) and the Vazhundhu Kattuvom Project, the monitoring of SGSY scheme has been transferred to the Managing Director, Tamil Nadu Corporation for Development of Women, which was merged under Rural Development Department in 2007.

(E) Total Sanitation Campaign (TSC)

The Government of India has restructured the Comprehensive Rural Sanitation Programme with effect from 1.4.1999 and launched the Total Sanitation Campaign (TSC). The Total Sanitation Campaign, a centrally shared programme, was designed to create awareness among the people on sanitation and to improve the sanitary conditions in rural areas. During 2005-06, 613,824 works including school and anganwadi toilets, Integrated Sanitary Complexes for women, sanitary parks, toilet linked biogas plants, etc. were executed in the State at a cost of Rs. 54.55 crores. The sharing pattern between the Centre and the State and contribution in the case of Panchayat/beneficiary oriented works varied according to the nature of activity or work. Under this programme a total of 13,064 sanitary complexes were constructed in the State during the period 2001-06.

With effect from 1.4.2006, the sharing pattern between the Centre and the State is as follows:

(a) 80:20 for Information, Education and Communication (IEC) activities, administrative costs, and rural sanitary marts.
(b) 60:20:20 for individual household toilets and solid and liquid waste management and community sanitary complexes, with 20 per cent contribution from beneficiaries/Panchayats.
(c) 70:30 for School and Anganwadi toilets.

Nirmal Gram Puraskar

Towards supplementing the efforts taken under Total Sanitation Campaign, the Government of India initiated a scheme called Nirmal Gram Puraskar in June 2003 under which cash awards are given to clean villages. The new approach aims at maintenance of clean environment and open defecation-free Village Panchayat. The Village Panchayats with less than 5000 population are awarded Rs. 2 lakhs and more than 5000 population are given Rs. 4 lakhs as Nirmal Gram Puraskar, i.e. clean village award.

(F) Member of Parliament Local Area Development Scheme (MPLADS)

The basic objective of the Scheme is to fill in the infrastructural gaps in the Parliamentary Constituencies so as to ensure total development. A sum of Rs. 2 crores is allotted per Member of Parliament per year for taking up development works identified by the concerned MP. The District Collector gives administrative sanction for the works. The guidelines contain a 'negative list' of works not permitted under this scheme and also an illustrative list of works that may be taken up. Under the scheme, all maintenance works of any type are prohibited. Desilting of ponds, rivers, tanks, canals etc. are also treated as maintenance activities and cannot be taken up under MPLADS. In the case of Lok Sabha, the scheme is implemented in the districts falling within the constituency of the concerned MP. In the case of Rajya Sabha, the MP can suggest works in one or more districts within the State from which he is elected. As far as the nominated MPs are concerned, they can suggest works anywhere in India.

During 2005-06,3884 works were completed by expending Rs. 87.09 crores out of allocation of Rs. 114 crores. For 2008-09, an amount of Rs. 114 crores is allotted for works under MPLADS.

(G) Pradhan Mantri Gram Sadak Yojana (PMGSY)—Rural Road Connectivity

This is a 100 per cent centrally assisted scheme. The Government of India launched this scheme in December 2000 to provide all weather roads to all rural habitations with a population of 1000 and above by the year 2003 and to all habitations having a population of 500 to 1000 by the year 2007. Now, Government of India have extended time bound plan to upgrade rural infrastructure in the areas of irrigation, roads, housing, water supply, electrification and telecommunication connectivity under the Bharat Nirman plan using the PMGSY funds. As part of the Programme, Government of India planned to connect every habitation of over 1000 population or over 500 in hilly and tribal areas with all weather roads by the end of 2008-09.

(H) National Project on Biogas Development

This is a 100 per cent Centrally Sponsored Scheme which envisages provision of a subsidy of Rs. 2,100 to general category, Rs. 2,800 to SC/ST and small farmers and Rs. 3,500 to those in hilly areas for establishing bio-gas units. The entire cost of the scheme is borne by the Government of India. During 2005-06 an amount of Rs. 36.30 crores was disbursed as subsidy for establishing 1,593 bio-gas plants. The tentative allocation for 2008-09 is Rs. 62 lakhs.

Conclusion

All the State and Centrally Sponsored Schemes are directed towards building infrastructure and its maintenance, housing scheme and some irrigation works. Panchayats are not enabled to engage in taking up productive works which would serve people in sustainable manner like collective farming in common lands, recruitment of people for maintenance of village assets, etc. The role of Panchayats has been reduced to the minimum level in the process of implementing the schemes and programmes of the State and Central Governments. It is time to make a cost benefit analysis of the Panchayats. Panchayats have their own cost for their creation and functioning and the cost is to be linked with value of service delivery done by the Panchayats.

Conclusion

Everywhere in Tamil Nadu collectively Gram Panchayat Presidents declared that they wanted to resign their positions due to paucity of funds in Panchayats to meet the felt needs of the people and to manage the Panchayats. Further, they were under severe pressure from the officials to carry out the scheme targets but they were not given the needed power to take decisions at Panchayat level. Against this background, this study was undertaken. Further with aim of generating a report from the field for the 13th Central Finance Commission, first it was decided to look into the principles and framework of the state government on Panchayat Finance in Tamil Nadu through the policies, recommendations of the State Finance Commissions, Action Taken Reports, and steps taken by the State Government to implement the decisions taken by the State Government. All these aspects have been covered in the first article.

Primarily the resource base of the Panchayats have to be improved and streamlined. It means the taxing power of the Panchayats has to be strengthened. They should have their own resource mobilizing domain to augment their resource and otherwise local institutions or Panchayats will become expenditure institutions. Secondly, the taxing power should be well within the framework of public finance. Thirdly, both the Centre and State Governments have to share their resources meaningfully to the Panchayats commensurate with the responsibilities assigned to them. Fourth, Panchayats should be oriented to mobilize resources and manage the same perceptively to perform the assigned duties and responsibilities with a sense of responsiveness to the local populace.

With the above stated objectives Panchayat finance was analysed the financial status of the Panchayats in Tamil Nadu by conducting intensive field study. From the three articles included in this volume the following conclusions are derived. They are: First, the very basic definition of 'power' is being contested and confused in the government literature in Tamil Nadu. As per the definition of the dictionary one understands that it is the authority to influence or authority to decide. In Tamil Nadu context power means to help, assist, and advise the authority. If any one is asking about power devolution in Tamil Nadu, officials used to inform that the state government has given 732 powers to three-tier rural local bodies. How the officials calculate the number? is a question. It is nothing but the Government orders passed on different subjects based on the recommendations of the High Level Committees. In the Government orders it has been stated that the Panchayat Council or Gram Sabha is authorized to advise, facilitate, help, support the selection of beneficiaries and implementation of the schemes and programmes of the State and Central Governments. Beyond that there is no meaningful devolution of powers to Panchayats.

Further, the State Government has not taken cognizance of the poor financial conditions of the Panchayats. Over a period of time the financial flow has been reduced drastically and it is not being looked into by the State Government. Financial autonomy has been curtailed. Further the tax domain of Panchayat has also been reduced. Even statutory grants are arbitrarily decided by the State Government for its own scheme and thereby the autonomy of the Panchayats is questioned.

Though the State Government has constituted State Finance Commission, honestly the accepted recommendations have not been implemented. As a result Panchayat financial condition has become worsened. In the name of regularizing the accounting system, Panchayat discretion in spending money has been removed. There is no data generation mechanism at the ground which ultimately act as a barrier for proper decision making at higher level. Financial management system in a standardized form should be in place for official financial management. The State Government has violated many of the established norms of financial autonomy of the Panchayats. Further, there is no information flow to Panchayats from the perspective of resource allocation from each and every department to local body areas through the department exactly in time. As a result Panchayats are not in a position to track the Panchayat finance. While implementing the schemes and programmes of the State Government and Central Government there is no flexibility at the implementation level. Thus, at the ground, a new financial management system is necessary with a clearcut perspective to increase the resource base of the Panchayats. Moreover Panchayats should be given power to tax and spend. Panchayats should not be made as spending agencies. The State and Central Governments' share of resource to Panchayats has to be increased.

Annexures-I

Annexure IA

ANAITHU GRAMA ANNA MARUMALARCHI THITTAM—DETAILED GUIDELINES FOR THE IMPLEMENTATION OF THE SCHEME DURING 2008-09

Rural Development and Panchayati Raj (SGS.1) Department

G.O. (MS) No. 88, Dated 5.6.2008

Read

1. G.O. (Ms) No. 115, Rural Development and Panchayati Raj Department, dated 11.9.06.
2. G.O. (Ms) No. 97, Rural Development and Panchayati Raj Department, dated 13.6.07.
3. G.O. (Ms) No. 208, Rural Development and Panchayati Raj Department, dated 31.12.07.
4. From the Director of Rural Development and Panchayati Raj, D.O.Lr. No. 33430/08/AGAMT-1, dated 24.5.08.

Order

1. The Government have launched the Anaithu Grama Anna Marumalarchi Thittam (AGAMT) from the year 2006 onwards which aims at substantial mobilization of resources into one-fifths of the Village Panchayats each year and improvement of infrastructure in the State over the period of five years. Under this Scheme, in order to improve the basic infrastructure facilities in the Panchayats, priority has been given to the Village Panchayats in which the per capita income is very low. Based on this, the list of one-fifth of Village Panchayats in each Block has been prepared according to ascending order of per capita income

and improvement of rural infrastructure is being taken up over a period of five years since 2006-07 in these Panchayats.

2. In the Government order second read above, guidelines were issued to implement various components under AGAMT 2007-08. Subsequently, in G.O. 3rd read above and in Government letter dated 6.3.08, amendment have been issued for the guidelines for purchase of books and fixing qualification for appointing Honorary Librarians.

3. The Director of Rural Development and Panchayat Raj in his D.O. letter fourth read above has stated that the AGAMT Scheme will be taken up in 2,521 villages during the year 2008-09. Hence, at the rate of Rs. 20 lakhs per Village Panchayat, a total of Rs. 504.20 crores may be allocated for the scheme. In addition, 1 per cent of the allocation, i.e. Rs. 5.042 crores may be allocated for Information, Education and Communication (IEC) component and monitoring. Totally, an amount of Rs. 509.242 crores is to be allocated for AGAMT 2008-09. For this, an amount of Rs. 472.278 crores has been provided in Budget Allocation for 2008-09. The balance amount of Rs. 36.964 crores may be provided from out of the Infrastructure Gap Filling Fund, provided out of the share of Village Panchayats from out of State Finance Commission Devolution Fund. Further, he has sent revised detailed guidelines for implementation of AGAMT for the year 2008-09 for approval of the Government.

4. The Government have carefully examined the proposal of Director of Rural Development and Panchayat Raj above and decided to accept them and issue orders as follows:
   (i) The detailed guidelines for implementation of various components under AGAMT 2008-09 are given in the annexure to this order.
   (ii) The amount of Rs. 5.042 crores earmarked (1% of the total allocation) of IEC activities will also be utilized to monitor the quality of works through independent agencies and to give Awards to District

Collectors and Project Officers of District Rural Development Agencies for good work undertaken to implement AGAMT Scheme.

(iii) The balance amount of Rs. 39.964 crores (Rs. 509.242 crores—Rs. 472.278 crores = Rs. 39.964 crores) required for the AGAMT Scheme 2008-09 will be provided from out of the Infrastructure Gap Filling Fund provided out of the share of the Village Panchayats from out of the State Finance Commission Devolution Fund.

5. This order issues with the concurrence of Finance Department *vide* its U.O. No. 1651/FS/P/08, dated 2.6.08.

(By order of the Governor)

K. Ashok Vardhan Shetty,
Special Commissioner and Secretary to Government

Annexure

Guidelines for Anaithu Grama Anna Marumalarchi Thittam—2008-09 G.O.(Ms) No.88, Rural Development and Panchayat Raj, dated 5.6.2008.

The Government launched the Anaithu Grama Anna Marumalarchi Thittam (AGAMT) from the year 2006-07 onwards. The scheme aims at substantial injection of resources into one-fifths of the Village Panchayats each year and improvement of rural infrastructure in the State over a span of five years. Under this Scheme, in order to improve the basic infrastructure facilities in the Panchayats, priority has been given to the Village Panchayats in which the per capita income is very low. Based on this, the list of one-fifth of Village Panchayats in each Block has been prepared according to the ascending order of per capita income and improvement of rural infrastructure is being taken up over a period of five years since 2006-07.

2. Based on the ascending order of per capita income, the list

of Village Panchayats in each District/Block to be taken up under AGAMT during 2008-09 has already been communicated to the districts. This list is inviolable and cannot be modified under any circumstances. Each Village Panchayat would get a direct State assistance of Rs. 20 lakhs. Out of this, Rs. 15 lakhs is for the tied component and Rs. 5 lakhs is for the untied component. The permissible limits of expenditure under the tied component are indicated in G.O. (Ms) No. 97, Rural Development and Panchayat Raj Department, dated 13.6.07, and are reproduced below against the relevant components. It is clarified however that this ceiling can be exceeded by drawing on a part of the untied component. For example, the ceiling for the school sports centre component is Rs. 1.5 lakhs. However a school sports centre can be developed for Rs. 2 lakhs by taking Rs. 50,000 from the untied component of Rs. 5 lakhs.

3. Committee for selection and finalisation of the location of works

For each of the AGAMT Villages, a Committee consisting of the following members will be given the responsibility for the selection of the works and finalisation of the exact location of the works.

(a) Village Panchayat President concerned.
(b) Block Development Officer (Village Panchayats).
(c) Assistant Engineer (RD)/Block Engineer of the concerned Block.
(d) Village Administrative Officer concerned.

The Village Panchayat President is the person who possesses local knowledge and hence his views about selection and location of works should be given due weightage.

The BDO (VP) should ensure that the Scheme guidelines have been followed while submitting proposals for administrative sanction.

The Assistant Engineer (RD)/Block Engineer should ensure that the technical specifications are adhered to and the values of the proposed works have been correctly arrived at.

The VAO will help in identifying suitable sites for the proposed works with reference to Revenue records.

This Committee should visit each AGAMT Village, spending at least one day in each Panchayat. Since selection of the right works is the key, the Committee should not do a cursory job, but should visit all the habitations, meet with a cross-section of people including other elected representatives and SHGs, assess the infrastructural needs of the Village Panchayat and inspect all the proposed sites. The Assistant Engineer (RD)/Block Engineer must take the necessary measurements for preparing detailed estimates for works during this visit itself. The selected works should be got approved by a Special Grama Sabha convened for this purpose.

The administrative sanction of the works will be accorded by the District Collector. The proposals for administrative sanction should be signed jointly by the concerned Village Panchayat President, BDO (VP), Assistant Engineer (RD)/Block Engineer. The proposal for the administrative sanction should necessarily be accompanied by (i) the resolution of the Special Grama Sabha; and (ii) a map of the Panchayat Village and the various items of work to be taken up under the Scheme (together with the location of the Village Panchayat office) should be clearly marked on the map. The concerned Village Panchayat President, BDO (VP), Assistant Engineer (RD)/Block Engineer should jointly sign the map. Collectors and POs, DRDA should ensure that the proposals are not prepared by the officials, by-passing the Village Panchayat Presidents and the Grama Sabha.

The works taken up under AGAMT scheme funds can be broadly grouped into *two* categories, namely:

A. Compulsory works
B. Optional works

The guidelines for the above works are as under:

(A) Compulsory Works

There are five components under this category:

(A-1) One Pond/Oorani/Tank per Village

It should be undertaken at a cost of Rs. 3 lakhs to Rs. 5 lakhs out of the tied component. The minimum cost of Rs. 3 lakhs is prescribed to ensure that piece-meal work is not done; and instead, a composite work, including desilting of inlet and outlet channels, construction of bathing ghats and retaining wall, etc. is taken up. To select and carry out works under this component, the following guidelines should be followed:

(a) **Selection of pond:** A Pond/Oorani, which is predominantly used by the people of the village, should be accorded the top most priority. Private ponds/ooranis should not be taken up. Other things being equal, ponds/ooranis within the village should be given priority over the ponds, which are farther away from the village.

(b) **Taking up New pond works/Temple Tanks/MI Tanks:** Some Village Panchayats may not have a pond/oorani. In such cases, a new pond/oorani work may be taken up if land is available. If this is not possible, then Temple tanks/Minor irrigation Tanks available may be taken up.

(c) **Use of Machinery:** Unlike other Centrally Sponsored schemes, under this scheme use of machinery is permitted for rendering quicker and more thorough execution.

(d) **Design of work:** AGAMT pond works must have a distinctive design. Deepening of the pond should be taken up till the removal of the silt is complete. A minimum depth of 2 metres should be dug up to ensure substantial retention of water in the pond/oorani and further deepening of the pond may also be encouraged if there is a possibility of this as per the site condition. The dug-up earth should be deposited on the outer bank of the pond and consolidated to prevent erosion of the bund and also to avoid the desilted earth entering the pond again during rainy season.

A baby pond, which is half the length and half the breadth of the main pond, should be compulsorily dug up in the pond/oorani taken up under this scheme. If the pond is very large, the size of the baby pond may be decided according to the local conditions. The baby pond should be dug up to a depth of minimum 1 metre beneath the level of main pond. The four sides of the baby pond should be lined with random rubble masonry/rough stone packing to prevent caving-in when the pond is full of water. Baby pond is not necessary in case of M.I. Tanks.

Desilting of inlet and outlet channels of the pond/oorani should be taken up along with the desilting of pond/oorani.

(e) **Bathing ghat:** A bathing ghat, on the most widely used side, must be compulsorily provided. A channel from the baby pond may be extended to the bathing ghat steps in order to ensure availability of water at the footsteps of the bathing ghat even during the dry season.

(h) **Retaining wall:** Subject to availability of funds, one or more sides of the pond may be provided with retaining walls of random rubble masonry/rough stone dry packing.

(i) **Other facilities:** A light and a few concrete sitting benches may be provided along the bund of the pond based on the requirement of the site conditions.

(A-2) Sports Centre

(a) There are 2 types of sports centres

(i) **School sports centres:** For this component the ceiling under the tied component is Rs. 1.5 lakhs. This should be taken up only in Government or aided High/Higher Secondary schools having enough open space. It need not be taken up in the elementary or middle schools. The following facilities shall be provided (if not already available):

1. A volleyball court with all accessories.
2. A ball-badminton court with all accessories.
3. A tennis court for the girls with all accessories.
4. Football and hockey goal posts with kits and other accessories.

5. Cricket kits with mat and practice net.
6. Basketball court with accessories. Plain ground will suffice; concrete flooring need not be provided.
7. Long jump and high jump pits with accessories.
8. Javelin, discus, shot-put.
9. Pull-up bars, parallel bars, multiple sets of weights, dumbbells, bench press, etc.
10. Table tennis table with accessories.
11. Chess boards and Carrom boards (4 sets each).

(ii) **Community sports centres:** If the Government/aided High/Higher Secondary School is not located in the Village Panchayat, then a Community sports centre should be provided in a suitable Public land. For this, the ceiling under the tied component is Rs. 1 lakh. The following facilities shall be provided:

(a) A volleyball court with all accessories.
(b) A ball-badminton court with all accessories.
(c) A tennis court for the girls with all accessories.
(d) Long jump and high jump pits with accessories.
(e) Pull up bars, parallel bars multiple sets of weights, dumbbells, bench press, etc.
(f) Chess boards and Carrom boards (4 sets each).
(g) Seesaw, Slides and Swings for young children (2 sets each/per village).

(b) Site availability is the key factor in location of sports centres. Where no site or adequate site is available, the village community can always be persuaded to donate land for this purpose.

(c) Layout Plan: For each and every Sports Centre, a layout plan should be prepared based on the site condition. This is necessary to ensure that the equipments are not installed in a haphazard fashion. It should be ensured that the area meant for the practice of javelin, discus and shot-put throws should be in one end of the layout in such a way that any of the above missiles thrown do not injure the other players. Also, the location of the pull-up bars, parallel bars, seesaw, slides and swings should be such that these should not be abutting the boundary of the volleyball court or ball-badminton court, so as to be causing obstacle to the players playing these games. In addition, the layout plan for each Sports Centre should be realistically planned in order to ensure optimum usage for all players. The Centre should also be preferably laid in North-South direction so that the players do not face sun directly when playing.

(d) Purchase of Sports Materials: For purchase of Sports materials, a Model Bid Document will be communicated separately by the Director of Rural Development and Panchayat Raj.

(e) Repairs and Replacement of Sports Material and Sports Consumables: Government have permitted the Village Panchayats to spend up to Rs. 10,000 from the General Fund of the Village Panchayats towards repairs and replacement of sports materials and consumables such as balls, bats, nets, etc., in Sports Centres. This expenditure is applicable both to the Community Sports Centres and School Sports Centres.

(f) Display Board: A Display Board indicating AGAMT Sports Centre should be prominently displayed on the site. This board should also contain the total cost of the Centre, the sports items available on site and also the fact that Rs. 10,000 per annum is available with Village Panchayat for repairs and replacement of sports materials and consumables in the sports centre.

(A-3) Library

Site availability is a key factor in location of libraries. Where no site or adequate site is available, the village community can always be persuaded to donate land for this purpose.

To carry out works under this component, the following guidelines should be followed:

(a) Building

An existing public building preferably of at least 400 square feet plinth area should be identified for setting up the library. It should be close to the Village Panchayat office to facilitate easy monitoring. Where there is no public building available, if any suitable building is available on rent, it may be considered. If an existing building is not available then a suitable new building of Standard Type Design, not exceeding 400 square feet plinth area preferably close to the Village Panchayat office, may be constructed. In new buildings, bookshelves and lofts should be provided in the walls as far as possible. Article 243G, along with the XI Schedule of the Constitution of India and Section 112 of the Tamil Nadu Panchayats Act, 1994 provide for the power of Village Panchayats to open and maintain libraries/reading rooms in the villages. Hence, running of libraries comes within the function of the Village Panchayats and such a responsibility is independent of any other library being available in the village through the Local Library Authority or any other department. Also, the Village Panchayat Presidents cannot take up the supply of furniture and books to libraries run by the Local Library Authorities. Hence, it has been decided that the AGAMT library under the control of the Village Panchayat has to be set up in each village of the State.

The existing building selected for library may require suitable repairs. It is essential to ensure that the library is free from roof-leakage during the rainy season.

Buildings with asbestos cement sheet roofing should be strictly avoided. It should be ensured that such existing public buildings, which are now converted into libraries under AGAMT Scheme, should essentially have weathering course tiles on the roof-top to prevent leakage of water during the rainy season and consequent damage to books. Hence, necessary provision of funds should be made for providing weathering course tiles and other suitable repairs to such buildings. Also provision for closed windows should be provided instead of window-mesh to prevent rain-water intrusion.

(b) Furniture

A typical library constructed with the type design communicated by this office will have rectangular tables and PVC moulded chairs for the benefit of the people coming to the library. In addition, bookracks for placing the books, which open on both sides without glass or sliding doors, should be procured for keeping the books. The dimensions (length, breadth, width, etc.) of the table, book racks etc., should be carefully decided on a library to library basis depending on the size of the building available in each case. Wherever possible, the existing unutilized furniture may be used or contributions from the public may be invited for donating the furniture. The cost for furniture should not exceed Rs. 50,000 out of the tied component.

While procuring furniture for library building, it should be borne in mind that all buildings selected for libraries are not of uniform size. Furniture should be building-specific, which means the size of the building should be taken into consideration in determining the size of the furniture and space required for the movement of the public.

(c) Books

1. *Procurement of Books for Libraries*: The books required for the libraries will bc selected at the State level by a Committee of eminent personalities in this field. Calling for expression of interest for supply of books from publishers and dealers for AGAMT libraries and placing of orders will be done by the Director of Rural Development and Panchayat Raj, Chennai. The District Collectors will make the payments from AGAMT funds. New books for at least Rs. 50,000 shall be purchased for the library.
2. The District Collector should encourage donation of such second-hand books to the AGAMT libraries, which are good and useful for the readers. However, text-books and guides should be avoided.
3. *Magazines*: The money available under AGAMT funds is exclusively for the purchase of books and not for magazines and newspapers as such. However, the District's Collectors and the Project Officers should ensure that they get subscriptions of newspapers and magazines for 3 to 5 years from corporate houses, service

organisations such as Rotary/Lions Clubs and philanthropists for the AGAMT Libraries.

4. Books, newspapers and magazines available in the existing libraries such as Ayyan Thiruvallur Noolagam should be pooled for the AGAMT library.
5. The World Map, Map of India, Map of Tamil Nadu and the District Map should be displayed prominently within the library building. One quotation from Thirukkural relating to education or learning should also be painted on a wall of the library.

(d) Appointment of Honorary Librarians

AGAMT libraries are to be manned by Honorary Librarians. Honorary Librarians are to be appointed on contract basis initially for a period of two years, at a consolidated pay of Rs. 750 per month, to be paid out of the Village Panchayat's General fund. The Honorary Librarian should be appointed only once the library building is fully completed, furniture bought and books procured for the library. Detailed guidelines for appointing Honorary Librarians in Anaithu Grama Anna Marumalarchi Thittam Libraries are issued in G.O. Ms. No. 177, Rural Development and Panchayat Raj (SGS-2) Department dated 25.10.2007.

(A-4) Burial Ground/Cremation Ground

Every burial ground/cremation ground taken up under this scheme should be provided with:

(a) **Approach road:** A cement concrete pavement up to the entrance gate, in the case of burial ground, and upto the cremation platform for a length of 50 metres or less as per the site condition shall be laid under this scheme based on necessity..

(b) **Compound wall:** A brick compound wall without a gate covering the entire perimeter may be taken up under this scheme. If the perimeter is very large, at least the side having the main entrance should be compulsorily taken up and the other corners earmarked with Pre-cast Cement Concrete Pillars with strong foundation. Further pillars may be put up at suitable intervals on the other sides of the burial ground in order to make the boundary well earmarked. On no account barbed wire/chain link fencing should be provided.

(c) **Cremation shed:** It should be constructed by adopting the following indicative size and dimensions:

- It should be 12 feet long × 6 feet wide and the platform should be raised to a height of 2 feet.
- It should only have a RCC roof supported by four pillars and have chimney facilities on the roof. GI sheet/Asbestos cement sheet are strictly banned.
- Flooring of the platform may be of sand/earth/fire resistant bricks.
- The platform should have a 4 feet wide cement concrete pathway.
- This can be modified into a waiting shed in case of villages where cremation is not in practice.

(d) **Water facility:** A hand pump shall be provided in the burial ground/cremation ground. Provision of water supply through extension of pipeline and putting up of a tap at the burial ground should be avoided for the sole reason that water in many places will not be available at the public fountains at late hours when the burial/cremation normally takes place in the villages and putting up of water supply pipeline instead of a hand pump will be a wasteful exercise.

(e) **Lights:** Lights may be provided based on necessity. Since the maintenance of solar lights in remote areas in the villages is found to be difficult and also the solar light materials in isolated places are prone to thefts, the solar lights should not be installed in burial/cremation grounds.

Burial ground is a popular component of the AGAMT Scheme. In case of requirement of additional burial grounds within the AGAMT village, more number of such burial grounds/

cremation sheds can be taken up from the untied component of the AGAMT Scheme as per the discretion of the Village Panchayat.

(A-5) Water Supply

For this component under the tied component, a minimum of Rs. 1 lakh should be provided and based on needs, additional allocation can also be made.

(a) Repair of defunct bore well/power pumps/mini power pumps/public fountains can be taken up under this scheme.
(b) Repair of OHTs, which can be put to use can be taken up.
(c) Any other works such as flushing and fishing, which would help in restoration of the existing source, supply and distribution of water, can be taken up.

(B) Optional Works

The following optional works can also be taken up under this Scheme:

(B-1) Cement Concrete Pavements

For this component the ceiling under the tied component is Rs. 3 lakhs. As per G.O. Ms. No. 74, Rural Development and Panchayat Raj Department dated 11.7.2006, the cement concrete pavement works should be undertaken by following the norms:

Habitations with less than 500 Population	: Upto 250 Mtrs.
Habitations with 501-1000 Population	: Upto 750 Mtrs.
Habitations with 1001-3000 Population	: Upto 1500 Mtrs.
Habitations with more than 3000 Population	: Upto 3000 Mtrs.

Works should be proposed by observing the above norms in the AGAMT Village Panchayats.

(b) Guidelines for Selection of Works

(a) Pavements having residential units on both sides of the pavement should be given priority.
(b) Streets or lanes in low-lying areas prone to waterlogging during the rainy seasons should be given priority.
(c) If a part of a street has been covered with cement concrete pavement and a part is still uncovered then such uncovered streets should be taken on priority.
(d) If there are any EB/telephone poles in the middle of the street, they should be shifted to the edges before laying the cement concrete pavement.
(e) Piecemeal works may be avoided.

(c) Design criteria to be followed for Laying the Cement Concrete Pavement

(a) The riding surface of the cement concrete pavement should be laid by taking into account the floor levels of the houses in order to ensure that the surface run off does not enter into the residential units.
(b) Both sides of cement concrete pavement should be filled up with unscreened gravel as this avoids stagnation of water on both sides and prevent breaking of edges apart from preventing skidding of two-wheelers and pedestrians. Gentle camber may be provided so that the water may drain.
(c) Cross drainage provision must be given to avoid the water-logging and stagnation on the sides of the pavement.
(d) Dummy duct with a pipe provision may be provided wherever necessary.
(e) Expansion joints should be provided at an interval of about five metres (5m) with bituminous pad.

(B-2) Installations of Street Lights

(a) Need-based extension of streetlights in newer habitations, extension areas, Adi-Dravidar and Tribal habitations and IAY housing colonies may be taken up.

Additional street light poles in areas where the existing coverage is felt to be inadequate may also be taken up.

A flat rate of Rs. 9,500 per new pole for such works will be charged by TNEB after 13.3.2007 and so the practice of preparing detailed estimates in each case by TNEB has been given up. For selection of the works under this component the following guidelines should be kept in mind.

(a) Totally uncovered habitations/streets should be given priority.
(b) Among uncovered habitations/streets, priority should be given to those having more number of houses.
(c) A fluorescent tube light should be installed.
(d) Based on necessity, street lights may be extended to approaches to the burial ground, village tanks under use by the public, roads leading to sandy and other community infrastructures and in case of fishing habitations to the main road leading to the seashore.
(e) In remote areas/hilly areas, solar lamps could be considered.

(b) **Installation of Sodium Vapour lamps:** As per G.O. Ms. No. 74, Rural Development and Panchayat Raj Department dated 11.7.2006; the norms for installation of Sodium Vapour Lamp have been indicated.

Habitations with less than 500 Population	Upto 2 SVL per habitation
Habitations with 501-1000 Population	Upto 4 SVL per habitation
Habitations with more than 1001 Population	Upto 6 SVL per habitation

The Selection Committee should propose Sodium Vapour lamps in habitations in accordance with the ceiling prescribed in the G.O.

Within the ceiling prescribed, the top most priority should be given to the place having maximum congregation of persons in a village (which may vary from place to place) depending on the location of the community facilities such as bus stand, village shandy/fish auction hall, PDS shop, Panchayat office, rural sports centre etc.

DGS&D rates are available for Sodium Vapour lamps and fluorescent tube lights. Procurement should be made from DGS&D approved companies or their authorized agents.

(B-3) Fish pond

Fish ponds should generally be provided in all AGAMT villages. Only in such cases where the Assistant Director (Fisheries) and the Panchayat President jointly certify that there is no scope of undertaking a fish pond in the concerned village, this component of AGAMT scheme can be dispensed with. For the development of one pond under this component, a ceiling of Rs. 25,000 has been prescribed. To select and carry out works under this component, the following guidelines should be followed:

(a) **Identification of minor irrigation tank/pond for fish culture:** Based on the report of baseline survey on the facilities available in the AGAMT village, the minor irrigation tank/pond suitable for fish culture should be identified. This may preferably be done in the pond/tank other than the pond/tank taken up for improvement as per A (1) above.

(b) **Supply of fingerlings:** Quality fingerlings for fish culture may be obtained in consultation with the Fisheries Department.

(B-4) Shandy

This is an optional item of work. Only if the AGAMT Village Panchayat is already hosting a shandy attracting large number of persons from the surrounding villages, then depending on the number of shops that are usually put up during such shandies, the following works may be taken up:

(a) Permanent platforms may be put up in the place where shandies are held.

(b) Approach path, water supply, lighting facilities etc. shall be provided to such places.

(c) Place for parking bullock carts/vehicles may be earmarked.

(d) Only tiled/RCC roofing should be put up for the village shandies. Asbestos Cement Sheet roofing should be avoided.

4. Maintenance of Assets Created

All assets created under AGAMT scheme are to be maintained by the Village Panchayat concerned.

5. Works not Permitted under AGAMT Scheme

The works not permitted under MLACDS will not be permitted under this scheme also.

6. Dovetailing and Preparation of Village Plans

Apart from the schemes under the Rural Development and Panchayat Raj department, many schemes are implemented by other departments at the district level such as Drought Prone Area Programme and Wasteland Development Programme and other programmes of Agriculture Department, schemes through Horticulture Department, Veterinary and Animal Husbandry, Dairy Department, Sericulture, Highways and Rural Roads, Public Works Department, health camps by Health and Family Welfare department, Labour department, Social Welfare department and Education department etc. By this time, the list of the AGAMT 2008-09 villages should have been communicated by the Collector to all the other Heads of Departments (HODs) at the district level. If it has not been done so far, this may be communicated immediately. The district level heads should focus on these Village Panchayats and ensure that the schemes are effectively dovetailed to bring about all-round development of the AGAMT village. The indicative target allocation for each

AGAMT Village Panchayat after such dovetailing shall be Rs. 1 crore. It is clarified that schemes like free colour TVs, gas stoves, 2-acre land etc. shall not be included for this purpose.

Two booklets—one for the district as a whole and another for each AGAMT Village Panchayat—should be prepared to show the works taken up under various schemes after the dovetailing. The District-level booklet should be formally released at a function with the local Minister. Copies of the individual Village-level booklet should be furnished to the Village Panchayat Presidents concerned as well as the BDOs (Village Panchayats).

7. District Level Committee

For the purpose of dovetailing of schemes and activities of different district level departments in AGAMT villages as proposed above and for monitoring the progress, a District Level Committee will be formed. The Committee will meet once a month, take stock of the progress and problems, provide guidance to the implementing agencies and remain in overall charge of the programme implementation in the district. The District Committee will comprise the following:

1. District Collector: Chairman
2. Project Officer, DRDA: Member Secretary
3. Project Officer, Mahalir Thittam: Member
4. Divisional Engineer (Highways): Member
5. Divisional Engineer (Rural Roads): Member
6. Superintending Engineer/EE (TNEB): Member
7. Superintending Engineer/EE (TWAD): Member
8. Superintending Engineer/EE (PWD)/WRO Wing: Member
9. Executive Engineer (PWD)/Buildings Wing: Member
10. Assistant Director (Inland Fisheries): Member
11. District Sports Officer: Member
12. District Library Officer: Member
13. Chief Education Officer: Member
14. Deputy Director (Horticulture): Member
15. Deputy Director (Health Services): Member
16. Joint Director/Dy. Director (Veterinary): Member
17. Joint Director/Dy. Director (Agriculture): Member

8. Flow of Funds

The District Collectors shall maintain a separate bank account and the BDO (VP) shall maintain a separate bank account for the AGAMT scheme. The amount meant for the libraries and the sports components should be retained at the district level and the funds for the remaining components should be released to the BDO (Village Panchayats). There is no need to open accounts for AGAMT at the Village Panchayat level and it is enough if the District Collector and the Block Development Officer (Village Panchayats) maintain separate Bank accounts for AGAMT at the District level and Block level respectively. In order to prevent mixing up of funds meant for one Village Panchayat with that of another, the Block Development Officer (Village Panchayats) shall maintain a ledger with separate page(s) for each Village Panchayat to indicate the receipts and expenditure pertaining to the scheme.

9. Tendering Procedure

Mode of execution: BDO (Village Panchayats) is the tender inviting authority for all works other than the purchase of Sports materials, furniture for libraries and library books. For inviting and accepting tenders, the procedure prescribed in G.O. Ms. No. 203 R.D. & P.R. (PRI) Department dt. 20.12.2007 should be followed.

The Project Officer, DRDA is the tender inviting authority for the purchase of Sports materials and furniture for AGAMT libraries.

As per provisions of G.O. Ms. No. 186 R.D. & P.R. (SGS-2) Deptt. dt. 16.11.2007, in respect of works, the estimate of which is Rs. 5 lakhs and below, if there is no response for three consecutive calls or if the rate quoted by the contractors is exorbitant or unacceptable or if the works are abandoned midway by the contractor concerned, these may be entrusted by the District Collector to the Village Panchayat concerned for departmental execution. In respect of works, the estimate of which is more than Rs. 5 lakhs, if there is no response for three consecutive calls or if the rate quoted by the contractors is exorbitant or unacceptable or if the works are abandoned midway by the contractor concerned, these may be entrusted by the District Collector to the Village Panchayat concerned for execution by inviting open tenders.

10. Information, Education and Communication

One per cent of the total annual allocation will be earmarked for Information, Education and Communication activities pertaining to this scheme. This amount will also be utilized to monitor the quality of works through independent agencies and to give Awards to District Collectors and Project Officers of District Rural Development Agencies for good work undertaken to implement this scheme.

11. Documentation

The District Collector should document various processes of this Scheme implementation starting from selection of works to completion of works. Documenting the works before and after implementation and documenting deliberations, photographs and videos etc. will be prepared for comparison and impact of the scheme. Success stories of community-based infrastructure will be prepared from beneficiary point of view.

12. The Secretary to Government RD&PR Department may in consultation with Director of RD&PR, change any of the above guidelines based on the exigencies that will arise then and there.

K. Ashok Vardhan Shetty,
Special Commissioner and
Secretary to Government

Annexure-IB

BRIEF GUIDELINES OF RURAL INFRASTRUCTURE SCHEME G.O. MS. No. 111, RD. Deptt. Dated 27.06.2008

Undertaking of Cement Concrete Roads, Noon Meal Centres/ Kitchen Sheds, Anganwadis, Public Distribution Shops, Culverts/ Causeways, Cremation Sheds, Upgradation of Roads upto B.T. standard, Compound Walls for Schools, Extension of Street lights, Purchase of new motors for Drinking Water Supply in Village Panchayats, Construction of Overhead Tanks and similar other works which could be taken up under the erstwhile SGRY Scheme (and are not specifically prohibited here) have been permitted under the Scheme.

The following categories of works are prohibited to be taken up under Rural Infrastructure Scheme:

1. Taking up of works in urban areas.
2. Other Departmental works except erection of new Street Lights through TNEB.
3. Construction of office and residential buildings for the Central and State Governments, their departments, Government Agencies/Organizations, and Public Sector Undertakings.
4. All kinds of repairs, maintenance and renovation works.
5. Individual beneficiary oriented works such as houses, upgradation of kutcha houses, repair to houses.
6. Purchase of movable items and accessories.
7. Desilting of ponds, tanks, channels and rivers.
8. Laying of Metal road.
9. Construction of Drainage.
10. Construction of Community Centres.
11. Extension of Pipeline.
12. Construction of Library building.

13. Acquisition of land or payment of compensation for land acquired.
14. Reimbursement of expenditure on completed or partly completed works.
15. Any revenue or recurring expenditure like Electricity Charges and fuel.
16. All works involving commercial establishments.
17. Execution of work within the places of religious worship and on the lands belonging to or owned by any religious faith/group.
18. Construction of monuments, memorials, statues, idols, arch gates/welcome gates.

Execution of Works

Works taken up under the scheme should be executed through tendering process.

Funding

A sum of Rs. 350 crores has been allocated for the year 2008-09 for implementation of Rural Infrastructure Scheme.

Total Allocation for Rural Infrastructure Scheme 2008-09

1.	Village Panchayats	Rs. 200 crores
2.	Panchayat Unions	Rs. 100 crores
3.	District Panchayats	Rs. 50 crores
	Total	Rs. 350 crores

The funds have been allocated to the Village Panchayats, Panchayat Unions and District Panchayats based on the following criteria:

(a) Village Panchayats

Out of the total amount of Rs. 200 crores allocated to the Village Panchayats, a minimum grant of Rs. 1 lakh was released to each Village Panchayat (i.e. 12,618 × Rs. 1 lakh = Rs. 126.18 crores) and the balance amount of Rs. 73.82 crores has been released to the Village Panchayats based on their population.

(b) Panchayat Unions

Out of the total amount of Rs. 100 crores allocated to the Panchayat Unions, a minimum grant of Rs. 10 lakhs was released to each Panchayat Union (i.e. 385 × Rs. 10 lakhs = Rs. 38.50 crores) and the balance amount of Rs. 61.50 crores was released to the Panchayat Unions based on their population.

(c) District Panchayats

Out of the total amount of Rs. 50 crores allocated to the District Panchayats, a minimum grant of Rs. 50 lakhs was released to each District Panchayat (i.e. 29 × Rs. 50 lakhs = Rs. 14.50 crores) and the balance amount of Rs. 35.50 crores has been released to the District Panchayats based on their population.

During the year 2008-09, 33,705 works have been taken up at an estimated cost of Rs. 34,972.73 lakhs.

District-wise Works taken up details under Rural Infrastructure Scheme

Sl. No.	District	Allocation	No. of Works Taken up	Estimate Amount (Rs. in Lakhs)
1	2	3	4	5
1.	Kancheepuram	1569.34	1394	1569.34
2.	Tiruvallur	1385.31	1103	1385.00
3.	Cuddalore	1589.64	1310	1581.17
4.	Villupuram	2566.24	1785	2559.17
5.	Vellore	2074.11	2184	2074.00
6.	Tiruvannamalai	1935.30	1607	1935.30
7.	Salem	1430.41	1363	1430.10
8.	Namakkal	991.15	1009	993.40
9.	Dharmapuri	899.16	1465	896.78
10.	Krishhagiri	1106.77	1380	1106.77
11.	Erode	1259.21	1726	1276.90
12.	Coimbatore	1398.66	1264	1399.26
13.	The Nilgiris	275.09	232	275.09
14.	Thanjavur	1492.82	1416	1495.37

(Contd.)

(*Contd.*)

1	2	3	4	5
15.	Nagapattinam	1139.75	945	1137.94
16.	Tiruvarur	1019.14	966	1019.14
17.	Tiruchirappalli	1224.38	1018	1208.85
18.	Karur	582.15	489	586.71
19.	Perambalur	466.58	441	388.95
20.	Ariyalur	491.07	743	557.32
21.	Pudukottai	1259.87	1211	1259.87
22.	Madurai	1197.74	1141	1202.62
23.	Theni	496.51	555	496.38
24.	Dindigul	1099.10	1071	1099.10
25.	Ramnad	1005.86	916	1003.03
26.	Virudhunagar	1141.00	1523	1141.00
27.	Sivagangai	1005.58	935	997.41
28.	Tirunelveli	1337.95	1181	1337.90
29.	Thoothukudi	1047.86	901	1047.85
30.	Kanniyakumari	512.23	431	511.01
	Total	34999.98	33705	34972.73

Additional Guidelines

The guidelines issued for the implementation of Rural Infrastructure Scheme for the year 2008-09 will be followed for the year 2009-10 also, with the following changes: (Commissioner of Rural Development and Panchayat Raj and Panchayat Raj D.O.Lr No.331133/08 dt. 21.02.2009)

(i) Cement Concrete road works should not be taken for more than 1/3rd of the allocation to each Village Panchayat, Panchayat Union and District Panchayat.

(ii) Not less than 1/3rd of the allocation should be utilized for stabilization of NREGS works like construction of Bathing ghats, Retaining walls in the ponds, tanks, etc. It is also classified that:

- (a) Repair of sluice, weirs in the ponds/tanks taken up under NREGS are allowed to be taken under this Scheme.
- (b) WBM road works from earthen roads, formed only under NREGS are also permitted now in this Scheme.

Annexure-IC

NAMAKKU NAAME THITTAM—GUIDELINES FOR THE IMPLEMENTATION OF THE SCHEME FOR THE YEAR 2008-09

Rural Development and Panchayati Raj (SGS.1) Department

G.O. (MS) No. 87 Dated: 05.06.2008

Read

1. G.O. (Ms) No. 172, Rural Development and Panchayat Raj Department, dated 15.10.2007.
2. From the Director of Rural Development and Panchayat Raj, D.O.Lr. No.30525/NEDM.1, dated 24.5.08.

Order

In the G.O. first read above, orders have been issued for the revival of 'Namakku Naame Thittam' from 2007-08 and a sum of Rs. 50 crores have also been sanctioned for 2007-08. Detailed guidelines for the implementation of the scheme were also issued in the above Government Order. In the D.O. letter second read above, the Director of Rural Development and Panchayat Raj has sent detailed guidelines for the implementation of the 'Namakku Naame Thittam' during 2008-09 and requested the Government for issue of order.

2. The Government have carefully examined the detailed guidelines sent by the Director of Rural Development and Panchayat Raj and decided to accept them. Accordingly, the detailed guidelines for the implementation of 'Namakku Naame Thittam' during 2008-09 are given in the annexure to this G.O. and these guidelines come into effect immediately.

3. The Government have sanctioned a sum of Rs. 50 crores for the implementation of 'Namakku Naame Thittam' for the year 2008-09. Out of the amount of Rs. 50 crores sanctioned for the scheme, the Government direct that 25 per cent of the amount be retained at the Directorate of Rural Development and Panchayat Raj for sanction of special schemes by the Director of Rural Development and Panchayat Raj, and the Director of Rural

Development and Panchayat Raj is empowered to release the balance amount in two instalments to Districts as per population, and Collectors are empowered to release funds to rural and urban areas on priority basis of works from the funds released to the districts.

4. As entrusting the works without calling tenders is against the sprit of Tamil Nadu Transparency in Tenders Act, 1998, the Government have already ordered in the G.O. first read above that the procedure laid down under Tamil Nadu Transparency in Tenders Act, 1998 should be followed in entrusting the works under 'Namakku Naame Thittam'. Therefore, the Government direct that in respect of works where the Government contribution is more than 50 per cent, the provisions of the Tamil Nadu Transparency in Tenders Act, 1998 shall be adopted, and in respect of works in which the Government contribution is 50 per cent or less of the value of the work, the contributors may be given chance to execute the work themselves, and in case the contributors do not want to execute the works themselves, the Collectors are directed to follow the provisions of the Tamil Nadu Transparency in Tenders Act, 1998.

5. This orders issues with concurrence of Finance Department *vide* its U.O. No.1652/FS/P/08, dated 2.6.08.

(By order of the Governor)

K. Ashok Vardhan Shetty,
Special Commissioner and Secretary to Government.

G.O. (MS) NO. 87, RURAL DEVELOPMENT AND PANCHAYATI RAJ (SGS.1) DEPARTMENT, DATED 05.06.2008. GUIDELINES FOR IMPLEMENTATION OF NAMAKKU NAAME THITTAM 2008-09

1. Namakku Naame Thittam will be implemented both in rural and urban areas

2. Suggested List of Works that may be Taken Up

The following works may be taken up under Namakku Naame Thittam 2008-09.

- Construction of buildings, laboratories, toilets and compound walls/fencing to Government, Adi-Dravidar, Panchayat Union and Kallar Reclamation Schools, Government Colleges and Government Hostels.
- Construction of buildings, compound walls and fencing to Government Hospitals, Primary Health Centres, Sub-centres, Veterinary Dispensaries, Livestock Centres and libraries.
- Construction of libraries in urban areas, Noon Meal Centres, Kitchen Sheds, Anganwadies and Public Distribution Shops in rural and urban areas.
- Creation of community assets like drinking water sources, cement concrete roads and threshing floors in rural and urban areas.
- Maintenance of all community assets (including white washing, painting etc.).
- Construction of bridges, culverts, upgradation of gravel/ WBM roads to BT standard, renewal of worn out BT roads, improvement of streets and lanes with brick or metal stones or cement slabs or cement concrete.
- Formation, improvement and maintenance of Parks, Play-grounds, Traffic Islands, Fountains, Street lights.
- Purchase of Furniture, Computers and accessories for Government and Panchayat Union Schools, Libraries and buildings for the use of the public. Old Computers and

accessories should not be purchased. Books used in Libraries may be got as donation.

- Construction of class rooms, laboratories and toilets in 100 per cent Government-aided and 100 per cent Tamil medium schools.

3. Negative List/Prohibited Works

The following works under the **'negative list'** (prohibited works) cannot be taken up under the NNT unless specifically included in the exceptions:

(1) Construction of office and residential buildings belonging to Central and State Governments, including Public Sector Undertakings, co-operatives and societies.
Exception: Construction of buildings, compound walls for all types of Government Hospitals, Primary Health Centres and Government Veterinary Hospitals; Construction of Public Distribution Shops, Direct Procurement Centres, Milk Producers' Co-operative Societies and Bulk Chilling Centres can however be taken up.

(2) Purchase of all movable items, equipments and furniture.
Exception: Purchase of furniture and equipments for Government Schools, Panchayat Union Schools, Adi-Dravida Schools, Kallar Reclamation Schools; Government Colleges, Government Hostels; Government Hospitals, Primary Health Centres and Government Veterinary Hospitals is permitted.

(3) Any work in Government-aided and Self-financing Schools and Colleges.
Exception: Construction of class rooms, laboratories and toilets in 100 per cent Government aided and 100 per cent Tamil medium schools can be taken up. If the School is partly Self-financed and partly aided or if it is partly Tamil Medium and partly English Medium, it is not eligible. The assistance by way of Government Grant under this scheme to an eligible aided school should not

exceed Rs. 10 lakhs in a particular year. Once a Government aided School eligible as above has been assisted, irrespective of the amount assisted, it shall be ineligible for further assistance under this scheme for a period of 3 years.

For such cases, apart from Collector making his own enquiries, the following certificates should be obtained from the District Elementary Education Officer or Chief Education Officer of the district concerned before undertaking the works.

(i) The school has 100 per cent Tamil Medium Classes/ Sections. There are no English Medium Sections.

(ii) *The School is 100 per cent Government aided School. No self-financing course/classes are run in the above school in the same campus or different campuses under the same management.*

(4) All works involving commercial establishments/units.

(5) Grants and loans, contribution to any Central and State/ UT Relief Funds.

(6) Acquisition of land or any compensation for land acquired.

(7) Reimbursement of any type of completed or partly completed works or items.

(8) Assets for individual/family benefits.

(9) All revenue and recurring expenditure.

(10) Works within the places of religious worship and on land belonging to or owned by religious faiths/groups.

(11) Desilting of ponds, ooranis, rivers, tanks, canals, channels and the like.

(12) Gravel/WBM roads (roads upto BT standard only should be taken up).

(13) Installation of High Mast Lights.

4. Conditions Stipulated

The suggested list of permissible works may be taken up subject to the following conditions:

(a) No permanent structure should be constructed without prior permission of the owner of the property.

(b) No rights can be claimed by the contributing person/ entity over the property/use of property.

(c) The names of the contributors who execute the work may be put in the name board at the place of execution of the work with the permission of the District Collector. The name of the scheme 'Namakku Naame Thittam' should be displayed in not less than two-thirds of the size of the name board. The name board may be permitted to be put up by the contributors in such a manner that it does not affect the aesthetic value of the site and the contributors do not claim any right or lease over the property.

(d) If the Collector feels that the contributors have not shown any interest on the work or that some conditions have been violated, the order issued for execution or maintenance of the work shall be cancelled or permission shall not be given for continuing the work.

5. Procedure for Selection of Works under Namakku Naame Thittam

- The need for taking up of works under Namakku Naame Thittam may originate from individual, group, institutions, companies or from the community.
- After identification of the work to be executed, an application specifying the nature of work, acceptance letter for contributing one-third of the amount by means of Demand Draft should be given to the District Collector or Project Officer, District Rural Development Agency.
- The contributions given by the local bodies, Universities and Public Sector Undertakings shall not be accepted under this Scheme.
- The District Collector will ascertain the actual need and feasibility of the work to be taken up.
- If permission of the local body or the Department concerned is necessary to execute the work, the Collector

shall obtain the permission before according administrative sanction.

- If the assets to be created have to be maintained by the local bodies or the department concerned, the District Collector should obtain concurrence from the department concerned.
- If requests are received for various works for a limited amount available under the scheme, the District Collector shall give priority for the works which are of maximum benefit to the community.

6. Execution of Works

(i) Administrative sanction should be accorded only after preparation of the estimate by the local bodies or the department concerned as per the schedule of rate approved by the competent authority or as per the latest schedule of rate of the Public Works Department. A minimum of one-third of the estimated cost of the work should be received by means of Demand Draft in favour of the District Collector to Namakku Naame Thittam Account. The balance amount will be released by Government from the Namakku Naame Thittam fund. Further, if the guidelines of other schemes of the Centre and the State are in tune with this Scheme, the funds of those schemes may also be dovetailed with the public contribution.

(ii) To facilitate larger participation of the people in this scheme, if the public or contributors opt to execute the work themselves or through their agency, willingness should be given by them in writing while applying for the work under Namakku Naame Thittam. The District Collector will examine the request and permit the contributors or the agency to execute the work if the public contribution is 50 per cent or more of the estimate of the work.

(iii) If the agency/institution does not come forward to execute the work, the work shall be implemented through tender as per the provisions of the Tamil Nadu Transparency in Tenders Act, 1998.

(iv) The District Collector will decide the Technical Authority for supervision of the work. The agency may be the local body or the department concerned. The District Collector will release the funds required to the Agency concerned.

(v) (a) The work order will be issued to the local body/ Line Department/Contributor/private institutions or the person from any one of the above agencies executing the work.

(b) Even though the works are executed by the private bodies/Associations or the Public, the funds will be at the disposal of the local body/Department concerned supervising the work.

(c) The bills will be sanctioned as per the measurement and check measurement by the competent Technical Authority and as per the guidelines for payment for works under other Government Schemes.

(d) In case of school buildings including the High School/Higher Secondary Schools, in addition to the supervision as above, the Public Works Department or the Corporation or Municipality or the Technical wing of the executing Department should issue the structural stability certificate. The technical wing shall prepare the completion report for the building work.

(vi) In respect of works taken up with 100 per cent public contribution, if the beneficiary association/contributors concerned express willingness to execute the work themselves, work can be entrusted to them without insisting on the advance cash contribution under Namakku Naame Thittam. However, the work should be executed as per the type design and stability aspects of the building, subject to the measurements of the works.

7. Maintenance of Assets Created under NNT

It is preferable that the local body or the contributor concerned on behalf of the Department themselves maintain the works/assets created under Namakku Naame Thittam. In order to continuously maintain the assets created under this scheme, the local people should form a user group run on self-generated resources. The local people should be encouraged to plan, execute and maintain the works based on local needs.

8. Additional Funds to the Districts and Funds for Special Schemes

(i) (a) If additional funds are required by the Districts to take up special schemes under Namakku Naame Thittam, proposals for such schemes should be sent to the Director of Rural Development and Panchayati Raj. Before sending proposals for additional funds and funds for special schemes from the Director of Rural Development and Panchayati Raj, the entire amount already allotted to the District should have been utilized.

(b) If required, the Director of Rural Development and Panchayati Raj will, in consultation with the Secretary, Rural Development and Panchayati Raj Department, re-allot the unutilised funds available with the Districts as on 28th February to districts with better performance and requiring additional funds for implementation of works.

(ii) (a) The funds received from Government and the Public will be deposited in a Savings Bank Account opened for Namakku Naame Thittam Scheme.

(b) All contributions received by the District Collectors should be by means of Demand Draft in the name of "District Collector's Namakku Naame Thittam Account". Receipt should be given for all contributions received.

(c) A register should be maintained for the contributions received in cash. The accounts and the register should be maintained by the Project Officer, District Rural Development Agency.

(d) The District Collector shall release 75 per cent of the funds including the public contribution to the local body/line department concerned, along with Administrative sanction. The remaining amount will be released only after receipt of utilization certificate.

(iii) In case of the work proposed not being taken up for certain reasons, the District Collector will order refund of the entire amount or part amount in accordance with the quantum and value of the work undertaken. In such cases, the contribution amount will be refunded to the contributor in full or part without any interest.

9. Information, Education and Communication

The District Collector should take steps for communication and publicity of the salient features and success stories of Namakku Naame Thittam through the local newspapers and electronic media. The District Collectors may utilize one per cent of the allocation under this scheme for IEC activities and documentation.

10. Chennai Corporation

As regards the Corporation of Chennai, the Commissioner of Chennai Corporation will execute all the works under Namakku Naame Thittam on behalf of Collector, Chennai. Accordingly the Commissioner of Chennai Corporation will accord administrative sanction for the works.

11. The Secretary to Government, Rural Development and Panchayati Raj Department is empowered to modify the guidelines of Namakku Naame Thittam, whenever necessary, in consultation with the Director of Rural Development and Panchayati Raj.

K. Ashok Vardhan Shetty,
Special Commissioner and
Secretary to Government

Annexure-ID

PERIYAR NINAIVU SAMATHUVAPURAM—ESTABLISHMENT OF FURTHER 29 SAMATHUVAPURAMS IN 2008-09—DETAILED GUIDELINES

Rural Development and Panchayati Raj (SGS.1) Department

G.O. (MS) No. 59 Dated: 16.4.2008

Read

From the Director of Rural Development and Panchayati Raj, D.O.Lr.No.749/08/G1, dated 24.3.2008.

Order

To promote social justice and spread Thanthai Periyar's message of social equality, 145 Samathuvapurams were established in the State where all communities live in unity and brotherhood. In the Governor's Address made in the Legislative Assembly on 23.1.2008, among others, it has been announced that "an even better way of spreading Thanthai Periyar's message of social equality would be to establish another 95 Samathuvapurams in his name."

2. The Director of Rural Development and Panchayati Raj in his D.O. Letter read above has stated that during 2008-09, the Government may take up one Samathuvapuram each in 29 districts (except Chennai and the Nilgiris where Samathuvapurams need not be taken up due to non-availability of suitable land in these districts) and requested the Government to issue orders. He has also sent proposals for issuing detailed guidelines to implement this scheme.

3. The Government have carefully examined the proposal of Director of Rural Development and Panchayati Raj above and direct that the establishment of Samathuvapurams one each in 29 districts (except Chennai and the Nilgiris) be taken up

during 2008-09. Orders regarding sanction of fund for this scheme for the year 2008-09 will be issued, separately. Meanwhile, the Director of Rural Development and Panchayati Raj/District Collectors are directed to take up preliminary works for establishing 29 Samathuvapurams as indicated in the guidelines for this scheme (given in the annexure to this order).

4. This order issues with the concurrence of Finance Department *vide* its U.O.No.1052/FS/P/08, dated 1.4.2008.

(By order of the Governor)

K. Ashok Vardhan Shetty,
Special Commissioner and Secretary to Government

G.O. (Ms) No. 59, RD&PR (SGS.1) Deptt., dated 16.4.2008
Guidelines for Construction of Samathuvapuram 2008-09

(1) Area of Site

- While selecting the site for Samathuvapuram, an approximate area of 8 to 9 acres of land should be selected in the rural area of the district.

(2) Selection of Site

- The site so selected should be abutting a bus route road and should not be too far from the District/Division/Taluk/Block Headquarters. Preferably the Samathuvapuram should be selected in a Block that has not so far been covered with Samathuvapuram in the previous years.
- Villages with higher population may be preferably selected for construction of Samathuvapuram.
- The nearest residential habitation should be preferably within 1 to 2 km from proposed Samathuvapuram. In no case, the site selected should be in an isolated place where the beneficiaries may hesitate to go and reside.
- The selected site should be suitable for construction of residential buildings and should not be in a low lying or swampy area prone to flooding during rainy season. Also,

the above site should not be a hilly or rocky land or land having HT power line running over the site rendering the site unsuitable for construction of houses. There should be little or no cost on land levelling or land filling of Samathuvapuram site.

(3) Categories of Land Permitted

- Subject to the conditions specified in para 2 above if vacant unobjectionable poramboke lands are available, the same may be located thereon. Wherever such lands are not available, private lands may be taken up for acquisition through private negotiation. No proposals be sent for land transfer of objectionable poramboke lands like pond/oorani/channel/grazing lands for Samathuvapuram.
- Among the private lands, preference should be given for dry lands, though wet lands are also permitted to be acquired for the purpose of Samathuvapuram through private negotiation only if dry lands are not available.

(4) Procurement of Land

- In case of private lands, the land may be acquired by private negotiation by a Committee headed by the District Collector and consisting of the District Revenue Officer (as Member Secretary), DIG (Registration) and PO, DRDA. The Committee will fix the price of land not exceeding 150 per cent of the guideline value or the market value of the land whichever is lower, as per the existing procedures/guidelines.
- In extraordinary circumstances, when the negotiated value of the land in the above case exceeds 150 per cent and the Committee is unable to reduce it to below 150 per cent due to high market rates prevailing in the vicinity, in order to fast track the acquisition of the land, the proposal may be sent to the Director of Rural Development and Panchayat Raj with full justification. A State Level

Committee consisting of the Secretary to Government, Rural Development and Panchayat Raj Department, Secretary to Government, Revenue Department, Secretary to Government, Finance Department and the Director of Rural Development and Panchayat Raj, (who will be the convener) is empowered to approve the value of land based on the recommendations of the District Collector and on the merits of the case.

(5) Sub-division of the Site

- After the land is transferred or acquired, it will be sub-divided into individual house-site plots for the beneficiaries and the layout of the site will be prepared in accordance with the rules of Town and Country Planning within the shortest possible time.
- Provision should be made for each house site to be of 5 cents of area. The roads having a width of 7 m should be provided as per the provisions of the Town and Country Planning rules and the layout of the site be prepared accordingly.
- Construction of Samathuvapurams is to be done within 12 months period and delays should be avoided. The approval of the layouts by the Town and Country Planning authorities usually involves delays in the entire process. Hence, a blanket exemption of requirement of approval as done for Tsunami Housing from the Town and Country Planning Department for the layouts of the Samathuvapurams will be obtained separately from the Government and communicated.

(6) Type Design and Construction of the Houses

- Samathuvapuram houses will be constructed by the Government. Each house should have a separate toilet and an appropriate disposal system like septic tank with soak pit as shown in the model type design of Samathuvapuram houses.

(7) Village Panchayat(s) from which Beneficiaries are to be Selected

The beneficiaries for Samathuvapuram will be selected as per the following criteria:

- As far as possible, the beneficiaries should be selected from the village in which Samathuvapuram is being constructed.
- If sufficient number of eligible beneficiaries are not available in the concerned Village Panchayat, the beneficiaries from the adjoining village having the highest population (amongst the neighbouring Panchayats of Samathuvapuram Village Panchayat touching its boundary) will be considered for being selected for Samathuvapuram. If sufficient number of beneficiaries are not available even from the neighbouring Village Panchayat with the highest population, another adjoining Village Panchayat with the next highest population may be taken up and this process may be extended till the 100 beneficiaries for the Samathuvapuram are selected as per eligibility norms.

(8) Caste-wise Distribution of Samathuvapuram Beneficiaries

- Allotment of the houses to the beneficiaries will be in the following proportions:
  SCs - 40
  BCs - 25
  MBCs - 25
  Others - 10
- Pattəs should be issued to the beneficiaries upfront and they should be given in such a manner that families of all communities live adjacent to each other in an inter-mixed manner and the following allocation criteria for a set of 20 houses each should be followed in general:

Category	*House No.*
SCs	2, 4, 7, 10, 12, 14, 17, 20
BCs	1, 5, 9, 11, 15
MBCs	3, 6, 13, 16, 19
Others	8, 18

- If the demographic profile of the District is such that sufficient number of persons belonging to SC/BC/MBC/ other communities are not available in the Samathuvapuram village or its vicinity, the Director of Rural Development and Panchayat Raj, based on the recommendation of District Collector, is authorised to modify this ratio suitably without detriment to the spirit of Samathuvapuram.

(9) Selection Committee

- The following persons shall comprise the Committee for selection of beneficiaries for Samathuvapuram:
  1. Project Officer, DRDA, who will be the Chairman of the Committee
  2. Block Development Officer (Block Panchayat)
  3. Tahsildar of the Taluk
  4. President of the Village Panchayat where Samathuvapuram is located
  5. Concerned VAO(s)
  6. One Panchayat Level Federation of Women Self-Help Groups member from the Samathuvapuram village
- In case the beneficiaries are also selected from village(s) adjoining the Samathuvapuram village, the Selection Committee members in Sl. Nos. 4, 5 and 6 will be pertaining to that particular Village and they will form part of the Selection Committee for selection of the beneficiaries.
- The above Committee will seek applications from those eligible who will be willing to stay at Samathuvapuram on permanent basis. While selecting the beneficiaries for Samathuvapuram, the persons living in houses with (i) mud walls with thatched roof, (ii) brick walls with

thatched roof, (iii) mud walls with tiled roof, and (iv) brick walls with tiled roof will be given priority in the above order as such persons are likely to be poorer. The beneficiaries list will have to be finally approved by the District Collector.

- Persons residing in houses with RCC roof will not be eligible for Samathuvapuram houses.
- No such persons who have been the beneficiaries of IAY houses or other housing schemes such as Fishermen Free Housing Scheme, Tribal Housing through Adi-Dravidar and Tribal Welfare Department will be eligible for getting house under Samathuvapuram.
- Reservation of 3 per cent will be done horizontally across all communities for selecting beneficiaries with over 70 per cent and above physical disability or mentally retardation, as certified by the competent authority. Wherever deemed necessary allotment may be made in the name of parents of the disabled.

(10) Issuance of Patta

- Patta should be given jointly in the name of the husband and wife, except in the case when one of them is not alive.
- The beneficiaries selection should be done upfront before the construction of a house is started. The allotment of house sites and consequently the houses to the beneficiaries should also be done upfront so that each beneficiary is aware of the place where his/her house is being constructed and the beneficiary is involved in the construction process from the beginning itself. Once 100 beneficiaries are finalized, the individual house number will be allotted by draw of lots, based on the mix of communal rotation as prescribed in Para 8 above.

(11) Undertaking to be Given

- An undertaking from the beneficiaries with regard to

the following points is to be got before allocation of the house:

(1) That the house will neither be sold or mortgaged or litigated by them upto 30 years from the date of allotment, nor will they use the house for non-residential purposes.

(2) That they will reside in the house permanently and if they fail to reside in the house initially or shift residence continuously for a period of more than 2 weeks or rent it out or sub-let it, then the house allotment is liable for cancellation and re-allotment to the other eligible person.

(3) That no damages will be caused to the houses and no encroachment in the public place in Samathuvapuram will be done by them.

(4) That they will use common facilities like drinking water, roads and public distribution shop without any discrimination, on caste or creed lines.

(12) Essential Infrastructure

The following essential infrastructure should be provided in the site of Samathuvapuram, besides the 100 houses:

1. Street lights
2. Drinking water with OHT
3. BT/CC roads
4. Public Distribution Shop
5. In addition to the above essential infrastructure, the statue of Thanthai Periyar should be installed in each Samathuvapuram.

(13) Implementation of Schemes

The Block Development Officer (Block Panchayat) will implement the scheme. However, the Project Officer, DRDA will call for the tenders by grouping the works in the following Packages:

1. **Package-I:** 100 houses and the Public Distribution Shop
2. **Package-II:** Roads pertaining to Samathuvapuram
3. **Package-III:** Drinking Water Supply works.

The work of installation of street lights will be entrusted to the Tamil Nadu Electricity Board. Payment will be made by the BDO (Block Panchayat) concerned based on the satisfactory completion of works.

14. The Secretary to Government, Rural Development and Panchayat Raj Department is empowered to modify any of the above guidelines in consultation with Director of Rural Development and Panchayat Raj based on the exigencies that may arise from time to time in the implementation of the scheme.

K. Ashok Vardhan Shetty,
Special Commissioner and
Secretary to Government

Annexures-II

Annexure-IIA
GUIDELINES FOR INDIRA AWAAS YOJANA (IAY)

[EFFECTIVE FROM 01.04.2004]

Ministry of Rural Development
(Department of Rural Development)

RURAL HOUSING PROGRAMME

Introduction

Housing is one of the basic requirements for human survival. For a normal citizen owning a house provides significant economic and social security and status in society. For a shelterless person, a house brings about a profound social change in his existence, endowing him with an identity, thus integrating him with his immediate social milieu. A housing programme for the rehabilitation of refugees was taken up immediately after partition by the Ministry of Refugee Rehabilitation and this lasted till around 1960. Approximately 5 lakh families were housed in various centres mainly located in Northern India. A Village Housing Scheme was also launched as part of the Community Development Movement in 1957, in which loans to individuals and cooperatives were provided up to a maximum of Rs. 5000/- per house. However only 67000 houses were built under this scheme by the end of the Fifth Plan (1980). In 1972-73, the Estimate Committee of the Lok Sabha in its 37th Report pointed out that "the Committee is distressed to note that although 83 per cent of India's population lives in villages and about 73 per cent of the rural population reside in unsatisfactory kutcha structures, the problem of rural housing has not received the close attention of the Government". Following this, certain initiatives were undertaken by Government including the launching of the House Sites-cum-Construction Assistance Scheme which began as a Central Scheme in the 4th Plan and was transferred to the State Sector with effect from 1.4.1974 on the recommendation of the National Development Council (NDC).

The genesis of the Indira Awaas Yojana (IAY) can be traced to the programmes of rural employment, which began in the early 1980s. Construction of houses was one of the major activities under the National Rural Employment Programme (NREP), which began in 1980, and the Rural Landless Employment Guarantee Programme (RLEGP), which began in 1983. There was, however, no uniform policy for rural housing in the states. For instance some states permitted only part of the construction cost to be borne from NREP/RLEGP funds and the balance was to be met by beneficiaries from their savings or loans obtained by them. On the other hand, others permitted the entire expenditure to be borne from NREP/RLEGP funds. Further, while some states allowed construction of only new dwellings, others permitted renovation of existing houses of beneficiaries. As per announcement made by the Government of India in June 1985, a part of the RLEGP fund was earmarked for the construction of houses for SCs/STs and freed bonded labourers. As a result, Indira Awaas Yojana (IAY) was launched during 1985-86 as a sub-scheme of RLEGP. IAY thereafter continued as a sub-scheme of Jawahar Rozgar Yojana (JRY) since its launching in April 1989. 6 per cent of the total JRY funds were allocated for implementation of IAY. From the year 1993-94, the scope of IAY was extended to cover below the poverty line Non Scheduled Caste/Scheduled Tribe families in the rural areas. Simultaneously, the allocation of funds for implementing the scheme was raised from 6 per cent to 10 per cent of the total resources available under JRY at the national level, subject to the condition that the benefits to Non-Scheduled Caste/Scheduled Tribe poor should not exceed 4 per cent of the total JRY allocation. IAY was de-linked from JRY and made an independent scheme with effect from 1st January, 1996.

Since 1999-2000, number of initiatives have been taken to improve the Rural Housing (RH) Programme by making provision for upgradation of unserviceable kutcha houses and by providing credit with subsidy for certain sections of the poor. Emphasis has also been laid on use of cost affective, disaster resistant and environment friendly technologies in rural housing.

(I)
BROAD OUTLINES AND OBJECTIVES

1.1 Indira Awaas Yojana (IAY)

The ***Indira Awaas Yojana (IAY)*** is a flagship scheme of the Ministry of Rural Development to provide houses to the poor in the rural areas.

1.2 Objective

The objective of the Indira Awaas Yojana is primarily to help construction/upgradation of dwelling units of members of Scheduled Castes/Scheduled Tribes, freed bonded labourers and other below the poverty line non-SC/ST rural households by providing them a lump sum financial assistance.

1.3 Funding Pattern

The Indira Awaas Yojana is a Centrally Sponsored Scheme funded on cost-sharing basis between the Government of India and the State Governments in the ratio of 75:25. In the case of Union Territories, the entire funds under this Scheme are provided by the Government of India.

1.4 Target Group

The target groups for houses under the IAY are below poverty line households living in the rural areas belonging to Scheduled Castes/Scheduled Tribes, freed bonded labourers and non-SC/ST BPL rural households, widows and next of kin to defence personnel/paramilitary forces killed in action residing in rural areas *(irrespective of their income criteria)*, ex-servicemen and retired member of paramilitary forces fulfilling the other conditions.

1.5 Earmarking of Funds for SC/ST Beneficiaries

Funds available under the Scheme in a district are earmarked for various categories as under:

(i) At least 60 per cent of the total IAY allocation during a financial year should be utilized for construction/upgradation of dwelling units for SC/ST BPL households.
(ii) A maximum 40 per cent for non-SC/ST BPL rural households.
(iii) 3 per cent of the above categories for physically and mentally challenged persons.

If any particular category is exhausted or not available in a district, allocation can be utilized for other categories as per priorities given in the Guidelines after it has been certified to this effect by the Zilla Parishad/DRDA concerned.

1.6 Strategy for the implementation of the Programme

The Programme will be implemented through the Zilla Parishads/DRDAs and houses will be constructed by the beneficiaries themselves.

(II) IDENTIFICATION AND SELECTION OF BENEFICIARIES

2.1. Identification of beneficiaries

The District Panchayat/Zilla Panchayat/District Rural Development Agencies (DRDAs) on the basis of allocations made and targets fixed shall decide the number of houses to be constructed/upgraded Panchayat-wise under IAY, during a particular financial year. The same shall be intimated to the Gram Panchayat concerned. Thereafter, the Gram Sabha will select the beneficiaries from the list of eligible BPL households, restricting this number to the target allotted as per the Programme Guidelines. Selection by the Gram Sabha is final. No approval by a higher body is required. Zilla Parishads/DRDAs and Block Development Offices should, however, be sent a list of selected beneficiaries for their information.

2.2. Priority in Selection of Beneficiaries

Prioritization of beneficiaries will be as follows:

(i) Freed bonded labourers

(ii) SC/ST households

- SC/ST households who are victims of atrocity
- SC/ST households, headed by widows and unmarried women
- SC/ST households affected by flood, natural calamities like earthquake, cyclone and man-made calamities like riot.
- Other SC/ST households

(iii) Families/widows of personnel from defence services/ paramilitary forces, killed in action.

(iv) Non-SC/ST BPL households.

(v) Physically and mentally challenged persons.

(vi) Ex-servicemen and retired members of the paramilitary forces.

(vii) Displaced persons on account of developmental projects, nomadic/semi-nomadic, and de-notified tribals, families with physically/mentally challenged members.

The selection of the beneficiaries will be subject to the condition that the households of all the above categories except (iii) are Below Poverty Line (BPL).

2.3. Involvement of Beneficiaries

The beneficiaries should be involved in the construction of the house. To this end, the beneficiaries may make their own arrangements for procurement of construction material, engage skilled workmen and also contribute family labour. The beneficiaries will have complete freedom as to the manner of construction of the house. Zilla Parishads/DRDAs can help the beneficiaries in acquiring raw material on control rates, if they so desire or request the Zilla Parishads/DRDAs in this regard. This will result in economy in cost, ensure quality of construction, lead to greater satisfaction and acceptance of the house by the beneficiary. The responsibility for the proper construction of the house will thus be on the beneficiaries themselves. A Committee may be formed, if so desired, to coordinate the work. The Committee shall be sensitized to incorporate hazard-resistant features in the design of the houses.

2.4. Allotment of Houses

Allotment of dwelling units should be in the name of female member of the beneficiary household. Alternatively, it can be allotted in the name of both husband and wife.

(III)
UNIT COST OF THE INDIRA AWAAS YOJANA HOUSES

3.1. Unit Cost for Construction of IAY Houses and Upgradation

The ceiling on grant of assistance per unit cost under the Indira Awaas Yojana for construction of new house and upgradation of unserviceable kutcha house is given as under:

	Plain Areas	*Hilly/Difficult Areas*
(a) Construction of house including Sanitary latrine and smokeless Chulha	Rs. 25,000	Rs. 27,500
(b) Upgradation of un-serviceable households	Rs. 12,500	Rs. 12,500

3.2 Construction of Sanitary Latrines and Smokeless Chulhas

Sanitary latrine and smokeless chulha will be provided with each

IAY house. Latrine could be constructed separate from the IAY house on the site of the beneficiary. Wherever possible, efforts should be made to dovetail funds from Total Sanitation Campaign (TSC) for providing sanitary latrine so that more money could be made available for construction of the IAY house. In case, the beneficiary is unable to construct sanitary latrine, due to some reasons, an amount of Rs. 600/- would be deducted from the assistance to be provided for construction of the new IAY house or for upgradation of an unserviceable kutcha house. Similarly, where smokeless chulha is not possible, deduction will be made of Rs. 100/-.

3.3 Loan for IAY Beneficiaries

In addition to the assistance provided under the IAY, loan for construction of IAY houses or for upgradation of unserviceable kutcha houses can be obtained from the banks/other financial institutions. It will be the responsibility of the State Governments/ DRDAs concerned to coordinate with the financial institutions to make available the credit facility to those beneficiaries who are interested.

3.4 Credit-cum-Subsidy for construction/upgradation of Rural Houses

Upto 20 per cent of the total funds can be utilized for upgradation of existing kutcha houses and towards subsidy for construction of houses with credit from Banks/Financial Institutions. Credit-cum-subsidy will be provided subject to the following conditions:

(i) Rural households having an annual income of upto Rs. 32,000/- only.

(ii) Ceiling of subsidy under the Scheme Rs. 12,500 per household.

(iii) The upper limit of construction loan under this scheme will be Rs. 50,000 only. Credit arrangement will be as mentioned in para 3.3.

3.5 Location of the Indira Awaas Yojana

The Indira Awaas Yojana dwelling units should normally be built on individual plots in the main habitation of the village. The houses can also be built in a cluster within a habitation, so as to facilitate the development of infrastructure, such as, internal roads, drainage, drinking water supply etc. and other common facilities. Care should always be taken to see that the houses under the IAY are located close to the village and not far away, so as to ensure safety and security, nearness to work place and social communication. To the extent possible, the site should not be located in disaster prone areas for example frequently floodable areas.

(IV)
CRITERIA FOR ALLOCATION AND RELEASE OF FUNDS

4.1 Criteria for Allocation of Resources

Central assistance under the Indira Awaas Yojana will be allocated to the States/UTs on the basis of poverty ratio and housing shortage, with each of these variables being given equal weightage. The poverty ratios prepared by the Planning Commission are used for this purpose, while housing shortage is determined on the basis of the last Census. The proportions of rural SC/ST population and housing shortage in a district to the total rural SC/ST population and housing shortage in the State/UT are the criteria of inter-district allocation of the Indira Awaas Yojana funds within a State/UT. Both these variables are given equal weightage in the inter-districts allocation. The targets for the Blocks within a District will be decided on the same principles. Diversion of resources from one district to another is strictly prohibited. Upto 20 per cent of the total funds can be utilized for upgradation of existing kutcha houses and towards subsidy for construction of houses with credit in accordance with Paras 3.1 and 3.4.

4.2 Release of Central Assistance to Zilla Parishads/DRDAs

The Indira Awaas Yojana funds are operated by the Zilla Parishads/DRDAs at the district level. Central assistance will be released every year to the Zilla Parishads/DRDAs, in two instalments, subject to the fulfilment of the following conditions:

(a) The first instalment amounting to 50 per cent of the total allocation for a particular district is released in the beginning of the financial year. This is subject to condition that the second instalment during previous year was claimed and released without any condition. However, if any specific conditions had been imposed at the time of release of the last instalment of the previous year, its compliance will have to be ensured before release of the first instalment.

(b) The second instalment for the districts will be released on receipt of request from the DRDAs as per Proforma at *Annexure - I* on fulfilment of the following conditions:

(i) 60 per cent of the total available funds, that is opening balance of the year *(in case of proposal for the first instalment, opening balance of the previous year)* plus the amount received including the State share *(if the State share has not been released against the first instalment, notional State share will be taken into account for the purpose of calculation of total availability)* and other receipts should have been utilized at the time of submitting the proposal for the second instalment.

(ii) The opening balance of the District should not exceed 15 per cent of the funds available during the previous year. In case, the opening balance exceeds this limit, the Central share of the excess will be deducted proportionately at the time of release of the second instalment.

(iii) The State Government has made sufficient provision in their Budget to match the Central financial assistance.

(iv) The State Government should have released all its contribution (including that of the previous years) due, up to the date of the application. In the event of shortfall in State share, corresponding amount of Central share *(i.e. three times the shortfall of State share)* will be deducted from the amount of Central share of the second instalment of the current year.

(v) Submission of Audit Reports for the IAY for the last year and submission of Action Taken Report on the comments made in the audit report of the previous year. The Audit Report should consist of Bank Reconciliation Statement and a Certificate from the Chartered Accountant that while auditing the district account of the IAY, the accounts of all Implementing Agencies such as block-wise expenditure etc have been taken into account.

(vi) Submission of Utilization Certificates of cash component from DRDAs based on reports received from the other Implementing Agencies such as Block Development Office etc. for the previous year should be submitted in the prescribed Proforma as per ***Annexure II.***

(vii) Submission of non-diversion and non-embezzlement certificate.

(viii) Annual Plan should have been approved by the Zilla Parishad or the Governing Body of the DRDA as the case may be.

(ix) All pending progress/monitoring reports should have been sent.

(x) Any other condition imposed from time to time will also have to be complied with.

(xi) All documents must be checked/enclosed with the proposal as per the Checklist. ***(Annexure III)***

(c) In case of districts/UTs having limited working season or any peculiar problem such as Kinnaur, Lahaul and Spiti, Leh, Kargil, Andaman and Nicobar Islands and Lakshadweep and any other areas as decided, the entire

Central assistance may be released in one instalment. The State shall also release its share in one instalment. In the case of these districts, to which funds are released in one instalment, funds will be released only on fulfilment of the conditions laid down.

4.3 Cuts to be imposed on Late Receipt of Proposals

4.3.1 The proposal for release of second instalment by the Zilla Parishad/DRDA complete in all respects should be submitted latest by 31st December every year.

4.3.2 To maintain financial discipline, a mandatory deduction(s) on account of late submission of proposal by the State Government shall be imposed depending upon the date of receipt of complete proposal for release of second instalment under the IAY. Under the system, there will be progressive deductions for proposal(s) received in the month of January and February @ 10 per cent and 20 per cent respectively on the total Central allocation for the year. Incomplete proposals will not be accepted. The date on which last information is received from the State shall be treated as date of receipt of the proposal.

4.3.3 Notwithstanding the above provision *(Para 4.3.2)*, State should submit the proposal for the second instalment before 15th February every year. Acceptance of proposal(s) after 15th February up to 28th February will be considered only in exceptional circumstances. Proposals will not be accepted after February. However, if the proposal received in the month of March is accepted under special circumstances, 30 per cent cut in the allocation will be imposed.

4.3.4 Zilla Parishads/DRDAs are required to complete all the incomplete houses sanctioned/taken up in the previous years first *(with the funds available during the current year)* even if there is a deduction while releasing the 2nd instalment in the previous year due to unavoidable circumstances. The targets fixed at the time of allocation of funds to the districts/states during the current year would be adjusted accordingly keeping in view the deduction/additional release, if any, during the previous year.

4.4 Earmarking of Resources under the IAY

4.4.1 5 per cent of the total allocated funds under IAY will be kept apart to meet the exigencies arising out of natural calamities and other emergent situations like riot, arson, fire, rehabilitation under exceptional circumstances etc.

Proposals for this purpose have to come from State Governments/Admn. of UTs showing the extent of damage and the estimated fund requirement in respect of the proposed IAY houses provided assistance has not been obtained from other sources. Funds to be released for this purpose shall not exceed Rs. 50 lakhs per district. The relief will be as per the norms with regard to per unit ceiling of assistance for IAY house prescribed under the scheme.

4.4.2 The unutilized amount, if any, of this provision of 5 per cent of the funds of the scheme, will be utilized for allocation to the better performing States/Districts. The Ministry of Home Affairs or any other Ministry/Department handling the natural calamity or other emergent situation will also be informed about the allocation of these funds, in order to avoid any duplication in relief work. Physical and financial progress reports of the funds so spent have to be furnished by the State Governments concerned on the work done within the provision of the allocation made for these contingencies.

4.5 Maintenance of Accounts

Zilla Parishads/DRDAs will follow the accounting procedures prescribed by the Ministry of Rural Development. The finalized accounts of the previous year shall be got approved by the General Body of the concerned DRDA on or before 30th June and got audited on or before 31st August of the same year. Copies of the Audit Report as accepted by the General Body of the concerned DRDA shall be sent to the State Government and Central Government on or before 30th September of the year. The above procedure will be in addition to any other procedures to be followed and requirements to be fulfilled by the DRDA as per the Articles of Memorandum of the Association.

4.6 Release of State share to DRDAs

The State Government shall release its share to the Zilla Parishads/DRDAs within one month after the release of Central assistance and copy of the same should be endorsed to Ministry of Rural Development.

4.7 Separate Bank Account for the Indira Awaas Yojana

The IAY funds *(Central share as well as State share)* shall be kept in a nationalized/scheduled or cooperative bank or a Post Office in an exclusive and separate savings bank account by the DRDAs.

4.8 Utilization of Interest Earned on Deposits

The interest amount accrued on the deposits of the IAY funds shall be treated as part of the IAY resources.

4.9 Drawal of Funds by the DRDAs

Drawal of funds from the accounts shall only be made for incurring expenditure under the IAY.

4.10 Payment to Beneficiaries

Payment should be made to the beneficiary on a staggered basis depending on the progress of the work. The entire money should not be paid to the beneficiary in lump sum. Installments of payment to be linked to the progress of work can be decided by the State Government or at the District level.

(V)
MISCELLANEOUS

5.1 Ban on Contractors or Departmental Construction

No contractor shall be involved in the construction of dwelling units under the IAY, by the Zilla Parishad/DRDA/Implementing

Agency. If any case of construction through contractors comes to notice, Government of India will have the right to recover the releases made to the State for those IAY houses. The house should also not be constructed by any Government department. Government departments or organizations can, however, give technical assistance or arrange for coordinated supply of raw materials such as cement, steel or bricks if the beneficiaries so desire. The spirit of the IAY is that the house is not to be constructed and delivered by any external agency. On the other hand, the house is to be constructed by the beneficiary himself/herself.

5.2 Appropriate Construction Technologies and Local Materials

Effort should be made to utilize, to the maximum possible extent, local materials and cost effective disaster resistant and environment friendly technologies developed by various institutions. Zilla Parishad/DRDA should contact various organizations/institutions for seeking expertise information on innovative technologies, materials, designs and methods to help beneficiaries in the construction/upgradation of durable, cost effective houses and disaster resistant houses. Help of Building Centres may also be taken to get the information on cost effective technologies/materials and conducting training for rural artisans. The State Governments may also arrange to make available information on cost effective environment friendly technologies, materials, designs etc., at district/block level. This information should only be for guidance and any other suitable location specific technology can be adopted by the beneficiaries.

5.3 Type Design

No type design should be prescribed for the IAY dwelling units, except that the plinth area of the houses should not be less than 20 sq.mts. The layout, size and type design of the IAY dwelling units should depend on the local conditions and the preference of the beneficiary. The houses, should be designed in accordance with the desire of the beneficiaries, keeping in view the climatic conditions and the need to provide ample space, kitchen, ventilation, sanitary facilities, smokeless chullha, etc. and the community perceptions, preferences and cultural attitudes. The barrier free concept may be incorporated in the houses meant for the physically challenged, with a view to facilitating their smooth and free movement in the house. In areas frequented by natural calamities such as fire, flood, cyclones, earthquakes, etc., incorporation of disaster resistant features in design should be encouraged.

5.4 Fuel Efficient Chulhas

It should be ensured that each Indira Awaas Yojana dwelling unit is provided with a smokeless chulha, which is a fuel-efficient alternative, smoke free, healthy for clean environment and more convenient to use.

5.5 Drinking Water Supply

The availability of drinking water supply should be ensured by the agencies responsible for the implementation of the Indira Awaas Yojana.

5.6 Environmental Improvements and Social Forestry

Plantation of trees in the entire habitation or around the individual house may be taken up simultaneously. Trees may be planted near the housing clusters so that, in due course, enough trees are available nearby, to enable the beneficiaries to source fuel/fodder/small timber. Such plantations can be taken up under the social forestry programme. Some of the popular indigenous species whose plantation can be undertaken include Neem (*Azadirachta indica*); Mahuva (*Madhuca indica*); Amla (*Emblica officianlis*); Coconut (*Cocos nucifera*); Deodar (*Credrees deadora*); Mango (*Magnifera indica*); Oak (*Quercus & Spp.*); Rose wood (*Dalbergia latifolia*); Chandan (*Santalum album*); Pipal (*Ficus religiosa*) etc. This list is merely illustrative, and not exhaustive. Species may vary with region, location and geo/agroclimatic conditions. Cultivation of fruits and vegetables at household level in the houses may also be encouraged for improving nutritional status.

5.7 Training

Officers dealing with the IAY at the State, District and Block levels must be trained in various disaster resistant features to be adopted in the houses and they should ensure that this is complied with during their field visits. In addition, local carpenters and masons should be trained for skill upgradation and use of low cost technology and local material under the SGSY. The awareness among the beneficiaries must be created about the disastrous resistant and environment friendly technology through exhibitions of low cost technologies at the district and block level, seminars, workshops etc. The services of State Institutes of Rural Developments (SIRDs), Extension Training Centres may be taken up for this purpose.

5.8 Involvement of Non-Governmental Organizations

Suitable local Non-Governmental agencies with proven good track record wherever available may be associated for assistance in construction of dwelling units under the Indira Awaas Yojana. The supervision, guidance and the monitoring of construction can be entrusted to these non-governmental organizations. In particular, non-governmental organizations should be made use of to popularize the use of sanitary latrine and smokeless chulhas, as well as innovative technologies, materials designs, etc for cost effective construction. If necessary, funds can be utilized for this purpose from the earmarked funds for training or by dovetailing with the total sanitation campaign.

5.9 Inventory of Houses

The implementing agencies should have a complete inventory of houses constructed/upgraded under the IAY, giving details of the date of start and the date of completion of construction of dwelling unit, name of the village and Block in which the house is located; occupation and category of beneficiaries and other relevant particulars.

5.10 Display of IAY Board and Logo

Completion of a dwelling unit in no case should take more than two years. On completion of an IAY dwelling unit, the Zilla Parishad/DRDA concerned should ensure that for each house so constructed, a display board is fixed indicating the Government of India Rural Housing logo, year of construction, name of the beneficiary etc. The expenditure on this account can be met from the funds available under the scheme accruing due to interest. The cost of each logo should not exceed Rs. 30/-.

(VI)
MONITORING & EVALUATION

6.1 Monitoring

Officers dealing with the IAY at the State headquarters should visit districts regularly and ascertain through field visits whether the programme is being implemented satisfactorily and whether construction of houses is in accordance with the prescribed procedure. Likewise, officers at the district, subdivision and block levels must closely monitor all aspects of the IAY through visits to work sites. A schedule of inspection which prescribes a minimum number of field visits for each supervisory level functionary from the State level to the block level should be drawn up and strictly adhered to. The State Government should prescribe the periodical reports/returns through which it should monitor the performance of IAY in the districts and also get appropriate reports and returns prescribed, to be collected by the Zilla Parishads/DRDAs. The monitoring of the programme at the State Level will be the responsibility of State Level Vigilance and Monitoring Committee for Rural Development Programmes. A representative or nominee of the Ministry of Rural Development, Government of India should invariably be invited to participate in the meetings of the Committee. The following reports and returns should be submitted to the Government of India by the State/UTs separately in respect of the Indira Awaas Yojana *(separately for new construction/upgradation)*: -

(i) a monthly progress report to be furnished by Telex/Fax/ E-mail/Nicnet in **Proforma–I(a) to I(c)**, on or before 10th of every succeeding month.

(ii) A detailed Annual Progress Report to be submitted by 25th April of the succeeding financial year in **Proforma-II(a) & II(b).**

6.2. Evaluation Studies

The Central Government may conduct periodic evaluation studies on the implementation of the Indira Awaas Yojana. These Evaluation studies may be got conducted by reputed institutions and organizations on the implementation as well as the issues thrown up by the Concurrent Evaluation, conducted by the Government of India. The States/UTs may also conduct Evaluation Studies on their own regarding the implementation and impact of the programme in their State. Copies of the reports of these evaluation studies conducted by the States/UTs should be furnished to the Government of India. Remedial action should be taken by the States/UTs on the basis of the observations made in these evaluation studies and also in the Concurrent Evaluation conducted by or on behalf of Government of India.

6.3. Transparency in Implementation of Indira Awaas Yojana

6.3.1 This requires greater transparency in the implementation of the IAY at various levels and hinges on the assumption that people should have access to information about implementation of these programmes in all their aspects. Disclosure of information should be the rule and withholding of information an exception. List of items (illustrative not exhaustive) on which information should invariably be made available to people to bring about greater transparency at village, block and district level is given below.

6.3.2 Village Level

(i) List of people below poverty line in the village.
(ii) List of disaster resistant construction features suitable for the region/locality.
(iii) List of beneficiaries identified during preceding year and current year including details of SC/ST, women beneficiaries and physically/mentally challenged persons under Indira Awaas Yojana.
(iv) Allocation made to the village under Indira Awaas Yojana.
(v) Guidelines of Indira Awaas Yojana/criteria of selecting beneficiaries.
(vi) Display of Indira Awaas Yojana signboard/logo on the allotted houses.

6.3.3. Block Level

(i) Details of houses taken up at Block level with cost, sources of funds and implementing agency.
(ii) Distribution of funds village-wise for the scheme.
(iii) Allocation/availability of funds and progress in implementation of the Indira Awaas Yojana.

6.3.4 District Level

(i) Distribution of the IAY funds block-wise/village-wise for the scheme.
(ii) Criteria for distribution of funds to blocks/villages including norms for its selection under the Indira Awaas Yojana.

(VII)
USE OF LOW COST TECHNOLOGY

7.1 There is a felt need for standardizing, popularizing and replicating cost-effective, disaster resistant and environment-friendly housing construction technologies, designs and materials and also developing ideal sustainable rural human settlements consistent with geo-climatic variations and natural disaster proneness. There is also a need for skill upgradation of rural artisans and other functionaries engaged in the field of rural housing and Habitat Development for adoption of cost effective technologies, materials etc. For adoption of such technologies necessary low cost material is also required to be reduced.

7.2 Development of Low Cost Rural Housing Technology through RBC

Under the Programme, efforts may be made to develop appropriate technologies and capacity building at the grassroots level in order to provide affordable house to the rural poor. This objective can be achieved by making use of the already established Rural Building Centres (RBCs) either by the Ministry or by HUDCO for transfer of technology, dissemination of information, skill upgradation through training, production of cost-effective and environment-friendly material/components, assistance and guidance to rural households/IAY beneficiaries in adoption of cost effective technologies/materials in construction of their houses.

7.3 Monitoring of the on going Projects for their Successful Completion

The implementation of the already sanctioned ongoing projects of Innovative Stream for Rural Housing and Habitat Development and Rural Building Centres (RBCs) shall be monitored by the Ministry of Rural Development. The implementing Agency will be required to furnish the physical and financial progress of the project on quarterly basis regularly in the **Proformas–III & IV** respectively. Further, it shall be open to the Ministry of Rural Development to get the projects verified by HUDCO/NLM/Area Officers/any other agency to facilitate the releases of fund to implementing agencies and completion of the projects. The Ministry of Rural Development can get these projects evaluated at any time and by any agency, if it so desires.

Annexure-IIB

GUIDELINES FOR SAMPOORNA GRAMEEN ROZGAR YOJANA (SGRY)

[EFFECTIVE FROM 01.04.2002]

Ministry of Rural Development
(Department of Rural Development)

Preamble

Creation of employment opportunities with food security has been an important objective of developmental planning in India. The relatively higher growth of population and labour force has led to an increase in the volume of unemployment and under-employment from the one Plan period to another. The Government of India aim at bringing employment through wage and self-employment into a larger focus with the goal of reducing unemployment and under-employment to a negligible level and of providing food security against hunger. Such an approach is necessary, because it is realized that larger and efficient use of available human and other resources is the most effective way of alleviating poverty, reducing inequalities, improving nutritional levels and sustaining a reasonably high pace of economic growth.

To make a dent on the prevailing poverty, unemployment and slow growth in the rural economy and to provide food security, it is necessary to provide a demand driven infrastructure at the village level to facilitate faster growth in the rural areas and to increase opportunities of employment through access to the market oriented economy.

To provide a greater thrust to additional wage employment, infrastructural development and food security in the rural areas, the Hon'ble Prime Minister of India announced on 15 August 2001, launching of an ambitious New Scheme with an annual outlay of Rs.10,000 crores. Accordingly the Ministry of Rural Development reviewed the hitherto on-going Schemes of the Employment Assurance Scheme (EAS), (the only additional wage employment Scheme for rural areas), the Jawahar Gram Samridhi Yojana (JGSY) (a rural infrastructure development Scheme) and by merging them into one Scheme, launched the New Scheme of the Sampoorna Gramin Rozgar Yojana (SGRY) w.e.f. 25 September, 2001.

(I)
BROAD OUTLINE AND OBJECTIVES

1. Objectives

1.1 The Sampoorna Grameen Rozgar Yojana (SGRY) will have the following objectives:

(a) Primary Objective

The primary objective of the Scheme is to provide additional wage employment in all rural areas and thereby provide food security and improve nutritional levels.

(b) Secondary Objective

The secondary objective is the creation of durable community, social and economic assets and infrastructural development in rural areas.

1.2 Status

The programme will be implemented as a centrally sponsored scheme on cost sharing basis between the Centre and the States in the ratio of 75:25 of the cash component of the Programme. In the case of UTs the Centre would provide entire (100%) funds under the Scheme. Foodgrains will be provided to the States/ UTs free of cost.

1.3 Target Group

The SGRY will be open to all rural poor who are in need of wage employment and desire to do manual and unskilled work in and around his village/habitat. The Programme is self-targeting in nature.

While providing wage employment, preference shall be given to agricultural wage earners, non-agricultural unskilled wage earners, marginal farmers, women, members of Scheduled Castes/ Scheduled Tribes and parents of child labour withdrawn from hazardous occupations, parents of handicapped children or adult children of handicapped parents who are desirous of working for wage employment.

1.4 Programme Strategy

(i) 5 per cent of the funds and foodgrains under the Sampoorna Gramin Rozgar Yojana will be retained in the Ministry for utilisation in the areas of acute distress arising out of natural calamities or for taking up preventive measures in the chronically drought or flood affected rural areas. Savings from 5 per cent could be allotted by the Ministry to better performing Districts.

(ii) A certain percentage of the allotted foodgrains under the SGRY will be reserved for the Special Component to be used in any Central or State Government Scheme with wage employment potential to meet exigencies arising out of any natural calamity.

(iii) The remaining funds and foodgrains under the SGRY will be available in two streams from the Department of Rural Development:

(a) **First Stream:** The First Stream will be implemented at the District and Intermediate Panchayat levels. 50 per cent of the funds and foodgrains will be available under the First Stream and will be distributed between the Zilla Parishad and the Intermediate Panchayats in the ratio of 40:60.

(b) **Second Stream:** The Second Stream will be implemented at the Village Panchayat level, and 50 per cent of the funds and foodgrains will be earmarked for the Village Panchayats and distributed among them through DRDAs/Zilla Parishads.

(iv) The Programme will be implemented through the Panchayati Raj Institutions (PRIs).

1.5 Special Safeguards for the Weaker Sections and Women of the Community

(i) 22.5 per cent of the annual allocation (inclusive of foodgrains) under the First Stream of the SGRY both at the District and the Block levels shall be earmarked for individual beneficiary schemes of SC/ST families living below the Poverty Line (BPL).

(ii) Minimum 50 per cent of the allocation to the Village Panchayat (inclusive of foodgrains) shall be earmarked for the creation of need based village infrastructure in SC/ST habitations/wards under the second stream of the SGRY.

(iii) 30 per cent of employment opportunities should be reserved for women.

1.6 Definition of Panchayats

(i) Village Panchayat in these Guidelines means the lowest elected body and includes Gram Panchayats, Mandals, Nagar Panchayats or traditional village institutions like village Councils and Village Development Boards having statutory character.

(ii) Where the duly elected Village Panchayat is not in existence, its share of funds will be passed on to the Administrator/Administrative Committee which will be responsible for implementing the second stream of the SGRY in such Panchayat. The works to be taken up would, however, be decided at the village level itself by the Gram Sabha (Village Assembly) of the concerned Panchayat.

(iii) District & Intermediate Panchayats mean elected bodies at the District & the Block levels respectively and include similar traditional institutions having statutory characters where the Panchayat Act is not applicable.

(iv) Where the duly elected District or Intermediate Panchayat is not in existence, DRDA at the District level and the Administrator/Administrative Committee at the Block level will be responsible for implementing the first stream of the SGRY.

(v) Where the Panchayat Act is not applicable and traditional institutions also do not exist at the District and Block levels, DRDA at the District level and a committee consisting of the heads of the Village Councils etc. and chaired by the BDO at the Block level will be responsible for implementing the first stream of the SGRY.

1.7 Forest Villages

The forest villages, which are not part of any existing Village Panchayat will be treated as Village Panchayats.

(II)
FOODGRAINS UNDER SGRY

2. Foodgrains Should be Given as Part of Wages Under the SGRY

2.1 Distribution of foodgrains as part of wages under the SGRY (First & Second Streams) is based on the principle of protecting the real wages of the workers besides improving the nutritional standards of the families of the rural poor.

2.2 Foodgrains should be given as part of wages under the SGRY to the rural poor at the rate of 5 kg per manday. Should a State Government wish to give more than 5 kg of foodgrains per manday, it may do so within the existing State allocation (subject to a minimum of 25 per cent of the wages to be paid in cash). The State Governments and UT Administrations will be free to calculate the cost of foodgrains paid as part of wages, at a uniform rate which may be either BPL rate, or APL rate or anywhere between the two rates. The workers will be paid the balance of wages in cash, such that they are assured of the notified Minimum Wages. Higher utilization per manday and higher price fixation of foodgrains will result in saving of cash component which may be utilized to meet the material cost for creation of durable community assets.

2.3 The Central Government will provide foodgrains and cash component to the States and UT Administrations as per the criteria in order to generate additional wage employment. If there is a balance of foodgrains from the SGRY the same can be utilized for dovetailing with other Central/State Sector Schemes as per para 8.3.1 provided 100 per cent cash requirement is available from such schemes.

2.4 Distribution of foodgrains to the workers under the Programme will be either through PDS or by the Gram Panchayat or any other Agency appointed by the State Government. Distribution of foodgrains will be made to the workers, most preferably, at the work site. In the event of the workers belonging to one Habitation and should they choose to receive foodgrains in their Habitation, the same could be organized. While the State Government would have the option of utilizing the PDS, it will have to be ensured that effective safeguards are in place to avoid leakages. DRDA's/ZPs will make necessary arrangements for distribution of foodgrains among the concerned Agencies.

2.5 Distribution & Release of Foodgrains under the SGRY

(i) The Department of Rural Development will intimate to the Department of Food & Public Distribution the quantity of foodgrains to be released to the State, with the District-wise details. The Department of Food and Public Distribution will thereafter send an appropriate advice to the FCI under intimation to the Department of Rural Development and the Secretary (RD) of the State, to release foodgrains from its designated depots to the authorised agencies of the State Governments/ZPs/DRDAs.

(ii) The Department of Rural Development will release funds for the foodgrains directly to the FCI at the economic cost. The FCI will be required to send bills duly verified by the DRDA/ZP to the Department of Rural Development on the basis of statements of quantities of foodgrains allocated, lifted District-wise, signed jointly by the PD (DRDA)/CEO Zilla Parishad and District Manager, FCI.

(iii) At the District level the PD, DRDA/CEO, ZP will coordinate the release and lifting of stocks under the programme. No payment will be required to be made to the FCI at the depots by the DRDA or Authorized Agency for lifting the Foodgrains within the District-wise allocation communicated by the Ministry of Rural Development/Department of Food and Public Distribution.

2.6 Procedure for Lifting of Foodgrains from FCI Depots

2.6.1 DRDA/ZP will identify the nearest depot of the FCI from which they are proposing to lift the foodgrains so that there is economy in the transportation charges for lifting of foodgrains. The District office of the FCI will issue release authorization against the District allocation for the SGRY programme. It will be desirable if the ZP/DRDA informs the concerned District office of the FCI about the quantities of foodgrains likely to be lifted by them on a monthly or a quarterly basis. The FCI is obliged to issue foodgrains against the release even without such intimation if stocks of foodgrains are available with them. However, advance intimation is likely to help in ensuring adequate stocks in the concerned depots at the time they are needed. In the interest of administrative convenience, lifting of SGRY foodgrains for all the implementing agencies including the Intermediate Level Panchayats and the Gram Panchayats will have to be made either by the ZPs/DRDAs themselves or through their authorized agencies only.

2.6.2 Stocks once issued will not be taken back by the FCI. It would, therefore, be the responsibility of the ZP/DRDAs to ensure that the quality of wheat/common rice supplied to them conforms to 'Fair Average Quality' (FAQ). The concerned officers of the DRDAs/ZP should conduct inspection of the stocks before taking delivery of the same to ensure that foodgrains below FAQ are not accepted.

2.6.3 The normal procedure by way of joint sampling, as is done for the PDS, will operate. In case of any complaint, the sample from the field will be compared with the sample packet retained at the FCI Depot and action will be initiated against all responsible in this behalf, if any discrepancy is established.

2.7 Provision of Transportation Cost/Handling Charges

The State Governments/Union Territories will bear the transportation cost and other handling charges from their own resources. Any taxes/charges like sales tax, octroi etc. will be borne by the concerned States/UTs. Cash component cannot be used for transportation, payment of local taxes etc.

2.8 Disposal of Empty Gunny Bags

The gunny bags in which the foodgrains are received for distribution under the Programme will be disposed of in accordance with the prescribed procedure in the State and the sale proceeds of the same can be used for making payment towards the transportation cost/handling charges.

(III)
WAGES UNDER SGRY

3. Wages Under the Programme

3.1 The wages under the programme shall be paid partly in foodgrains and partly in cash.

3.2 Minimum Wages

Minimum Wages fixed by the State authorities shall be paid under the SGRY both for skilled and unskilled labour.

3.3 Equal wages shall be paid under the programme to both men and women workers.

3.4 Payment of wages shall be made on a fixed day in a week preferably a day before the local market day, in the presence of the Village Pradhan/Sarpanch or Panchas.

3.5 In case the executing Agencies do not pay the wages for a category of employment at the rate notified for the relevant schedule of employment under the Minimum Wages Act, the Zilla Parishad/Panchayat Samiti shall withhold further release of funds to that implementing agency and inform the fact to the concerned authority for suitable action against the erring official under the Minimum Wages Act and also inform the Central Government.

3.6 Where the Central Government finds that the above provisions are not being followed, it may withhold further release of funds under the programme to the concerned District.

(IV)
CRITERIA, ALLOCATION AND UTILISATION OF RESOURCES

First Stream

4.1 Allocation of Funds/Foodgrains from Centre to State/UTs and the Districts

(i) Under the Scheme, funds and foodgrains would be allocated to the States/UTs on the basis of proportion of the rural poor in a State to the total rural poor in the country or such other criteria as decided by the Central Government from time to time.

(ii) At the District level, the allocation of funds and foodgrains will be made on the index of backwardness formulated on the basis of the proportion of rural SC/ST population in a District to the total SC/ST population in the State and inverse of per capita production of the agricultural workers in that District. Equal weightage will be given to these two criteria, while allocating funds and foodgrains to the district.

4.2 Distribution of Funds Among Zilla Parishads/DRDAs and Panchayat Samitis

(i) **Zilla Parishads/DRDAs:** 40 per cent of the funds and

foodgrains earmarked under the First Stream will be reserved at the District level and shall be utilized by the Zilla Parishads/DRDAs preferably in the areas suffering from endemic labour exodus/areas of distress, as per the Annual Action Plan approved by the Zilla Parishads/ DRDAs.

(ii) **Panchayat Samitis:** 60 per cent of the funds and foodgrains earmarked under the First Stream would be allocated among the Panchayat Samitis (Intermediate Panchayats). While allocating the funds and foodgrains, equal weightage will be given to the proportion of SC/ ST population and of rural population of the respective Panchayat Samiti areas to those of the Districts. The works will be taken as per their own Annual Action Plan approved by the Panchayat Samitis. However, while selecting the work, to be taken up, preference will be given to the Areas which are backward, Calamity Prone or face migration of labour.

4.3 Earmarking and Utilization of Resources

4.3.1 Earmarking of Resources

There will be no sectoral earmarking of resources under the First Stream of the SGRY except that the 22.5 per cent of the annual allocation of the Zilla Parishad/DRDA and of the Intermediate Level Panchayat must be spent on individual beneficiary schemes for SCs/STs below the poverty line. Diversion of funds meant for SCs/STs to other works is not permitted.

4.4 Beneficiary Oriented Individual Programmes for SCs/STs

As indicated in the above Para, 22.5 per cent of the resources released to the Zilla Parishad and Intermediate Level Panchayat shall be used for individual works for SCs/STs. The illustrative list of such Economic Assets/Works which can be taken up for the benefit of identified individuals belonging to SCs/STs are as under:

(i) Development of allotted land in the case of allottees of ceiling surplus land, Bhoodan land, Government land.
(ii) Social forestry works, such as fuelwood and fodder plantations on the private lands belonging to SCs/STs.
(iii) Agri-horticulture, floriculture, horticulture plantation on the private lands belonging to SCs/STs below poverty line.
(iv) Work sheds or infrastructure for any self-employment programme.
(v) Open Irrigation Wells/Bore-wells for irrigation.
(vi) Pond excavation/re-excavation with primary support for pisciculture, and
(vii) Other sustainable income generating assets.

Assets for Improving the Quality of Life

(viii) Dwelling units.
(ix) Sanitary Latrine and smokeless chullahs.

Priority should be given to provide economic assets to individual beneficiaries for sustainable employment. Assets such as dwelling units, sanitary latrines, smokeless chullhas, etc. may be given lesser priority and should be considered under exceptional circumstances.

While providing assets to the individual poor, his/her participation in the work may be ensured.

4.5 Provision for Maintenance of Assets

The Zilla Parishads/DRDAs and Intermediate Level Panchayats are permitted to spend up to a maximum of 15 per cent of the funds on maintenance of the public assets created under the wage-employment programme sponsored by the Ministry of Rural Development from time to time within its geographical boundary.

4.6 Provision for Contingency

Up to 2 per cent of the funds released during the year under the First Stream can be spent by the Zilla Parishads on contingency for strengthening monitoring and coordination. In case the expenditure on contingency exceeds the prescribed limit, Central

Share of the excess amount will be deducted from the Second Instalment.

4.7 Unspent Resources of Administrative/Contingent and Maintenance Expenditure

Effort should be made by the Zilla Parishad and Intermediate Level Panchayats to incur only such expenditure on maintenance of assets, which are absolutely necessary. Strict economy should be observed in incurring such expenditure. Unspent balances under these heads will form part of the programme resources of the First Stream of the SGRY.

Second Stream

4.8 The Second Stream of the SGRY will be implemented at the Village Panchayat level for generation of supplementary wage employment and creation of demand driven community village infrastructure which includes also durable assets to enable the rural poor to increase opportunities for sustained employment.

4.9 Criteria and Procedure for Allocation/Release of Resources

4.9.1 Out of the total resources earmarked under the SGRY, 50 per cent of the funds are earmarked for the Second Stream of the SGRY. The entire resources released under the Second Stream would be distributed among the Gram Panchayats directly by the DRDA/Zilla Parishad.

4.9.2 While, during the current year (2001-02) the allocation and release of resources will continue as per the existing criteria for the JGSY, from the second financial year (2002-03) onwards, the allocation of funds would be made in a manner that each Panchayat receives at least a certain minimum of resources as to be decided from year to year.

4.9.3 The State and District-wise allocations will be made by the Ministry of Rural Development at the Central level. At the Panchayat level, the DRDA/Zilla Parishad will make the allocation to each Panchayat, as per the criteria given in Para 4.9.4 below.

4.9.4 The base year allocation will not get affected if there is subsequent increase or decrease in the number of Panchayats in each District. If there is increase in the number of Panchayats in any given year, the share of each Panchayat will be reduced proportionately. If there is decrease in the number of Panchayats, the share of each Panchayat will be increased proportionately. The proposed allocation criteria will be taken into account for working out State-wise allocation in the subsequent years subject to the following conditions:

(i) The year 2001-02 would be treated as base year for taking into account the number of Panchayats per District. Henceforth, the number of Panchayats District-wise as on 1.4.2001 would form the base for working out allocation in the subsequent years. The Government of India would allocate funds to the State/UTs based on the number of Panchayats in a District as on 1.4.2001.

(ii) The State Government would have no claim for additional allocation of resources if the number of Panchayats in a particular District is increased after 1.4.2001

(iii) In no case, the State Government/DRDAs/ZPs would be authorized to make any alteration or change in the above criteria for working out District-wise allocation or any diversion from one District to another District or from one Panchayat to another.

4.10 Earmarking of Resources

Minimum 50 per cent of the allocation to the Village Panchayat (inclusive of foodgrains) shall be earmarked for the creation of need based Village infrastructure in SC/ST habitations/wards under the second stream of the SGRY.

4.11 Provision for Maintenance of Assets

Village Panchayats are permitted to spend up to a maximum of 15 per cent of the funds on maintenance of the public assets created under the wage-employment programme sponsored by the Ministry of Rural Development from time to time within its geographical boundary.

4.12 Provision for Administrative/Contingent Expenditure at the Gram Panchayat Level

Under the Second Stream of SGRY, Village Panchayats may spend up to a maximum of 7.5 per cent of the annual allocation of funds or Rs. 7500/- whichever is less during a year on the Administration/Contingencies and for technical consultancy.

4.13 Unspent Resources of Administrative/Contingent and Maintenance Expenditure

Effort should be made by the Village Panchayats to incur only such expenditure on maintenance of assets, which are absolutely necessary. Strict economy should be observed in incurring such expenditure. Unspent balances under these heads will form part of the programme resources of the Second Stream of the SGRY.

4.14 Release of Funds to Village Panchayats

(1) The resources to the Village Panchayats will be distributed by the DRDAs/ZPs within fifteen days of the receipt of the funds by the DRDAs/ZPs from the Central or the State Governments, as the case may be. The distribution of Central Share will not wait for the matching State share.

(2) In so far as forest villages are concerned DRDAs/ZPs will place the allocated funds and foodgrains at the disposal of the respective District level forest officials for taking up works under the programme in these villages. The forest authority at the District level will utilise these funds and foodgrains to take up works in the forest village through a committee of five members, consisting of at lease one SC/ST and a women, as per felt need of the village community.

(V)
RELEASE OF CENTRAL ASSISTANCE

5. Release of Central Assistance from the Department of Rural Development

5.1 Central Assistance (inclusive of foodgrains) will be released every year directly to the DRDAs/ZPs in two instalments, subject to the fulfilment of the following conditions:

5.2 First Instalment: The Districts, which obtained the second instalment of funds and foodgrains in the preceding financial year without any condition shall automatically receive the first installment under both the streams. Others shall have to submit the proposal for the 5.1. Instalment with necessary documents as mentioned under Para 5.4 or after fulfilling the conditions imposed while releasing the Second Instalment for the previous year.

5.3 In case of snow bound Districts, viz. Kinnaur, Lahaul and Spiti, Leh, Kargil and those Districts of North-Eastern States to be decided mutually between the Central Government and the State Government concerned, which have a limited working. season, the entire Central assistance shall be released in one instalment, after fulfilling the condition prescribed under Sub-para 5.4 below.

5.4 Second Instalment: The second instalment of Central assistance (inclusive of foodgrains) will be released on request from the DRDA/ZP separately under both the streams in the prescribed proforma as per **Annexure I** and *mutatis mutandis* and on fulfilment of the following conditions:

(i) 60 per cent of the total available funds, that is opening balance of the year (in case of proposal for the first instalment, opening balance of the previous year) plus the amount received including the State share and other receipts should have been utilized at the time of submitting the proposal for the second instalment.

(ii) 75 per cent of the foodgrains allocated as first instalment has been lifted and 60 per cent of the lifted foodgrains (including the balance) has been utilized along with a reconciled statement of the quantity lifted to be signed by the PD/DRDA/CEO, Zilla Parishads and FCI District Manager.

(iii) The opening balance of the District, i.e. the aggregate balances with the Zila Parishad and Panchayat Samitis in case of Stream I and of the Gram Panchayats in case of Stream II should not exceed 15 per cent of the funds available during the previous year. In case, the opening balance exceeds this limit, the Central share of the excess will be deducted proportionately at the time of release of the second instalment.

(iv) The allocation of foodgrains in the second instalment will be reduced by the quantity which remained unlifted in the previous year. The cash component of Central share accordingly will be reduced proportionately.

(v) The State Government has made sufficient provision in their Budget to match the Central financial assistance.

(vi) The State Government should have released all its contribution (including that of the previous years) due, up to the date of the application. In the event of shortfall in State share, corresponding amount of Central share will be deducted from the amount of Central share of the second instalment of the current year.

(vii) Submission of Audit reports for the SGRY for the last year and submission of Action Taken Report on the comments made in the audit report of the previous year.

(viii) Submission of Utilization Certificates (Cash and foodgrains) from DRDAs/Zilla Parishads based on reports received from Intermediate Level Panchayats (Stream – I) and Gram Panchayat (Stream – II) for the previous year should be submitted in the prescribed Proforma as per **Annexures II (a) and II (b)**.

(ix) Submission of non-diversion and non-embezzlement certificate.

(x) Certificate that the Zilla Parishads, the Intermediate Level Panchayats & Village Panchayats have prepared the Annual Action Plan. In the case of Village Panchayats the certificate should show that the plan has been got approved by the Gram Sabhas.

(xi) Certificate by the DRDA/Zilla Parishad to the effect that Intermediate Level Panchayats & Village Panchayats have been disbursed the funds as per their entitlement according to these guidelines within 15 days of their receipt in the DRDA/ZP from the Central/State Government.

(xii) All pending progress/monitoring reports should have been sent.

(xiii) Details of expenditure incurred in respect of SC/ST sector, i.e. 22.5 per cent funds and foodgrains earmarked at the Zilla Parishad and Intermediate Level Panchayats and 50 per cent of annual allocation of Village Panchayats for SC/ST habitations respectively during the previous year should be furnished. In case of shortfall in expenditure on SC/ST sector in either of the stream, proportionate deduction (i.e. 75 per cent of shortfall) will be made from the II instalment of Central Share.

(xiv) Certificates to the effect that :

- (a) No work started more than two years ago remains unfinished.
- (b) All conditions laid down in the guidelines are being fulfilled.

(xv) Certificate regarding maintenance of muster rolls.

Any other condition imposed from time to time will also have to be complied with.

5.5 In case of the districts, to which funds are released in one instalment, they will be released on fulfilment of the conditions laid down in Para 5.4 .

5.6 For the sake of convenience, a check list to be furnished along with the proposal is given in **Annexure III.**

5.7 Release of State Share to DRDAs/ZPs: State Government shall release its matching share to the DRDAs/ZPs within a fortnight after the release of Central assistance (cash component).

5.8 Release of funds to the Intermediate Level and to Village Panchayats

5.8.1 The funds and foodgrains to Intermediate Level Panchayats (under stream–I) and resources to the village panchayats (under stream–II) will be distributed by the DRDAs/ZPs within fifteen days of the receipt of the funds by the DRDAs/ZPs from the Central or the State Government, as the case may be. Distribution of Central Share should not wait for matching State share.

5.8.2 In so far as forest villages are concerned DRDAs/ZPs will place the allocated funds at the disposal of the respective District level forest officials. The forest authority at the District level will utilize these funds /take up works in the forest village through a committee of five members consisting of at least one SC/ST, woman and as per felt need of village community in respect of works taken up by the Village Panchayats.

5.9 Diversion of Resources: Diversion of resources from one District to another will not be permitted. Similarly, diversion of resources from a Intermediate Level Panchayat to another Intermediate Level Panchayat will also not be permissible except as provided under Para 5.11.

5.10 Carryover Funds Not to Exceed 15 Per cent: The District/Intermediate Level Panchayats and village panchayats should spend the funds and foodgrains made available to them during the year in which they are made available. If the carryover funds is more than 15 per cent of the funds and foodgrains available during the previous year, a cut will be imposed for this District. The Zilla Parishads/DRDAs should ensure that such of the Gram Panchayats and Intermediate Panchayats which did not have an excess carry over are not affected by the cut and are given full allocation. The Opening Balance of the EAS and JGSY for the year 2001-02 will be carried forward in the account of First and Second Stream of the SGRY respectively for being utilized as per the Guidelines for the Ist and IInd Stream of SGRY.

5.11 Cuts to be Imposed on Late Receipt of Proposals

5.11.1 The proposal for release of second instalment by the DRDA/ZP complete in all respects should be submitted latest by 31. December every year.

5.11.2 To maintain financial discipline, a mandatory deduction(s) on account of late submission of proposal by the State Government shall be imposed depending upon the date of receipt of proposal for release of second instalment under the SGRY (First Stream). Under the system, there will be progressive deductions for proposals(s) received in the month of January and February @ 10 per cent and 20 per cent respectively on the total Central allocation (inclusive of foodgrains) for the year. Incomplete proposals will not be accepted. The date on which last information is received from the State shall be treated as date of receipt of the proposal.

5.11.3 Notwithstanding the above provision (Para 5.11.1), State should submit the proposal for the second instalment latest by 15th February every year. Acceptance of proposal(s) after 15th February upto 28th February will be considered only in exceptional circumstances. Proposals will not be accepted after February under any circumstances. However, if the proposal received in the month of March are accepted under special circumstances, 30 per cent cut in the allocation will be imposed.

5.12 Opening of Bank Accounts: The SGRY funds (Central share as well as State share) shall be kept in a nationalized bank or a Post Office in an exclusive and separate savings bank account by the Zilla Parishads/DRDAs/Intermediate Level/Village Panchayat.

5.13 Utilization of Interest Earned on Deposits: The interest amount accrued on the deposits of each streams shall be treated as additional resources for that stream and should be utilized as per these Guidelines.

5.14 Drawal of Funds

5.14.1 Drawal of funds by the DRDAs/Zilla Parishads from the SGRY (First Stream) accounts shall only be made either for distribution of funds among the Intermediate Level Panchayat or for utilisation under their share of funds and drawal for **IInd stream** for distribution of funds among the village panchayats.

5.14.2 Stream I: The amounts for payment from the account of the village/Intermediate Level Panchayat should be drawn through a cheque. The cheque shall be signed by the BDO or an officer of equivalent rank. Release of every amount should be authorized in the meeting of the Intermediate Level Panchayat.

5.14.3 Stream II: However, in case of village panchayats the cheque shall be signed by the Head of Panchayat along with another person who has been specially authorized by the village panchayat by a Resolution. The other person must be a member of the village panchayat or Secretary of the panchayat. Payment of every amount should be authorized in the meeting of village panchayat and the Gram Sabha should be informed about it in the following meeting.

Drawals for any other purpose shall not be authorized.

5.15 Utilization of Savings: Savings under the First and Second stream of the SGRY at the Central level of funds/ foodgrains from the allocation of a State/UT can be reallocated by the Ministry to better performing Districts. Such savings which cannot be absorbed within the State can be reallocated by the Ministry to better performing Districts according to the guidelines of the Ministry of Rural Development.

5.16 Miscellaneous Points

5.16.1 Ban on Contractors: The programme will be implemented departmentally only. Contractors are not permitted to be engaged for execution of any of the works under the programme. No middleman or any other intermediate agency should be employed for executing works under the programme. The full benefit of wages to be paid should reach the workers and the cost of the works should not involve any commission charges payable to such contractors, middlemen, or intermediate agency.

5.16.2 Muster Rolls: Muster rolls shall be maintained for every work separately, showing the details of wages paid to workers and foodgrains distributed. The muster rolls for all works should have entries showing the number and details of Scheduled Castes/Scheduled Tribes/Women and others who have been provided employment. Those responsible for the preparation of muster rolls should be responsible for these entries also. To prevent non-payment or under payment of wages or any manipulation, muster rolls should be maintained in stitched forms and all its pages must be numbered.

Muster rolls shall be made available for public on demand. However, for works taken up by the Village Panchayats under SGRY, muster rolls' copies duly certified by the Panchayat Sarpanch shall be placed before every Gram Sabha.

5.16.3 Records of the Assets Created: Each District, Block and Village Panchayat shall maintain complete inventory of the assets created under the programme giving details of the date of the start and the date of completion of the project, cost involved, benefits obtained, employment generated and other relevant particulars. Signboards should be displayed near the works giving these details. Photographic record of the work may also be kept of the various stage of implementation before start, during implementation and after completion.

5.16.4 Audit of Works: Both physical and financial audit of the works under the scheme are compulsory. This must be carried out at the end of the financial year by each district. The audit will be done either by Local Fund Auditors or by the Chartered Accountants listed in the panel of the State Government or AGs of the State or C&AG. The audit report together with action taken on the auditor's observations shall be furnished at the time second instalment of funds for the next financial year.

5.16.5 Social Audit: Immediately on finalization of works of the programme Zilla Parishad/DRDAs shall publicise and inform Gram Panchayats details of works to ensure transparency, accountability and social control. Gram Panchayats should place these details before the respective Gram Sabhas.

As regards Village Panchayats meetings of the Gram Sabha shall be held every quarter at a fixed date, time and place to consider the issues regarding the planning, execution, monitoring and supervision. These meetings shall be open to all members of the village community, who shall be free to raise any issue regarding implementation of the Yojana. The Gram Sabha should also be kept informed about the progress of the implementation of the scheme and all other related issues.

(VI)
PLANNING, WORKS AND EXECUTION

6.1 Annual Action Plan

6.1.1 Each Zilla Parishad/DRDA, Intermediate Level and Village Panchayat shall independently prepare and approve, before the beginning of each financial year, an Annual Action Plan equivalent in value of about 125 per cent of its share of funds allocated in the preceding year. No work can be taken up unless it forms part of the Annual Action Plan. The exercise of approval of Annual Action Plan should be completed by the end of February of the preceding financial year.

6.1.2 To ensure meaningful utilization of resources under the SGRY, routine division of resources among the wards of the Gram Panchayat and among the Constituencies of the Panchayat Samiti and of the Zilla Parishad is prohibited. Works included in the Annual Action Plan should be need based and properly prioratized. Looking to the priorities of works and the availability of resources only that many works should be taken up which can be completed within a year and in exceptional circumstances in a maximum period of two years.

6.1.3 While preparing the Annual Action Plan, completion of the incomplete works including those of the EAS/JGSY should be given priority over the taking up of new works. No work shall be taken up which cannot be completed in one year or at the most within two financial years.

6.1.4 As soon as the Annual Plan is finalized, the Zilla Parishads/DRDA and Intermediate Level Panchayats shall inform the concerned Gram Panchayats about the works selected for their areas.

6.1.5 Works to be taken up by ZPs/DRDA and Intermediate Panchayats should be labour intensive. Works requiring larger component of materials like cement, steel etc. should not be sanctioned unless the excess cost on material component is provided from other sectoral programme funds.

6.1.6 The Annual Action Plan prepared by the Village Panchayat should be thoroughly discussed in the meeting of the Gram Sabha. Similarly, the Annual Action Plan prepared by the ZPs/DRDAs and Intermediate Level Panchayats should be thoroughly discussed in their respective General Bodies. The Gram Sabha in respect of Village Panchayats and the General Bodies in respect of ZPs/DRDA and Intermediate Level Panchayats shall approve the Annual Action Plan. The approved Annual Action Plan should be intimated to the Panchayat Samiti and ZP/DRDA.

6.1.7 All works proposed to be dovetailed with State and/or other schemes should be included in the Annual Action Plan. In that case the cash component shall be met fully from those schemes and the corresponding foodgrain component from SGRY.

6.2 Administrative Sanction

The administrative sanction for the works under the Annual Action Plan will be given by the competent authority as decided by the State/UT.

6.3 Technical Sanction

The technical sanction would be accorded as per rules of the State Government/Union Territories.

6.4 Coordination and Supervision of Works

The Zilla Parishad/DRDA would be responsible for the overall coordination and supervision of the works. Subject to overall control of the ZP/DRDA, the Panchayat Samitis shall exercise supervision of the works taken up with the Panchayat Samiti component.

6.5 Works to be taken up under the First Stream of SGRY

6.5.1 In formulating the Annual Action Plan and while taking up the works, Zilla Parishads/DRDAs and Panchayat Samitis shall give priority to the works of soil and moisture conservation, minor irrigation, rejuvenation of drinking water sources and augmentation of ground water, traditional water harvesting structures, desiltation of village tanks/ponds etc. and such other schemes of individual nature which are necessary for Watershed development. However, since the nature of works is required to be such that they could be completed in one or two years, watershed development projects requiring commitment for a large period shall not be taken up. Other priority works may be construction of rural link roads, farm roads linking agricultural fields, drainage works and afforestation. Other than these, they should essentially take up works that result in creation of durable socio-economic assets such as schools, kitchen sheds for schools, dispensaries, community centres, Panchayat Ghars, development of hats (markets) etc.

However, while taking up these works, the Implementing Agencies may take into consideration the facilities being created under basic Minimum Services and other Centrally Sponsored Schemes or State Government's schemes.

6.5.2 While there is no ceiling on the cost of works to be taken up, their size and cost and nature should be such that they may be completed within a period of one year and in exceptional situations within a period of maximum two years. The works taken up must be kept within the overall Annual Action Plan (As per Para 6.4). The following works shall not be taken under the programme:

(a) Building for religious purposes such as temple, mosque, gurudwara, church etc.
(b) Monuments, Memorials, Statue, Idols, Arch Gate/ Welcome Gate.
(c) Bridges.
(d) Building for higher secondary schools.

(e) Building for colleges.
(f) Black topping of roads.

6.5.3 Works taken up under the programme should be of a durable nature and should meet technical standards and specifications, if any, for the concerned work/area.

6.5.4 Efforts should be made to utilise local materials and cost effective technology developed by various institutions.

6.5.5 The items of work approved by the Intermediate Level Panchayat for their share of funds in the manner prescribed above shall not be changed at the Zilla Parishad/DRDA.

6.5.6 In order to facilitate the technical scrutiny of the works, authorities at the Zilla Parishad/DRDA level may prepare and approve standard designs and cost estimates of those items of works which are common in nature.

6.6 Execution under First Stream

Implementing Authority

6.6.1 The Zilla Parishad/DRDA shall be the "Implementing Authority" for its share of resources released to the Zilla Parishad (ZPs)/DRDA and the Intermediate Level Panchayats (IPS) shall be the Implementing Authority for its share of resources released by the Zilla Parishad/DRDA. The ZPs/DRDAs and Intermediate Level Panchayats would be responsible for approval of Annual Action Plan for their respective share of resources and entrusting works to executing agencies.

6.6.2 The Zilla Parishad/DRDA shall be responsible for overall supervision and coordination of works and furnishing of necessary reports to the State and Central Governments.

6.7 Executing Agencies

6.7.1 The Executing agencies of the First Stream of SGRY within a District can be any line department, corporation of the State Government, Panchayati Raj Institutions (PRIs) at all three levels or well reputed NGOs as approved by the Zilla Parishad/DRDA.

6.7.2 It shall be the duty of the head of each executing agency in the District to scrupulously ensure the implementation of the works allotted by the Zilla Paishads/DRDA and Intermediate Level Panchayats. All executing agencies shall be responsible to the Zilla Parishad/DRDA/Panchayat Samiti for the proper maintenance of accounts of the expenditure incurred, measurement of physical work done, payment of wages to labour, submission of periodical statements of attendance, details of work and accounts for all works entrusted to them under the first stream of the SGRY.

6.7.3 The executing agencies may utilize one person from among the beneficiaries group as animator/leader/facilitator in maintenance of muster rolls, payment of wages, monitoring of quality of works etc. Such animator/leader/facilitator can be paid wages applicable to the skilled workers. If the animator/leader/facilitator is not from among the beneficiaries (one of the labour working on the scheme) then the executing agencies would be responsible for supervision, maintenance of muster rolls, payment of wages etc.

6.8 Maintenance of Employment Register under First Stream

6.8.1 Each Panchayat Samiti for its Samiti area shall maintain an Employment register for the works under the Panchayat Samiti component which would contain the details of number of persons employed including the number of SC/ST, gender of the workers and number of mandays generated for each work under the First Stream of the SGRY. This information should be based on the Muster Rolls which is maintained work-wise. This register would be open to the public for scrutiny. Copies of this register shall be made available to public on demand, after charging a small fee if necessary. The State/UT shall fix the fee. Display board should be put on the work site giving details of the work. Photographs of the works at various stages may also be kept.

6.8.2 The Zilla Parishad/DRDA shall similarly maintain the Employment register for the entire district for its own component.

6.9 Works to be taken up under Second Stream of SGRY

6.9.1 All works that result in the creation of durable productive community assets can be taken up under the programme as per the felt needs of the area/people by the Village Panchayat.

6.9.2 Priority shall be given in the following order:

(a) Infrastructure support for Swarnjayanti Gram Swarozgar Yojana (SGSY).
(b) Infrastructure required for supporting agricultural activities in the Village Panchayat.
(c) Community infrastructure for education(including kitchen sheds), health and internal as well as link roads (roads linking the village to the main road, even if it falls outside the Panchayat area is allowed to be constructed.
(d) Other socio-economic community assets.
(e) Desiltation, renovation of traditional village tanks/ponds.

6.9.3 While creating rural infrastructure, emphasis should be given on labour intensive works. Purely material oriented works are not to be taken up. It should be seen to it that works are sustainable and cost effective.

6.9.4 While there is no ceiling on the cost of works to be taken up under the programme, only such works should generally be taken up whose size and cost and nature are such that they are capable of being implemented at the local level and do not involve high level of technical inputs, etc. The works taken up must be kept within the overall Annual Action Plan. The following works shall not be taken up under the programme.

(i) Buildings for religious purposes such as temple, mosque, gurudwara, church etc.
(ii) Monuments, Memorials, Statues, Idols, Arch Gate/ Welcome Gate.
(iii) Bridges. (except culverts, small bridges on local "nalas" small streams).
(iv) Building for higher secondary schools.
(v) Building for colleges.

6.9.5 Works taken up under the programme should be of

durable nature and should meet technical standards and specifications, if any, for the concerned work/area. The village Panchayats may also take technical advice from the block officials or from reputed NGOs in the area, if needed.

6.9.6 Use of low cost technology and local materials shall be encouraged.

6.9.7 While fixing technical specifications, efforts should be made to utilize, to the maximum extent, local materials and low cost technology development by various institutions.

6.9.8 The items of works approved by the Village Panchayat/ Gram Sabha in the manner prescribed above shall not be allowed to be changed either at the block or the district level.

6.9.9 In order to facilitate the technical scrutiny of the Plan of Action of the Village Panchayat, the authorities at the DRDA/ ZP may prepare and approve standard designs and cost estimates of those items of works which are generally taken up by the Village Panchayats. It will help in quicker preparation of the Plan of Action by the Village Panchayats and also quicker approval by the Gram Sabha.

6.10 Execution under Second Stream

Implementing Agencies of Second Stream

6.10.1 The programme will be implemented through the Village Panchayats, who will be responsible for planning and execution of the Yojana. The technical supervision will be the responsibility of the DRDAs/ZPs. Execution of works can be entrusted to well established Self Help Groups under the Swaranajayanti Gramin Swarozgar Yojana (SGSY).

6.10.2 Forest Departments in the district will implemented the programmes in forest villages in consultation with the people of the concerned forest villages keeping in view of the SGRY guidelines and Forest (Conservation) Act, 1980, as amended from time to time

6.10.3 At the village level, the entire work relating to co-ordination, review, supervision and monitoring of the programme will be the responsibility of the Village Panchayat.

6.10.4 At the district level, the DRDAs/Zilla Parishads and at the intermediate level the Panchayat Samitis will have overall responsibility for guidance, co-ordination, supervision, periodical reporting and monitoring the implementation of the programme. The DRDAs/Zilla Parishads will also be accountable to the State Government to ensure that the returns/reports in respect of the works taken up for execution in the district are furnished in time.

6.10.5 The Panchayats will execute the work. The Panchayats will have the power to execute works/schemes upto Rs.1,00,000 with the approval of Gram Sabha. No other administrative or technical approval will be necessary. Preparation of cost-estimates for work/schemes up to Rs.1,00,000 will be the sole responsibility of the Gram Panchayats. But the Gram Panchayat should get the estimates of works prepared by technically qualified people and check measurement of work done with reference to estimates prior to payment. However, for works/schemes costing more than Rs.1,00,000 after taking approval of the Gram Sabha, the Gram Panchayat shall seek the technical/administrative approval of appropriate authorities.

6.10.6 In case of shortage of technical staff or otherwise, it shall be permissible for the Village Panchayat to have the projects technically appraised by even private technically qualified people. State Government should lay down norms for employment of such private technical qualified staff.

(VII)
MONITORING AND EVALUATION

7. Monitoring and Evaluation of the Programme

7.1 Monitoring

7.1.1 Vigilance and Monitoring Committees at the State, District and Panchayat Samiti level constituted for overseeing the various programmes of the Ministry of Rural Development will also be responsible to monitor the implementation of the works under the first and second streams of the SGRY.

7.1.2 Schedule for Inspection of Works: For effective

implementation of the programme, the officers at the District, Sub-Division and Panchayat Samiti levels must closely monitor all aspects of the programme through visits to work sites in the interior areas. A schedule of inspection, which prescribes the minimum number of field visits for each supervisory level functionaries from District to Panchayat Samiti level, should be drawn up by the Zilla Parishads/DRDAs, and strictly adhered to. A copy of the inspection schedule drawn should be sent to State and Central Governments for information.

7.1.3 The officers dealing with the SGRY at the State headquarters shall visit Districts regularly and ascertain through field visits that the programme is being implemented satisfactorily and that execution of works is in accordance with the prescribed procedures and specifications.

7.1.4 During the course of inspection, if any official comes across any irregularities, he/she should immediately bring it to the notice of the CEO, Zilla Parishad and the Project Director, DRDA so that appropriate action is taken.

7.2 Reports and Returns

7.2.1 It shall be open to the Central Government to prescribe reporting formats for Monthly and Annual Reports. The State may, if it so desires, call for such additional information in such formats, as it may deem fit. The DRDAs/ZPs will also be accountable to the State Government to ensure that the returns/ reports in respect of the works taken up for execution under both the streams of the SGRY in the Districts are furnished in time.

7.2.2 The following reports and returns will be submitted to the State/UTs by the Zilla Parishads/DRDAs:

(i) **A Monthly Progress Report** to be furnished in **Proforma I** for both the streams separately by the 10th of every succeeding month as per **Annexure IV.**

(ii) A detailed **Annual Report** to be submitted for both the streams separately by 25th April of the succeeding year. **Proforma II** will be used for this purpose as per **Annexure V.**

7.2.3 The State Government will consolidate these reports and returns received from the Districts and furnish the same to the Central Government, by the 25th of every succeeding month.

7.2.4 The reports would enable the authorities both at the Centre and the State/UT level to monitor the progress of the programme and to keep a close watch on the wage employment generated and quality of infrastructure created. It will also help the Government to take mid-course corrections.

7.2.5 The Central Government may develop a computerized information system for reporting under the SGRY. All implementing agencies, Zilla Parishads/DRDAs shall follow the prescribed system.

7.3 Evaluation

7.3.1 The States/UTs should conduct periodical evaluation studies on the implementation of the programme.

7.3.2 Evaluation studies may be given to the reputed institutions and organizations, on issues meriting detailed studies. These studies may be initiated by the Centre as well as the States/UTs. Copies of the evaluation studies conducted by the State should be furnished to the Central Government.

7.3.3 Remedial action shall be taken by the States/UTs on the basis of the observations made in these evaluation studies.

7.3.4 The Zilla Parishad/DRDA may also conduct studies from time to time. The Zilla Parishad/DRDA shall report the outcome of the studies to the State Government and the Central Government from time to time.

(VIII) CONVERGENCE WITH THE OTHER PROGRAMMES

8. Contributions by the Village Community

8.1 The village Community may be encouraged to contribute either physically or financially for the development of rural infrastructure. The PRIs may, subject to relevant laws, even raise additional resources through appropriate cess/tax to ensure people's participation by inculcating in them the feeling of community ownership.

8.2 Acceptance of Donations

8.2.1 The Panchayati Raj Institutions may accept donations from charitable institutions, NGOs, NRIs and individuals either to expand the programme or to ensure the durability of the assets requiring funds. These funds should be treated as additional and dovetailed with the SGRY funds to complete the works.

8.3 Convergence/Dovetailing with Other Programmes

8.3.1 Funds available from other sources like market committees, co-operatives, NGOs, NRIs and other institutions could also be dovetailed with the SGRY funds for similar purposes. The funds available with the PRIs from other sources such as National Finance Commission, State Finance Commission, State Departments, other Central and Centrally Sponsored Schemes, etc. can also be dovetailed for construction of durable community assets/works. However, SGRY funds should not be used as a substitute for Departmental Plan funds of different Departments and agencies. Funds from other programmes for the works permissible under the SGRY can be dovetailed with SGRY funds and not *vice versa*. Such works are required to be part of the Annual Action Plan.

8.3.2 If the State Governments are unable to utilize entire foodgrains with the cash component available under the SGRY, the balance of foodgrains can be utilized by dovetailing the cash component from their State Sector Schemes. However, the mandays generated under such circumstances will be the part of the SGRY Scheme and the same should be reflected in their Annual and Monthly Progress Reports and Annual Action Plans should be prepared keeping in view of the above factors.

(IX)
MISCELLANEOUS

9. Provision of Facilities at the Work-Sites

9.1 Wherever required, arrangement for providing facilities like drinking water, rest sheds for the workers and crèches for the children coming with working mothers should be made. Expenditure involved for providing these facilities should be met out of the non-wage component under the programme.

9.2 Rural Standard Schedule of Rates

9.2.1 The State Secretaries should evolve and publish "Rural Standard Schedule of Rates" to eliminate the role of contractors.

9.3 Redressal of Grievances

9.3.1 If there are any grievances with regard to the implementation of the SGRY by the implementing agencies including proper payment of wages, representation can be made to the CEO, ZP, DRDA or the Block Development Officer. It will be the responsibility of these functionaries to enquire into the representation and redress the grievances in an appropriate manner.

(X)
SPECIAL COMPONENT

10.1 There will be a Special Component of the SGRY for augmenting food security through additional wage employment in the calamity affected rural areas after due notification by the State Government and its acceptance by the Ministry of Agriculture. A certain percentage of the allotted foodgrains under the SGRY will be reserved for this purpose.

10.2 Foodgrains under the Special Component can be used in any Scheme of the Central or State Government being implemented for generation of wage employment in the District affected by a natural calamity and duly notified as such. The cash component of the wages and the material cost will be met from the Scheme under which the sub-component will be used.

10.3 For foodgrains to be provided to the State free of cost under the Special Component, Ministry of Agriculture, after obtaining district-wise proposals from the State Government concerned, will scrutinized a proposal and recommend the quantity to be authorised for release to the Department of Rural Development. Accordingly the Department of Rural Development will authorize the Department of Food and Public Distribution for releasing foodgrains district-wise. Any additional demand will have to be accompanied by the certificate that the 75 per cent of the released foodgrains has been lifted and that 60 per cent of the lifted foodgrains has been utilised. The Department of Food and Public Distribution will duly send an appropriate advice to Food Corporation of India (FCI) to release foodgrains at the District Headquarters from its existing depots under intimation to the Ministry of Rural Development as well as the Ministry of Agriculture and to the State Government.

10.4 FCI will release foodgrains without insisting on prepayment from the Collector/DRDA for lifting the requeired quantity of foodgrains within the district-wise release by the Department of Food and Public Distribution.

10.5 MORD will make payment to FCI directly against the lifting of foodgrains by the State on submission of bills by FCI to the Ministry duly verified by the Collector/Relief Commissioner and the SRM/DM indicating the quantity of foodgrains allotted and lifted.

10.6 Keeping in view the need to immediately respond to the exigencies of the situation, all the works to be taken up under this Programme will however be decided by the District Committee formed for this purpose under the Chairmanship of the District Collector.

10.7 The works for the Special Component will be executed in accordance with the Guidelines of that Scheme under which they are taken up. In other words, there will be no relaxation in the product output.

10.8 Signboards should be displayed at the work site giving the details of the cost of the work, date of completion, funds and foodgrains actually utilized, name of the Implementing Agency etc.

10.9 The assets created under the Programme would be maintained by the State Governments or any agency to be designated by them. No funds will be provided by the Union Government for their maintenance.

10.10 The provision under each respective scheme relating to Supervision and monitoring will continue to be applicable. The State Government shall issue necessary Guidelines designating appropriate authorities and detailing procedures to oversee the receipt, storage, transport and distribution of foodgrains under the Special Component.

10.11 The Relief Commissioner/Collector/DRDA of the State will submit the utilisation certificate to MORD and to Department of Agriculture & Cooperation (DOAC) . They will also submit the monthly progress report indicating the foodgrains allocated and utilized, works completed/uncompleted, mandays generated (district-wise/scheme-wise) under the Special Component by the 10th of every month. The **Proforma III** will be used for this purpose as per **Annexure VI.**

10.12 The Schemes in which the Special Component is used will continue to be monitored by the respective agencies which will also indicate the additionality of assets created on account of the additionality in terms of foodgrains.

10.13 The District Collector being the Chairperson of the District Relief Committee will be over all in charge for the purpose of supply of foodgrains and the need for additional employment generation under different Schemes in the calamity affected areas of the district.

10.14 For fixing price of foodgrains for distribution, transportation of foodgrains, wage payment, quality of foodgrains, the SGRY Guidelines are to be followed.

ANNEXURES

(Attached in separate MS-Word File)

Annexure II-C

GUIDELINES FOR SWARNJAYANTI GRAM SWAROZGAR YOJANA

Ministry of Rural Development

(I) ACTVITY CLUSTERS: PLANNING AND SELECTION

1.1 The objective of the Swarnjayanti Gram Swarozgar Yojana (SGSY) is to bring the assisted poor families (Swarozgaries) above the Poverty Line by ensuring appreciable sustained level of income over a period of time. This objective is to be achieved by *inter alia* organising the rural poor into Self Help Groups (SHGs) through the process of social mobilization, their training and capacity building and provision of income generating assets. The SHG approach helps the poor to build their self-confidence through community action. Interactions in group meetings and collective decision making enables them in identification and prioritization of their needs and resources. This process would ultimately lead to the strengthening and socio-economic empowerment of the rural poor as well as improve their collective bargaining power.

The poverty line varies from State to State. As per the latest (1999-2000) estimates of the Planning Commission, the poverty line in terms of per capita consumption expenditure per month in the rural areas varies from Rs.262.94 in Andhra Pradesh to Rs.367.45 in Himachal Pradesh. The State specific , Poverty lines (1999-2000) in terms of per capita expenditure per month is furnished in the **Annexure I.**

1.2 SGSY lays stress on the cluster approach. What this means is that instead of funding diverse activities, each block should concentrate on a few select activities (key activities) and attend to all aspects of these activities, so that the Swarozgaris can draw sustainable incomes from their investments. These key activities should preferably be taken up in clusters so that the backward and forward linkages can be effectively established. This would facilitate not only monitoring but more importantly provision of various services required by the Swarozgaris.

Selection of Key Activities

1.3 The success of SGSY will therefore depend, to start with, on the choice of activities. The key element is that the choice of activity should be based on the local resources, the aptitude as well as the skill of the people. It is also necessary that the products have ready market.

1.4 The choice of key activities should not be an arbitrary or an *ad hoc* decision but should be a carefully thought out process. The Block SGSY committee has a very important role to play in it. For identifying the key activities that can be taken up, the committee should ensure that this selection takes place through a participative process. For selection of key activities, a profile of the poor families, as reflected in the BPL Census should be analyzed. There will be poor families with assets, such as land. Efforts should be made to see that those having a minimum extent of land are enabled to cross the poverty line by making additional investment on their lands, such as wells or other irrigation facilities, pump sets etc. The experience over the years as well as Evaluation Studies have shown that investments on land based activities have resulted in generation of income on a more sustainable basis. The Block SGSY committee should, therefore, analyze the potential for farm activities on priority. Care must be taken to see that they also have access to short term credit and other inputs required in the farm sector to supplement the efforts under the Scheme. The next priority may be given to those who have an inherent skill. These would primarily be the rural artisans who form a significant segment of the rural society. Under the SGSY, rural artisans should be covered in a significant manner. Another category would be the unemployed educated youth. A number of them would have been trained under the erstwhile TRYSEM Programme. An inventory may be taken of such people to find out which activities are best suited for the area. Generally, the people who are assetless and skill-less are poorest of poor and get left out under the Programme. Such category of people may require small doses of multiple credit over a period of time coupled with emphasis on awareness creation, training and capacity building. The activities which are easier to handle and product is easily marketable could be identified for such category of people to ensure sustainable income, so that, they do not fall into debt trap.

1.5 The Block SGSY Committee may also look at the potential link plans prepared by NABARD as well as any other survey carried out by various banks, industrial/technical organizations, etc. The local Khadi & Village Industry officials as well as the District Manager of District Industry Centre may also be consulted.

1.6 The Block SGSY Committee must interact with as many sarpanches as possible and also discuss with groups of the rural poor such as the landless labour, the educated unemployed, those rural poor with lands, the artisan groups etc. Where self-help groups are in position, they should also be consulted. In their discussions, the Committee should explore various opportunities that are available (provided credit, technology, skill upgradation and marketing are assured) to enable the poor to cross the poverty line. While conducting this dialogue, the Block SGSY committee should be equipped with information relating to the performance of various activities in the village whether such activities are taken up under government programmes or otherwise. The committee should use that knowledge to supplement the traditional knowledge of the poor households and to facilitate the identification of suitable activities. In this process, the traditional wisdom of the poor families acquires value and the Block committee builds upon the traditional knowledge of the poor families with its knowledge base. It must be ensured that the consultation process is genuine and not perfunctory or token in nature.

1.7 In so far as on-farm activities are concerned, provision of irrigation facilities continues to be important. These facilities can be provided either in the form of open dug wells or bore/tube wells or through lift irrigation or check dams etc. In other words, the nature of source is not important for providing irrigation facilities under SGSY. Effort may be made to bring in as much of the land of the rural poor as possible under irrigation so that they can have sustainable incomes Minor irrigation investment will include cost of well, lifting device and land development—a composite investment. Working capital requirement can also be considered but would not be eligible for subsidy.

1.8 Minor irrigation projects may be group oriented or individual oriented. It is preferable to adopt as far as possible, a project approach under minor irrigation instead of spreading the investment in a scattered manner. Minor irrigation can also be the basis for activity clusters or formation of SHGs.

1.9 As regards the non-farm activities, care must be taken to identify only those activities which result in the production of goods/services that have a ready market.

1.10 Based on this consultation process, the committee may identify about 8-10 activities, which they may rank in the order of preference. This list should then be placed before the general body of the Panchayat Samiti (Block Panchayat). The Panchayat Samiti should be asked to give its recommendations. The list of selected key activities, along with the recommendations of the Panchayat Samiti, should then be forwarded by the BDO to the District SGSY committee for consideration. Before sending the list to the District SGSY Committee, the Block Committee should prepare a brief project report, keeping in view the guidelines.

1.11 The District SGSY committee will receive the block-wise proposals and will vet them. The committee will select about 10 activities per block. However, focus should be on 4-5 Key activities which are identified for training and micro-enterprise development in a cluster approach for larger number of Groups. In the process, scope for other potential activities should not be excluded. In doing so, the District SGSY committee will ensure that the infrastructure already available in the district—in terms of production, service, training facilities as well as market are utilized and that the choice of activity does not require a new effort in all directions—production as well as marketing. In other words, at least some of the key elements of the economic chain of the selected activity should be present and it is only the missing link that needs to be provided. Secondly, in choosing the activities, the district level committee will also ensure that Swarozgaris taking up the activity can realize appreciable incremental income sustained over a period of time which will help them to effectively cross the Poverty Line. DRDAs may ensure that the anticipated income as stipulated in the project is realized during the project period in order to enable the Swarozgaries to cross the Poverty. Generally, one time assistance/credit injection might not help the Swarozgaris to cross the poverty line. Therefore, multiple dose of credit would be necessary which should be ensured through continuous monitoring and follow up. The Committee will ensure that the views of Line Departments are taken into consideration so that the Line Departments have a commitment to the key activity being taken up in the respective blocks and provide required services to the Swarozgaris.

1.12 The District SGSY Committee should scrutinize the proposals for each key activity separately in consultation with the concerned experts including the line department officials. In fixing the unit costs for the farm sector, the costs fixed by the regional committees of NABARD should be taken into consideration. With regard to the loans for various purposes falling under ISB sector of SGSY, the responsibility of fixing the unit cost and other techno-economic parameters is of the committee.

1.13 It must be noted that identification of activities is critical for the success of the SGSY. It is therefore necessary that it should be done in careful manner. Care should however be taken that the market is either readily available or there is a potential for market creation for the products. This may require engaging the services of professionals in the field for market research and survey. A detailed timetable may be drawn up by each DRDA for each Block and the schedule publicized so that everyone is aware of the selection of key activities.

1.14 The District SGSY Committee is empowered to add or delete any activity in the list of selected key activities with due justification. Any of the selected activities can be replaced by a new one, if the scope of the former has been exhausted. The procedure for replacement will be the same as it is for making the original list of key activities. However, the number of selected key activities should not ordinarily exceed 10. The DRDAs shall prepare directory of selected key activities in the District, which will be consolidated at the State level for preparation of directory of selected key activities.

Preparation of Project Reports

1.15 For each key activity there should be a project report indicating various elements such as training, credit, technology, infrastructure and marketing. The project report should indicate how many people could be covered economically in a block under a key activity. The tendency to provide finance to a large number of similar units must be avoided so as to prevent creation of excess capacity.

1.16 The project report should also include the balancing infrastructure that needs to be provided and the costs involved. The district level committee should ensure that it is well within the limits of the money that is likely to be available under SGSY infrastructure. Care should be taken to avoid any attempt to create infrastructure for line departments without concomitant benefit to Swarozgaris. The test of SGSY will be in additional incomes accrued to Swarozgaris, the additional infrastructure being only an enabling factor. The project report should specifically include a chapter on the levels of investment required at individual Swarozgari's level or by a group. The economics for group lending should be shown distinctly from that of individual lending. The Project report shall be prepared for each activity and for each block separately. The project report should indicate that whether the key activity selected is for individual or group or both. The economics should also be clearly spelt out for each of these. The economics should indicate the details of investment required, the details of returns, the repayment schedule and the net income accruable to the Swarozgari.

1.17 The Committee should undertake the entire exercise in a careful manner and not as a routine exercise. All expenses relating to this exercise will be borne by the DRDA from its administrative expenses, which are provided for separately under the head 'DRDA Administration".

1.18 The line departments have an important role to play in the entire exercise, for they will be responsible for implementation and monitoring of respective sect oral activities. SGSY would need a very close collaboration between the implementing agencies and the line departments. Presently, this is lacking or at least is not taking place to the desired extent. This collaboration must start with the identification of key activities and preparation of project reports. The line departments will be responsible for planning and creation of the infrastructure required for making the key activities successful. In addition, once the bank has sanctioned the loan, the line departments must ensure that all facilities including technical guidance are provided to the Swarozgris. The line departments may also verify whether the Swarozgaris have the necessary skill requirement and take steps to train them. The line departments should also satisfy themselves about the quality of training that is being imparted. They should assist the DRDAs in ensuring that the Swarozgaris are duly trained in appropriate institutions. It shall be their responsibility to monitor the progress and whether Swarozgaris are able to derive the expected levels of income. In other words, the line departments must recognize that promotion of self-employment in their sector is as much their responsibility as that of DRDAs/ Panchayati Raj Institution/Banks and it should be an integral part of their day-to-day functioning.

1.19 On approval by the District SGSY Committee, the list of selected key activities as well as the project report of each key activity in respect of each block should be placed before the governing body of the DRDA. Where no DRDA exists, it should be placed before the Zilla Parishad. On approval, it should be circulated to the BDO and all the banks in the concerned blocks as well as the concerned line departments. All the banks in the district would be expected to follow the model set out in the respective project reports. Under any circumstances, under-financing of the key activity should not be allowed. This should be reviewed in the Block SGSY Committee constantly.

1.20 The major share of SGSY assistance will be for the key activities. A minimum of 75 per cent, both by number and funding, will be for the key activities identified in the block both as group assistance and individual assistance. However, assistance is not prohibited for other activities. There may be stray instances where a Swarozgari may like to take up an activity by himself/ herself and where the nature of activity is such that its economic return is assured. SGSY allows such activities but subject to a limit of 25 per cent of the total number and funding of Swarozgaris in any given year. It must be noted that this is only an enabling provision for exceptional cases and it is expected that the funding of key activities will be the norm. Therefore, the figure of 25 per cent is only the upper limit and should not be the norm.

Clusters

1.21 The key activities may be taken up for implementation preferably in clusters. It must be noted that the clusters are not mere geographic agglomerations but units where the backward and forward linkages can be effectively established. This will facilitate greater control of the progress of the programme, including setting up of infrastructure, raw-material distribution, technology transfer as well as quality control. It is not essential that SGSY should be implemented in each and every village of the Block. Advantage may be taken of the infrastructure already built up so that the results may be more definite. At the same time, care must be taken to see that maximum number of villages are covered under one or the other of the activity clusters.

1.22 the clusters will be taken up for each activity separately. The idea is to select a few villages every year under a key activity and concentrate the effort so that necessary linkages are available and also the monitoring becomes easy. It is not necessary that if a cluster of villages is taken up in a year, it should be given up the next year. More swarozgaris can be brought each year under the key activity in the identified clusters. However, in doing so, care must be taken to see that there is no undue concentration of a programme in only a few villages.

1.23 After the District SGSY committee communicates the list of selected key activities for the Block, the Block SGSY committee will identify the villages to be covered under each activity. This is an exercise that needs to be taken up before the beginning of each financial year. This process is for identification of geographical clusters of neighbouring villages for taking up each activity in a focussed manner. The list of cluster villages so selected may be placed before the Panchayat Samiti, so that members of the Panchayat Samiti are aware of the selection and also the principles that underline the selection of villages.

(II)
PROGRAMME INFRASTRUCTURE

2.1 Proper infrastructure is essential for the success of micro enterprises. The infrastructure may be either for production, processing, quality testing, storage or marketing. The lack of proper attention to this item has been one of the drawbacks of IRDP. Although provision had been made for expenditure on infrastructure, the investments made did not necessarily correspond to the needs of the self-employed.

2.2 SGSY will seek to ensure that the infrastructure needs for the identified activities are met in full, so as to enable the Swarozgaris to derive the maximum advantage from their investments. Planning for infrastructure will be made in close concert with the banks. As indicated earlier, the project report for each key activity should clearly identify the existing infrastructure and the additional infrastructure that needs to be created. It should be noted that the creation of additional infrastructure should be meaningful and should only be in the nature of providing the missing critical links. The proposals for infrastructure development should be drawn up by DRDA in consultation with Bankers and form part of the Annual Plan of the Block and District.

2.3 The provision of infrastructure is essentially the responsibility of the State Governments. Therefore, the States will strive to provide for necessary investments as part of their plan efforts of the respective departments. Where the plan funds of the line departments do not have adequate provision, recourse may be go to JGSY and EAS. Similarly, any other State or Centrally sponsored schemes can also be used for the creation of infrastructure. Resource to SGSY infrastructure fund should be as a last resort and only critical gaps in investments will be made under the SGSY.

2.4 The District SGSY Committee should review the infrastructure gaps and identify the areas of intervention for financing projects in activity clusters. Infrastructure needs and their fulfilment will be constantly and closely monitored by the DRDA, particularly the Governing Body of DRDA, to ensure that the infrastructure needs are met as per plan. Financing in sectors should be restricted where infrastructure is inadequate.

2.5 It should be noted that the funds available for providing infrastructure support under SGSY are primarily to bridge small gaps in infrastructure which can make the programme implementation more effective and not for creation of an altogether non-existent infrastructure in the area.

Funds for infrastructure development should, in no case be used to augment resources of the State Government for development of general infrastructure.

2.6 In order to meet expenditure on such critical infrastructure, SGSY will provide for a fund, which will be known as 'SGSY-Infrastructure Fund'. 20 per cent (25% in the case of North Eastern States) of SGSY allocation for each district will be set apart for this fund. DRDAs will maintain this fund in a separate account. The DRDAs are advised to utilize this fund to generate additional funding wherever feasible.

The following principles may be kept in view while framing the infrastructure proposals:

(a) The infrastructure activities should enable SGSY Swarozgaris to make full utilization of their assets. Marketing linkages should be given priority.

(b) The proposals should emerge out of the specific activities being taken up by the Swarozgaris and the location decisions should be made by the Blocks/DRDAs in consultation with Bankers.

(c) Only village or block or district level infrastructure should be planned. In no case should the proposals envisage development of infrastructure at the State or regional level.

(d) Only the fixed cost and not the recurring expenditure should be met out of SGSY funds. There should be an undertaking that the State Government or the organization concerned would meet the recurring expenditure on staff and other items.

(e) In the case of assistance for development of infrastructure to cooperative societies, it should be ensured that at least 50 per cent of the members are SGSY Swarozgaris.

2.7 The proposals should clearly spell out the time span envisaged for building up the infrastructure, its impact on the activities of the Swarozgaris in particular and economic environment in general, the agency charged with the implementation of the project and the monitoring system provided to see that projects are executed in given time at the given cost. The funds to the executing agency should be given in phases depending on the progress of the work. The decision on the phasing of the release should be taken by the DRDA.

Other Admissible items of Expenditure under the Programme Infrastructure

(i) Expenditure on account of premium for insurance and risk fund to cooperatives could also be met under this head.

(ii) Expenditure on account of commissioning studies for the purpose of local resource and skill based integrated projects, for the SGSY subject to a maximum of Rs. 50,000 per annum per District approved by Governing Body of the DRDA could also be made.

Monitoring of Expenditure on Infrastructure Projects

2.8 Given the magnitude of funds allocated for infrastructure development, it is imperative that expenditure under this head be monitored more rigorously. Accordingly, suitable formats will be prescribed for monitoring purposes. The Districts are required to send information in this format to the States every quarter. The data will be consolidated for all the districts by the State Government and sent to the Central Government on a quarterly basis.

(III) SWAROZGARIS

3.1 Under Swarnjayanti Gram Swarozgar Yojana (SGSY), the beneficiaries are known as Swarozgaris. The Swarozgaris can be either individuals or groups. SGSY lays emphasis on the group approach, under which the rural poor are organized into Self Help Groups. In either case, the list of BPL households identified through BPL census, duly approved by the Gram Sabha will form the basis for identification of families for assistance under the SGSY. The Self Help Groups should also be drawn from the BPL list approved by the Gram Sabha.

This chapter is about the Swarozgaris and the linkages with the banks. Part 'A' of this chapter is about the SHGs. Part 'B' is about individual Swarozgaris.

(A) Self Help Groups (SHGS)

3.2 SGSY will focus on organization of the poor at grassroots level through a process of social mobilization for poverty eradication. SGSY's approach to organize the poor stems from the conviction that there is a tremendous potential within the poor to help themselves and that the potential can be harnessed by organizing them. Social mobilization enables the poor build their own organizations (Self Help Groups) in which they participate fully and directly and take decisions on all issues concerning poverty eradication. Simultaneously, SHGs have the advantage the assistance—be it in terms of credit or technology or market guidance etc.—reaching the poor faster and more effectively.

Self Help Groups Go Through Various Stages of Evolution

3.3 Social mobilisation is not a spontaneous process; it has to be induced. DRDAs are expected to initiate and sustain the process of social mobilisation for poverty eradication by formation, development and strengthening of the Self Help Groups (SHGs). Issues that are key to poverty eradication should become entry points for DRDAs to organise the poor into SHGs. There could be different entry points for different SHGs depending on the local situation. The groups that are formed with thrift and credit as an entry point have demonstrated that the poor can secure greater access to credit and other support services for enhancing their income levels.

The process of SHG formation could be divided into phases. While the process of SHG formation cannot be standardized, a few Guidelines could be useful to the field level functionaries.

Self Help Groups go through various stages of evolution.

- **Group Formation** (formation, development and strengthening of the groups to evolve into self-managed people's organisation at grassroots level. In our society, members are linked by various common bonds like caste, sub-caste, community, blood relation, place of origin, activity etc. The facilitators must identify these natural groups which are commonly called 'Affinity Groups'. Identification of such Affinity Group is critical for the progress and success of the Self Help Group. This would require staying with the people for some period to facilitate proper understanding and establish rapport with them. Therefore, while forming Groups, facilitators must recognise the natural bonds and affiliations existing within the society.
- **Group Stabilization** through thrift and credit activity amongst the members and building their Group Corpus. The group takes up internal loaning to the members from their Group Corpus. The groups should save regularly and begin to lend to members. This provides the members with opportunities to acquire the skills to prioritize scarce resources, to assess the strength of each member, to time the loans and schedule of repayments and fix interest rates. The group institutionalizes the need to introduce sanctions for deviant behaviour, which could include delay in repayments, arriving late or absenting from meetings etc.

- **Micro Credit**, the Group Corpus is supplemented with Revolving Fund sanctioned as cash credit limit by the Banks or the group could also have access to credit under the Self Help Group-Bank Linkage Programme of NABARD.
- **Micro Enterprise Development**, Group takes up Economic Activity, of their choice for income generation. This phase would include Entrepreneurship Development as well as Skill Development training of the members of the Group to enable them to successfully implement the chosen activity. All the Groups, particularly Groups formed with members who are skill less, asset less, destitute and living under abject poverty might not graduate to the stage of Micro-enterprise within the time frame indicated in the Guidelines. Such groups may continue to remain in the Micro-Finance stage for a longer period of time and may require intensive training and capacity building inputs to enable them to reach higher levels of income generation.

Formation of Self Help Groups

3.4 SHG is group of rural poor who have volunteered to organise themselves into a group for eradication of poverty of the members. They agree to save regularly and convert their savings into a Common Fund known as the Group corpus. The members of the group agree to use this common fund and such other funds that they may receive as a group through a common management. The group formation will keep in view the following broad guidelines:

(i) Under the SGSY, generally a self-help group may consist of 10 to 20 persons. However, in difficult areas like deserts, hills and areas with scattered and sparse population and in case of minor irrigation and disabled persons, this number may be from 5-20. The difficult areas have to be identified by the State Level SGSY Committee and the above relaxation in membership will be permitted only in such areas.

(ii) Generally all members of the group should belong to families below the poverty line. However, if necessary, a maximum of 20 per cent and in exceptional cases, where essentially required, up to a maximum of 30 per cent of the members in a group may be taken from families marginally above the poverty line living contiguously with BPL families and if they are acceptable to the BPL members of the group. This will help the families of occupational groups like agricultural labourers, marginal farmers and artisans marginally above the poverty line, or who may have been excluded from the BPL list to become members of the Self Help Group. However, the APL members will not be eligible for the subsidy under the scheme. The group shall not consist of more than one member from the same family. A person should not be a member of more than one group. The BPL families must actively participate in the management and decision making, which should not ordinarily be entirely in the hands of APL families. Further, APL members of the Self Help Group shall not become office bearers (Group Leader, Assistant Group Leader or Treasurer) of the Group.

(iii) The group should devise a code of conduct (Group management norms) to bind itself. This should be in the form of regular meetings (weekly or fortnightly), functioning in a democratic manner, allowing free exchange of views, participation by the members in the decision making process.

(iv) The group should be able to draw up an agenda for each meeting and take up discussions as per the agenda.

(v) The members should build their corpus through regular savings. The group should be able to collect the minimum voluntary saving amount from all the members regularly in the group meetings. The savings so collected will be the group corpus fund.

(vi) The group corpus fund should be used to advance loans to the members. The group should develop financial management norms covering the loan sanction procedure, repayment schedule and interest rates.

(vii) The members in the group meetings should take all the loaning decisions through a participatory decision making process.

(viii) The group should be able to prioritise the loan applications, fix repayment schedules, fix appropriate rate of interest for the loans advanced and closely monitor the repayment of the loan instalments from the loanee.

(ix) The group should operate a group account preferably in their service area bank branch, so as to deposit the balance amounts left with the groups after disbursing loans to its members.

(x) The group should maintain simple basic records such as Minutes book, Attendance register, Loan ledger, General ledger, Cash book, Bank passbook and individual passbooks. The sample proforma for maintenace of above records by the group is in the **Annexure II** for guidance. These could be used with necessary changes/ modifications wherever required.

3.5 50 per cent of the groups formed in each block should be exclusively for the women. In the case of disabled persons, the groups formed should ideally be disability-specific wherever possible, however, in case sufficient number of people for formation of disability-specific groups are not available, a group may comprise of persons with diverse disabilities or a group may comprise of both disabled and non-disabled persons below the poverty line

3.6 By and large, the SHG will be an informal group. However, the groups can also register themselves under the Societies Registration Act, the State Cooperative Act or as a partnership firm. The SHGs can be further strengthened and stabilized by federating them at, say village or cluster of villages or block or District level depending upon the number of Self Help Groups and their spatial distribution. DRDAs may facilitate in planning of network of SHGs by federating them at appropriate level, once SHGs have reached the stage of maturity and have stabilized. This would facilitate regular interaction, pooling of surplus with the groups, exchange of experiences including flow of information from DRDAs and other departments, bulk access to Credit from various Micro-Finance Institutions and help them to plan for desired backward and forward linkages including marketing of their products.

3.7 Social mobilization and community organization is a process oriented approach as different from target oriented approach. The group formation should not be driven by any targets but lend itself to a 'process approach'. The members of the SHGs should fully internalise the concept of self help.

A large number of DWCRA groups have been formed and assisted by DRDAs in the past. Likewise, there are a number of Self Help Groups formed by NABARD, other Banks, Rashtriya Mahila Kosh (RMK), Non-Government Organisations (NGOs), Women and Child Development Department under the Swa-Shakti and Swayamsidha etc. The DRDAs should put in concerted efforts to strengthen and consolidate these groups as some level of synergy already exists and then take steps to form new groups. Further, there is a need to develop data base on the Self Help Groups formed and existing under various programmes in the district. The DRDAs may act as nodal agency for developing the data base, which should include Self Help Groups formed under all the schemes. This would ensure convergence of various Schemes as well as better planning for training and other requirements of SHGs.

Role of NGOs

3.8 The experience across the country has shown that group formation and development is not a spontaneous process. A facilitator working closely with the communities at grassroots level can play a critical role in the group formation and development. The quality of the groups can be influenced by the capacity of the facilitator. The facilitator may or may not be an official. In some cases, NGOs cannot only work as the facilitator but also help in training and capacity building of facilitators being used by DRDAs. DRDAs may support such sensitive support mechanisms in the shape of NGOs or Community Based

Organisations (CBOs) or Network of Community coordinators/ Animators or a team of dedicated functionaries of the Government who are fully engaged in the task of initiating and sustaining the group development process. The Community Coordinators/Animators could be from the community or may be from outside the area. They could be leaders/members of SHGs, or persons having experience or training in the field of community organisation and social mobilisation. The selection of Facilitator/Community Coordinator and their training and capacity building for involvement in formation, development and training of SHGs is critical for the success of the Programme. The District SGSY Committee may therefore select suitable Organisations/Societies/Individuals as facilitators/Community Coordinators in the Programme based on their past experience in SHG formation, community organisation or any other similar work involving participatory approach, communication skill, ability to stay with the people in the rural area etc. They would have to stay for a period of 2-3 years with the Group to ensure continuity as well as to enable the Groups to mature into a self-managed peoples organisation. Facilitators involved in the process of group formation and development should have a well defined exit policy and by which time community should either become self reliant or be willing to pay for their services for further continuance and management of the Group. The emphasis should be to form groups in geographical clusters to facilitate better training and management. A Community Coordinator/Animator could take up the responsibility of managing 10-15 SHGs in a geographical cluster consisting of 4-5 villages within a radius of 4-5 kms. The DRDAs may organise training and exposure programmes for the facilitators and should interact with them regularly to get feed back about groups.

The DRDAs may devise a Memorandum of Understanding (MoU) or contract to be used for entering into an agreement with NGOs/CBOs/Community Coordinators/Animators being involved as facilitators for group formation, development and training. The MoU should clearly define the role of facilitator in group formation and development. Further, payment to the facilitator should be specifically linked to the stage of development of the group and overall performance. The DRDA shall regularly monitor the progress of groups through periodic evaluations. The involvement of facilitators in the programme will be purely on contractual basis and DRDAs shall take all precautions to ensure that there are no legal obligation on the Government in future. A detailed instruction on operationalization of involvement of facilitators in the process of social mobilisation and group formation is being issued separately.

3.9 Whether the support machinery (SHG promotion institutions) is offered by NGOs or DRDA itself, what is critical is the capacity of the support machinery. DRDAs will have to play a very crucial role in facilitating development of the capacity to nurture and strengthen the groups.

Linkage with the Banks

3.10 During the stage of group formation, the SHG should be brought into contact with the local banks through opening of savings bank account preferably in their service area branch. This has a dual purpose. The SHG begins to realise the opportunities and also the mode of dealing with the banks. Likewise, the bankers get to familiarise themselves with the SHGs. Establishment of these linkages at the early stages will ensure the formation of strong SHGs, which will be mutually beneficial. Further, the group could also avail credit from the Bank as per their requirement under the Self Help Group–Bank Linkage Programme of NABARD. The BDO and the banker may visit the SHG as often as they can and explain to the members the opportunities for self-employment. They may also explain to them about the process of graduation into taking up full-fledged self-employment activity. Training and capacity building programmes for the SHGs in different stages of development may be organised periodically on a continuous basis at different levels (i.e. at the village, cluster of village, Block and District). For this, besides inviting experts in the relevant field from outside, the District should have their own team of trained resource persons taken from different fields. The DRDA should involve the Bank functionaries also in the training programme of SHGs.

Grading of the Self-Help Groups

3.11 The formation stage may last for about six months or more depending upon the literacy, awareness levels, socio-economic background of the people being organised, as well as the capacity of the facilitator involved in the process of social mobilization and Group formation. At the end of the formation stage, which may be about six months or more, it is necessary to subject each Self Help Group to a test to assess whether it has evolved into a good group and is ready to go into the next stage of evolution. This is done through a grading exercise. The objective of this exercise is to identify the weaknesses, if any, and help the group to overcome the same through training and capacity building inputs, so as to develop into a good group. Grading exercise thus should help to focus attention on weak groups so that DRDAs can assist them to overcome weaknesses and graduate into good groups. Grading of the group should also enable the DRDAs to establish linkages for the good groups with the Banks. In case the Self Help Group has been in existence prior to the SGSY under other Programmes and have completed six months from the date of formation and it is being brought under the SGSY, such groups may be subjected to first grading immediately, without waiting for another six months.

3.12 The DRDAs will have to play an effective role in grading exercise. The capacity of DRDA personnel will have to be enhanced to take this exercise professionally. Grading of the Self Help Groups could be done by the same agency that is involved in the promotion and development of SHGs or any independent agency contracted to undertake the grading exercise. The cost incurred for conducting grading exercise through an independent agency may be incurred under the Scheme. It is desirable that the grading exercise is undertaken by an independent agency as it will have objectivity and acceptance by financial institutions etc.

3.13 A number of Government and Non-Government Organizations, working with SHGs across the country have evolved very effective strategies for grading the SHGs. The grading criteria should be consistent with the characteristics that are agreed to be essential for strong, self-managed and vibrant

SHGs. In other words, clarity on the features to be promoted in an SHG should become the starting point for any grading exercise.

Following are the various processes that are involved in the grading:

- Development of exhaustive list of characteristics of a good group by DRDA in consultation with its partners if any, involved in promotion and development of SHGs.
- Development of criteria for grading of the groups with appropriate weightage for various parameters.
- Identification of a suitable agency to undertake the grading exercise.
- Intensive training to the investigators who will interact with the members of the group to assess the group on various parameters. This training can either be conducted by the agency identified for grading or by DRDA.
- Facilitate the agency to visit the groups for assessing the status of the groups.
- Obtain SHG-wise reports with the rating awarded and the reasons.
- Develop an appropriate SHG-wise action plan for strengthening the groups identified as 'weak' or average.
- Pursue with bankers for securing SHG linkage with such SHGs that are rated as 'good'.

3.14 Grading exercise should not be a questionnaire-oriented exercise where the members become passive participants. It should provide an opportunity for the members to assess their own performance to a participatory approach and the investigator assumes the role of the facilitator to the process.

3.15 DRDAs should ensure active participation of the bankers in the grading exercise. In this context, NABARD and local banks will have to be involved very closely right from the development of criteria for grading the groups. The criteria, the strategy and operational details of the grading exercise should be discussed in the District SGSY Committee.

3.16 Right from the beginning, it is necessary that the SHGs should be nurtured carefully. The grading exercise must therefore be carried out at different stages. To start with, the objective of the SHG in the first six months is to evolve as a viable group. Accordingly, the grading at the end of six months should be with reference to the objectives in the first stage of the evolution of the Self Help Groups. Grading exercise should be undertaken every quarter till such time that all the groups obtain good grade.

Capacity Building of the Self Help Groups

3.17 SHGs that are in existence for about 6 months and have demonstrated the potential of a viable group enters the third stage, wherein it receives the Revolving Fund of Rs.25,000 from bank as cash credit facility and also embarks on further capacity building of its entire team. DRDAs will arrange to provide the revolving fund to such groups, meeting their share from out of the SGSY Fund. Of this a sum of Rs.10,000 will be given to the Bank by the DRDA. Banks may charge interest only on the sum exceeding Rs.10,000. The subsidy of Rs.10,000 released by DRDA will be adjusted against the loan at the end of cash credit period on the request of the group. In case of default in the payment of loan or the group becoming defunct or dissolution of the group and in case the Bank fails to recover the entire dues in spite of all possible measure, i.e. personal contact, organisation of joint recovery camps with district administration, legal action etc. the process of forfeiture of subsidy for adjustment against dues may be taken up. After getting the approval of District SGSY Committee the concerned Bank may adjust the subsidy against the Swarozgaris dues. If the Bank is able to realise any amount subsequently over and above the amount due to it, the same may be returned to the DRDA.

The groups shall keep the following principles in view concerning the management of the Revolving Fund:

- The revolving fund is provided to the groups to augment the group corpus so as to enable more number of members to access loans and also to facilitate increase in the per capita loan available to the members.

- As the revolving fund become part and parcel of the group corpus, the groups should follow same norms for utilization as in the case of their own saving fund.
- The group should discuss the credit requirement of the members and advance loans from out of the corpus (savings + interest + revolving fund) to a few members and fix repayment schedule and interest rates. From the amounts recovered from the loanees, new members could be covered.
- The revolving fund imparts credit discipline and financial management skills to the members, so that they become creditworthy and bankable in the eyes of the bank.
- On receipt of the revolving fund, the group shall utilise the fund in the manner and for purposes it deems fit. The idea is that the group should develop the capacity to utilise funds it has received from outside. The revolving fund can be used by the group for purchase of raw materials, marketing or infrastructure support for income generating activities. It can alternatively be used for lending to individual members for their own purposes. The members shall inculcate the habit of prompt and full repayment of the loans taken by them from the revolving fund.

3.18 Those groups that have received fund under DWCRA or any other programme shall not be eligible to receive the revolving fund under the SGSY. However, there is no bar on such groups receiving credit and subsidy under group loaning under the SGSY, after they have demonstrated their functioning as a viable group.

At the end of six months from the date of receipt of the revolving fund the SHG will be subjected to another grading test to see if it has been functioning effectively and is capable of taking up an economic activity through higher levels of investment. However, for Minor Irrigation Schemes, relaxation of time for the second grading could be allowed if the group is found creditworthy and the project is viable. The decision in regard to the relaxation may be taken by the Block level SGSY Committee.

In case the Self Help Group has been in existence prior to the SGSY under other programmes and has completed one year from its date of formation and it is being brought under the SGSY, the group may be subjected to second grading directly to assess its eligibility for economic activity without subjecting it to first grading. It is important that the Bank should be satisfied about the grading of the SHG at this stage. Therefore, the choice of the agency carrying out the grading as well as the criteria should be to the satisfaction of the bank. In fact, it would be desirable that Bank functionaries are involved in the grading exercise of groups functioning in their service area.

At the end of the third stage, the SHG is broadly expected to demonstrate the following attributes:

1. The per capita loan amount availed by its members increases gradually over the years.
2. There is a shift from consumption loans to production loans.
3. The group is able to clearly identify its training needs to the members and give value to the training input received by its members.
4. The members are able to investigate into their poverty situation and are able to articulate clearly the opportunities for overcoming their poverty.
5. The group is able to develop a portfolio of opportunities (investment opportunities) for the members and has a clear plan of action for meeting the credit requirement of its members.
6. The group acquires the capacity to undertake participatory monitoring of assets created from the loans advanced to its members.
7. The group has implemented some community action programmes and is capable of continuing to do so independently.
8. The dependency on outside facilitating agency or matters related to group management would gradually come down and the groups emerge as self-managed in terms

of managing various aspects of group and financial management.

9. All members have total clarity on the activity, including the economics of the activity.
10. The members have clarity on the responsibility of each and every member and the management of the common activity.
11. The members have clear assessment of their training needs.
12. The members have evolved effective strategy for participatory monitoring of the common activity.

Taking Up of Economic Activities

3.19 Once the SHG has demonstrated that it has successfully passed through the second stage, it is eligible to receive the assistance for economic activities. This is in the form of loan and subsidy. There are two ways in which a SHG can receive this assistance:

1. Loan-cum-subsidy of SGSY to the individuals in a group, provided the prospective Swarozgaris in the group are capable of an willing to take up income generation activities under these sectors.
2. Loan-cum-subsidy to the group where all the members in the group want to take up a group activity. Ideally, under the group loaning, the group should take up single activity but if there is a necessity, the group could also take up multiple activities under the group loaning. In either case, loan will be sanctioned in ;the name of the group and the group stands as guarantee to the Bank for prompt repayment of loan.

Loan-cum-Subsidy to the Members of the Group

3.20 Through a few individuals are identified as beneficiaries under loan-cum-subsidy, it is essentially the group that is standing guarantee for the promote repayment of the loan to the bank.

The group also undertakes responsibility to closely monitor the asset management and income generation. The group also is expected to access services from the line departments concerned to enable the members to derive the expected income from the activities undertaken. Since the groups are constantly interacting with the banks, their initiatives to secure continuous line of credit to the Swarozgaris to access multiple dose of loan become critical. In any case, the members of the group who are assisted under SGSY's loan-cum-subsidy assistance want to avail the back-end subsidy nothing should prevent the members to do so. Considering multifarious support services Swarozgari is receiving by being member of a group it is natural that the group may like to charge a part of the subsidy provided to the Swarozgaris as individual contribution to the group corpus. The Swarozgari is expected to repay all the loan instalments to the banks through the group and the group may keep to itself part of subsidy component. In any case, this is an issue that has to be left to the decision of the group.

Loan-cum-Subsidy for the Group Activity

3.21 Group activities stand a better chance of success because it is easier to provide back up support and marketing linkages for group activities. The SGSY will primarily follow the group approach. The groups should demonstrate minimum levels of group dynamism, as detailed above, before considering for assistance with the loan-cum-subsidy for the group under the SGSY. The group is entitled to Subsidy of 50 per cent of the project cost subject to per capita subsidy of Rs.10,000 or Rs. 1.25 lakhs, whichever is less. DRDAs should conduct training programmes to the members and the representatives of the groups so that the groups become fully self-managed and evolve into strong self-managed groups. The cost of the group formation and development should be met from the funds provided under the SGSY. Considering the experiences of the NGOs involved in the development of SHGs in the country, it is estimated that an amount of Rs. 10,000 per group would be the investment required over 3–4 years. Rs. 10,000 per group as mentioned above for formation and development of Self Help Group, is the maximum ceiling, however, the actual amount may be decided by the District Level SGSY Committee based on the local prevailing situations.

Payment of the amount to the NGOs/CBOs/Community Co-ordinators/Animators will be made in four installments in the manner given below:

(a) 20 per cent of the funds at the beginning when the formation of Self Help Group is commenced by the NGO/CBOs/Community Co-ordinator/Animator. This money could be utilised during the formation stage. During this period the group should open an account in the service area Bank Branch and they should be imparted Basic Orientation training on the concept of Self Help Group, Group dynamics, maintenance of records and books of accounts, conducting group meetings and financial transactions;

(b) 30 per cent after the group qualifies for Revolving Fund or get linked to the Bank by way of availing Credit and continue to work satisfactorily;

(c) 40 per cent after the group take up an economic activity; and

(d) 10 per cent after the start of economic activity by the group and adherence to repayment schedule of the loan sanctioned by the Bank.

(B) Individual Swarozgaris

Identification and Selection

3.22 In the case of individual Swarozgaris, their selection will be as follows: Once the list of villages is finalized by the Block SGSY Committee every year, the concerned Sarpanches should be intimated. The individual Swarozgaris are to be selected in the Gram Sabha. It is possible that the Gram Sabha held at the Panchayat headquarters may not have the participation of all the BPL families. Therefore, in order to afford the maximum participation for the poor, a 3-member team consisting of the

BDO or his representative, the banker and the Sarpanch should visit each of the habitation in the Panchayat according to a schedule drawn up for this purpose and duly published. In each habitation, the team must then ascertain from the BPL families, the persons who can be covered under athe designated key activity. This process of identification of the potential Swarozgaris should be done carefully.

3.23 The selection of the Swarozgaris must be done in an open and transparent manner. The poor should have the confidence that if they fulfil the requisite conditions they would be able to avail of the facilities under the programme. It is possible that the number of such potential Swarozgaris would be more than the programme available to the bank/BDO. In such a case, the fact may be made known and the best of the potential entrepreneurs can be taken up for the final say. While SGSY is not a programme that targets only the poorest of the poor, it should be the endeavour of the committee to cover the relatively poorer among the BPL families provided however they are otherwise eligible.

3.24 In case the Committee is not sure of sufficient number of potential Swarozgaris being sanctioned the loan, it is open to the Committee to select a higher number and leave the final selection to the bank. The effort in this exercise is two-fold. On the one hand, while the bank is to be free to choose the swarozgaris, the effort is also to see that this is done in a transparent manner.

3.25 After the selection is made, the BDO shall arrange to have the applications filled by the selected persons. Since most of the potential Swarozgaris are illiterate and some of them would be very poor, it is necessary that the proforma prescribed by the banks should be simple, while, however, satisfying the legal requirements. It should also be in the local language. The DRDAs should particularly look into the matter and also take steps to familiarize the BPL families with the loan sanction process and the proforma so that the poor are not overawed by the process.

3.26 Once the banks have received the applications, they should sanction the application normally in 15 days and at any rate not later than one month. Every year the process of sanction by the banks should normally be over by July. Further details are given in Chapter-IV.

3.27 The list of Swarozgaris finally selected (for the year) should be got printed by the BDO and the copies made available to the Gram Panchayat for placing it before the next Gram Sabha. This list shall also be made available to the DRDA, other Block officials, bankers and all other concerned agencies.

3.28 Safeguards for the Weaker Section: The SGSY will particularly focus on the vulnerable groups among the rural poor. Accordingly, the SC/STs will account for a minimum of 50 per cent, women for 40 per cent and disabled for 3 per cent of the total swarozgaris assisted during the year.

(IV)
FINANCING THE INVESTMENTS: BANK CREDIT AND SUBSIDY

4.1 Financial assistance to Swarozgaris under SGSY comprises of two components viz., loan and subsidy. SGSY is a credit-linked scheme and credit is the key element. Subsidy is only a minor and enabling component. The major part of investment consists of bank credit from financial institutions comprising commercial banks, co-operative banks and regional rural banks. This chapter deals with the various aspects of the flow of credit and subsidy to the Swarozgaris.

Norms of Lending

4.2 The size of loan for project depends on the nature of project. The loan should, however, be a composite loan comprising both fixed and working capital. **SGSY has not investment ceiling other than the unit cost (i.e. investment requirement) worked out for the project.** The loan amount would be equal to the total project cost including the amount of subsidy admissible to the Swarozgari. Interest rates for SGSY loans will be as notified by RBI/NABARD from time to time.

Security Norms: The security norms will be as prescribed by Reserve Bank of India from time to time.

Sanction of Loans by the Banks

4.3 As indicated in Chapters III & IV, the BPL families that are best suited for taking up a particular key activity are identified each year. From the date the applications are received in the bank, the bank shall not take more than fifteen days to sanction the loan. The Bank will thereupon communicate this list to the Gram Panchayat, which shall place it before the Gram Sabha in its next meeting. The bank shall also communicate this list to the BDO as well as the concerned line department.

4.4 The bank will also consider the Groups for lending for a given activity. In such case too, the bank shall communicate the name of the selected group to the Gram Panchayat and others for action as above.

4.5 While sanctioning projects, the Bank Managers should ensure that the unit costs, terms of the loan and repayment schedule are as indicated in the project profiles for the concerned key activity. Part-financing and under-financing should not be resorted to under any circumstances. However, where the nature of the activity is such that the loan is to be released in stages, the disbursal may be made accordingly. If some cases are rejected, the reasons for rejection should be clearly recorded on the application form itself and the relevant application should be returned to the sponsoring authority immediately for their information and further action as they deem necessary.

4.6 As soon as the selection is made and the list communicated to the line departments, the latter will proceed to test whether the Swarozgari has the necessary skill or not (refer to Chapter VI).

4.7 As soon as the Swarozgari completes the basic orientation or the skill-training programme, the bank shall proceed to disburse the loan and subsidy amount to the Swarozgari. This shall invariably be done immediately, so that the money is available to him/her for purchase or creation of the asset. The entire amount sanctioned shall be disbursed unless the amount is to be disbursed in designated instalments. The Bank shall disburse the subsidy amount also as per the guidelines governing the back-ended subsidy.

Asset Creation by Swarozgaris

4.8 Swarozgaris will be given the full amount (Loan and Subsidy) and they will have the freedom to procure the asset themselves. The Swarozgari shall procure the asset within one month from the date of release by the bank of the money. He/she shall inform the BDO and the Bank of the fact of procurement of the asset. The Swarozgari should subsequently furnish to the bank a receipt of the items purchased. The assets procured should be of standard quality, and at economic prices. Both DRDA and banks should ensure through proper monitoring and verification that that quality assets have been procured.

4.9 In the case of Swarozgaris under the ISB sector, when a number of sundry items are to be bought, disbursement up to Rs.10,000 may be made in cash. This can be done either in one lump sum or in stages depending upon the items to be purchased. This will give the Swarozgaris requisite freedom to negotiate and settle the price for the asset and will also give him the satisfaction that he has purchased goods of his own choice. In all cases, necessary documents relating to acquisition of assets should be obtained by the bank and also followed up through visits by the field staff of bank within one month of disbursement.

4.10 In the event, the Swarozgari does not inform the bank of the fact of procurement, the bank shall inform the BDO who shall enquire into the reasons. If the non-procurement is due to the negligence of the Swarozgari, the bank, in consultation with the BDO, shall afford him reasonable opportunity of doing so after which the bank shall be free to cancel the loan and recover the money. The Swarozgari will be liable for civil as well as criminal proceedings that are likely to arise in such a case. In case of the SHGs, all the members will be liable.

4.11 On receipt of the news of procurement, the line department as well as the Bank shall verify the asset and satisfy themselves of its quality. Thereafter, the assets should be marked to check the misutilization or transfer of the assets. This is also necessary in the eventuality of filling insurance claim and physical verification of assets etc.

4.12 While providing for a key role to the Gram Panchayats,

SGSY accords certain discretion to bankers in the selection of Swarozgaris. The bankers are, therefore, expected to associate themselves in the entire gamut of activities so that development banking concept is taken to its logical end. The aptitudes of the Swarozgaris and their endowments should be weighed properly while selecting them for credit support. The Subsidy-Credit Ratio proposed by the Ministry from time to time should be taken as a floor ratio rather than an upper limit for credit sanction. In fact, SGSY guidelines do not provide for any ceiling for investment. The investment requirements have to be assessed based on the unit cost and the Swarozgari's needs and viability of the scheme.

Multiple Credit and Multiple Doses of Credit

4.13 SGSY will seek to develop close linkages with credit mechanism in such a manner as would promote multiple credit rather than a one time credit injection. Multiple doses of credit would mean assisting a Swarozgari over a period of time with a second and subsequent dose(s) enabling him/her to access higher amount of credit. The Swarozgari should have the confidence that so long as he/she proves her credit worthiness by way of proper utilization of the asset and prompt repayment, the bank will stand by him/her and will provide additional credit, whether or not this is backed by subsidy. As already indicated, while SGSY is a credit-cum-subsidy programme, the subsidy is only an enabling element and credit is the key component. The Swarozgaris will be allowed to stabilize and improve their credit absorption capacity and to increase their credit intake over the years either for the same activity or a new activity. The second/subsequent dose can be given even during the currency of first/earlier loan provided the bankers is satisfied about the financial discipline of the first/earlier dose. Subsidy entitlement for all doses taken together will not exceed the limit prescribed for that category.

Further Loan to Inadequately Assisted Beneficiaries under IRDP

4.14 As already indicated, assistance under the SGSY should be on multiple doses and not a one-time activity. This will facilitate gradual improvement in the income earning capacity of Swarozgaris. Such second and subsequent doses of credit can be extended to IRDP beneficiaries if they have failed to cross the poverty line because of no fault of theirs. The second and subsequent loans may be granted by the same bank that gave the initial loan or any other bank.

Principles and Procedure for Disbursement of Assistance

4.15 The funds received by the DRDAs will be kept in saving bank accounts. The DRDAs can open these accounts with the principal participating bank branches in the field. The funds deposited in the savings bank account will earn interest at the usual rates till the amount is disbursed to the Swarozgari. After assistance is disbursed to the Swarozgari, the participating bank will provide the particulars of the Swarozgari, the project and the amount of subsidy adjusted in his/her favour for the record of the Block/DRDA. These details should be made available tin the monthly report on the adjustment of subsidy prepared by the bank and sent to the Blocks/DRDAs. While computing the figures of advances and recoveries, the banks are to exclude the amount of subsidy received so as to reflect the factual position. The banks are to report separately the amount of recoveries under SGSY. The accounts of the Blocks/DRDAs with the participating banks should be reconciled every three months and a bank reconciliation certificate should be issued by the Chartered Accountant in this regard at the end of the year.

Subsidy

4.16 Subsidy under SGSY will be uniform at 30 per cent of the project cost, subject to a maximum of Rs.7500. In respect of SC/STs, however, these will be 50 per cent and Rs.10,000 respectively. For groups of Swarozgaris (SHGs), the subsidy would be at 50 per cent of the project cost subject to per capital subsidy of Rs.10,000 or Rs.1.25 lakhs, whichever is less. There will be no monetary limit on subsidy for irrigation projects.

Back-End Subsidy

4.17 Subsidy will be back-ended. Banks would disburse the full project cost including subsidy to the Swarozgaris as loan. The benefits of subsidy will also be available to Swarozgaris who prefer to avail themselves of required working capital in the form of cash credit. The operation of subsidy amount by the bank will be as follows:

(a) The subsidy admissible to the Swarozgaris under SGSY should be kept in the Subsidy Reserve Fund Account Swarozgari-wise instead of in term deposit in the name of the Swarozgari. Banks should apply no interest on the Subsidy Reserve Fund Account. In view of this, for the purpose of charging interest on the loan, the subsidy amount should be excluded. The balance lying to the credit of subsidy Reserve Fund Account will not form part of DTL for the purpose of SLR/CRR.

(b) In the case of Working Capital advances also, subsidy may be kept in the Reserve Fund Account as stated above without any interest being offered. However, the amount standing to the credit of the account should be withdrawn and credited to a Cash Credit Account of the SGSY Swarozgaris after a period of 5 years.

4.18 The repayment schedule of loan would be drawn in such a way that the subsidy kept under Subsidy Reserve Fund would be sufficient for adjustment towards that last few instalments. Swarozgaris will not be entitled for any benefit of subsidy, if the loan is fully repaid before a certain fixed period specified by NABARD depending upon the activity. The availability of the benefit of subsidy to Swarozgaris would be contingent on their roper utilization of loan as also its prompt repayment and maintaining the asset in good condition.

4.19 Banks will issue loan passbooks to Swarozgaris. These passbooks should, *inter alia*, contain details such as the date of sanction of loan, amount of loan sanctioned, subsidy to be adjusted in the final instalment of repayment, rate of interest, amount due under each instalment, due dates of instalments, etc. The banks may issue loan books to Swarozgaris in regional languages. Banks should ensure that the branch mangers fill in all the columns in the passbooks, as otherwise the purpose of issuing the passbooks will be defeated.

Repayment of Loan

4.20 All SGSY loans are treated as medium term loans with minimum repayment period of five years. Loan instalments will be fixed as per the unit cost approved by the NABARD/DLCC and there will be a moratorium on repayment of loan during the gestation period. Repayment instalments should not be more than 50 per cent of the incremental net income expected from the project. Number of instalments will be fixed in accordance with the principal amount, the interest liability and the repayment period.

4.21 Swarozgaris will not be entitled for any benefit of subsidy if the loan is fully repaid before a certain fixed period known as the lock-in period. The lock-in period for various activities under SGSY can be categorized broadly into three categories depending on the loan repayment period for 5, 7 and 9 years. The lock-in period corresponding to these repayment periods would be 3, 4 and 5 years respectively. If the loan is fully repaid before the currency period, the Swarozgaris will be entitled only to *pro rata* subsidy.

Measures for Affecting Recovery

4.22 Prompt recovery of loans will be an important aspect of SGSY, not only to ensure a discipline but more importantly as it reflects the success of the self-employment programme. All concerned must therefore ensure that the recovery is hundred per cent. To ensure this, the following measures shall be undertaken.

4.23 The Block SGSY Committee shall monitor, every month, the progress of different Swarozgaris. In particular, it should be seen whether the schemes have been grounded and whether they are giving the Swarozgari the intended income and also whether the Swarozgari is repaying the loan. Prompt action in case of defaults cannot be overemphasized. The bank shall furnish every month the list of defaulters, and the Block SGSY Committee shall go into the reasons. The line departments and the BDO shall contact the Swarozgari and take such remedial measures as are necessary. In case of groups, there shall be a periodic meeting of the SHGs to monitor the performance. In addition, the Gram Panchayats will also be given the list of defaulting Swarozgaris and requested to take suitable measures to see that the loans are repaid. In Panchayats with high default rates, the BDO/DRDA shall organize recovery camps. It is necessary that the DRDA keep a close watch over the repayment position in each Panchayat. In addition, the District administration shall assist the banks in the recovery through designated legal processes, including appointment of Special Recovery Officers. Enactment of the Model Bill as recommended by the Talwar Committee may be expedited.

4.24 The banks would take all possible measures, i.e. personal contact, organization of joint recovery camps with District Administration, legal action, etc. In case, even after this, the bank fails to recover the entire dues, the process of forfeiture of subsidy for adjustment against dues will be taken up. For this purpose, a notice will be issued to the Swarozgaris and he/she will be provided reasonable opportunity to show cause why his/her subsidy should not be forfeited. Thereafter, the concerned banks will place before the District SGSY committee a complete report on action taken and a proposal for forfeiture and adjustment of subsidy. After getting the approval of the Committee, the concerned bank will adjust the subsidy (including interest earned) against the Swarozgari's dues. However, if the bank is able to realize any amount from the Swarozgaris subsequently ovear and above the amount due to it, the amount will be returned to the DRDA.

4.25 Constant flow of information about every Swarozgari is necessary to ensure full recovery. Since the banks are also understaffed, they may engage the services of NGOs or individuals (other than government servants) as Monitor-cum-recovery facilitators, on a commission basis. A processing-cum-monitoring fee of 0.5 per cent of the loan amount may be charged to the Swarozgaris to meet this expenditure.

4.26 In order to ensure recovery discipline, with effect from 1.1.2001, any Panchayat that registers a recovery of less than 80 per cent under SGSY will not be eligible for consideration under SGSY. Likewise, any Panchayat Samiti registering a recovery of less than 80 per cent will see the further programme suspended in the Samiti.

4.27 In order to ensure that Panchayats/Panchayat Samitis do not meet with such a situation, they shall keep a close watch over the situation. The report of the Block SGSY Committee shall be placed by the BDO before the Panchayat Samiti. The District SGSY Committee shall also review the recovery position every month and ensure that steps are taken to recover the loans.

Incentives and Disincentives for Recovery Performance

4.28 In order to promote credit discipline among Swarozgaris and also to bring about a sense of accountability of the community, the following incentive and disincentive system is introduced.

(a) At the Swarozgari's level, prompt repayment will entitle him/her to waiver of the 0.5 per cent processing-cum-monitoring fee.

(b) At Gram Panchayat level and block level—a minimum of 80 per cent recovery should be ensured by Panchayats and block. Those Gram Panchayats and blocks that do not fulfil the required recovery performance will not be eligible for any allocation under SGSY in the subsequent year.

Observance of Non-Banking Day

4.29 Banks are required to observe one day in a week as non-banking day to enable the bank officials to go to the field and attend to the problems of Swarozgaris.

Risk Fund for Consumption Credit

4.30 To meet the small consumption needs of weaker sections of society, a Risk Fund for Consumption Credit can be created with (one per cent) (1%) of SGSY fund at District level. The scheme is intended to enable Commercial Banks, Cooperative Banks and Regional Rural Banks to provide consumption loans, not exceeding Rs.2000 per Swarozgaris from weaker sections of society. "Weaker Section" means all SGSY Swarozgaris, small and marginal farmers, landless agricultural workers, rural artisans and other people of very small means like carpenters, barbers, washermen etc. who form an integral part of the village community. Under this scheme, risk fund assistance is provided to the banks to the extent of 10 per cent of the total consumption loans disbursed by them during the year to the above mentioned target groups.

Refinance for SGSY Loans

4.31 Commercial banks (including Regional Rural Banks and Co-operative Banks) are eligible to get refinance from NABARD for the loans disbursed under SGSY, as per their guidelines. The eligibility for refinance is related to the recovery position of the banks. In addition, insurance cover to Commercial Banks and Regional Rural Banks is also available through the Deposit Insurance and Credit Guarantee Corporation.

Service Area Approach

4.32 The RBI has introduced Service Area Approach with effect from 1.4.1989. It is applicable to rural and semi-urban branches of Commercial and Regional Rural Banks. Under this scheme, each Bank branch has a designated service area comprising certain villages in which it will concentrate its activities for productive lending. The financing for SGSY in those villages is, therefore, to be done by the Bank Branches to which they have been allocated.

4.33 RBI has clarified that if some RRBs are not in a position to sanction the applications sent to them on account of constraint of funds, inadequacy of staff, etc., the designated branch of the Commercial Bank should extend financial assistance in such cases.

Insurance

Marking of Assets

4.34 The assets should be marked to check the misutilization or transfer of the assets. This is also necessary in the eventuality of filing insurance claim and physical verification of assets etc.

Insurance Cover for Various Assets

4.35 Insurance Cover at present is available for livestock assets given under IRDP (now SGSY). The General Insurance Corporation has agreed to provide this cover on the terms and conditions as reflected in the specimen Master Policy and Long Term Master Policy Agreement signed between the GIC and the State Government.

(i) Livestock Insurance

The coverage and premium rates are to be fixed in accordance with the Mater Policy Agreement.

(ii) Scope of Cover

The livestock policy provides indemnity in the even of death of animal/bird due to accident inclusive of fire, lightening, riot and strike, flood, cyclone, earthquake, famine or due to any fortuitous cause of disease contracted or occurring during the period of insurance subject to certain exclusions.

(iii) Sum Insured

The cost of the asset shall be treated as the sum insured for the settlement of claims. For permanent total disablement (PTD) claims 75 per cent of the sum insured shall be payable.

(iv) Claim Procedure

The claim procedure is simplified to secure expeditious disposal of claims. The Bank/DRDA shall forward a death certificate given jointly by any two of the following within 30 days from the date of occurrence:

1. Sarpanch/Upsarpanch of Village;
2. President or any other officer of the co-operative credit society;
3. Official of Milk Collection Centre or Government Veterinary Surgeon/Veterinary Assistant;
4. Supervisor/Inspector of Co-operative Central Bank;
5. Authorised nominee of DRDA;
6. Secretary of Panchayat;
7. Village Revenue Officer;
8. Village Accountant; and
9. Head Master of Primary School.

(v) Adjustment of Insurance Claim Money

The procedure of adjustment of insurance claim of animals will be as follows:

(a) Where the borrower has been regular in payment of interest/repayment of instalments and is willing to receive a replacement animal, the claim proceeds may be utilized to purchase a new animal.

(b) Where the Swarozgari was a wilful defaulter and has additional dues to the bank by way of interest, the claim proceeds would be adjusted to the bank loan liability and the balance may be paid to the DRDA. However, if the default was not wilful, replacement animal may be provide out of claim proceeds.

(c) Where the Swarozgari has been regular in payment of loan and interest but is unwilling to take a replacement animal he may be offered assistance for some other activity and claim proceeds utilized for financing the same. If he is unwilling to take any other activity, the claim money may be utilized by giving to the bank an amount equal to the balance outstanding in the loan account. The DRDA will also get subsidy amount proportionate to the balance loan outstanding and balance, if any, may be given to the beneficiary. Here, the Swarozgari is entitled to share the claim proceeds to the extent of loan repaid by him because he has utilized the asset properly and has paid the banks dues until the death of animal and has fulfilled the programmes objective to that extend.

(vi) Other Facilities

The General Insurance Corporation of India have informed that if any IRDP (now SGSY) beneficiary has other milch animals where not loan or subsidy is involved, such milch animals could also be insured at the concessional rates of premium, i.e. 2.25 per cent per annum or 1.69 per cent for three years. It has also intimated that IRDP (now SGSY) beneficiaries who have closed their loan account can insure the animals acquired by them through loan and subsidy at the concessional rates of premium for a further period of three years after closing the loan account it animals do not exceed the insurable age limit.

Expenditure on Premium

The expenditure on the premium is to be shared between the Government, bank and the beneficiary in the following proportions:

	When the banks do not participate	When the bank agrees to participate
Swarozgaris	1.25%	1.00%
Government	1.00%	0.75%
Bank	Nil	0.50%

The expenditure to be borne by the Government will be shared between the State and the Centre in the ratio of 75:25. It should be met out of SGSY funds but should not be included in the individual subsidy ceiling applicable to the beneficiary.

Group Life Insurance Scheme

4.36 A group life insurance scheme for Swarozgaris aged not less than 18 years and not more than 60 years was introduced w.e.f. 1.4.1988. This scheme is operative from the date on which the asset is disbursed to the Swarozgari till the Swarozgari completes the age of 60 years or a period of 5 years from the date of commencement of the cover, whichever is earlier. A sum of Rs.5000 shall become payable by LIC to the nominee of the deceased in case of natural death. In the event of death due to accident a sum of Rs.10,000 shall become payable by LIC.

(V)
SKILL UPGRADATION

5.1 It has been well recognized that for success of self-employment endeavours and also for their sustainability, the required skill to successfully run the enterprise is a prerequisite. SGSY proposes a number of measures for upgrading the capacity of Swarozgaris both in individual as well as group oriented activities.

5.2 While developing the project profiles for the identified key activities, the District SGSY Committee should in consultation with concerned technical personnel determine the Minimum Skill Requirement (MSR), in terms of both the technical and managerial skills. Once the person or group of persons has been identified for assistance, their training needs also should be ascertained with reference to MSR. The assessment regarding technical skills may be made by the line departments while that of the managerial skills may be made by the banker while scrutinizing the loan application. Such an exercise along with the Swarozgaris will help tin identifying those who have the MSR and therefore need only a basic orientation and those who need skill training. Keeping this in mind two types of training are contemplated under SGSY.

Basic Orientation Programme

5.3 Where the Swarozgari possesses the required skills, he/she may be put through a basic orientation programme after the loan is sanctioned and before it is disbursed. This mandatory programme may be organized at the block headquarters, not far from the place of residence. This basic orientation programme will seek to familiarize the Swarozgaris with SGSY and its objectives, the responsibilities of the Swarozgari, as well as the behavioural aspects. It will also seek to infuse confidence in the Swarozgari by drawing his/her attention to the success stories in the given key or allied activity, as well as alert him/her to the possible risks. This programme will include elements of book keeping, knowledge of market, identification and appraisal, acquaintance with produce costing and product pricing, familiarization with project financing by banks as well as some basic skills in the key activity identified. It will of a very short duration, and should not normally be more than two days. BDOs, Bankers and line departments can act as resource persons for this training. Training expenses like training material, honorarium to resource persons, travel and food expenses of Swarozgaris can be met by DRDA from SGSY Training Fund. No stipend will be admissible.

Skill Development Training

5.4 For the identified activities, Swarozgaris who need additional skill development/upgradation of skills appropriate training may be identified and suitable training programmes organized. Government institutions like engineering colleges, that is, Polytechnics, Universities and NGOs may be approached to imparting training. The objective of this training is to ensure that the Swarozgaris posses the Minimum Skill Requirement (MSR). Swarozgaris will be eligible for assistance only when they possess MSR and loans will be disbursed only when they have satisfactorily completed skill training.

5.5 For this training, Swarozgaris will be entitled for financial assistance if they require to undergo training for more than a week. The rate of assistance may be fixed locally. The bank will give this money to the Swarozgaris as a soft loan.

Identification of Training Institutions

5.6 Data on the available training Infrastructure should be collected so as to make an optimal use of the existing Infrastructure facilities at the District as well as the block levels. The facilities may include institutions, such as Polytechnics, Krishi Vigyan Kendras, Khadi and Village Industries Boards, State Institutes of Rural Development, Extension Training Centres, reputed voluntary organizations and any departmental facilities available in that area. Private institutions shall not normally be used for training, unless they are well known and have excellent infrastructural facilities that are otherwise not available. There is however no bar to utilize the private sector industrial units for appropriate training. The selected training institutions should have adequate facilities in terms of faculty, buildings, etc. The DRDA will be entitled to meet the expenses, incurred by the training institution for conduct of the training programme, from out of the SGSY-Training fund, but such expenses should not exceed Rs.15 per trainee per day.

SGSY Training Fund

5.7 Upto 10 per cent of SGSY funds will be set aside as training fund and will be utilized to provide both orientation and training programmes to the Swarozgaris, as indicated above. A separate Head of Account should be opened for this purpose.

5.8 The DRDA will be entitled to meet the expenses, incurred by the training institution for both Basic Orientation and Skill Development Training from out of the SGSY Fund. The Basic Orientation Training may include topics on concept of Self Help, group dynamics, conflict resolution, conduct of group meetings, maintenance of records, awareness about social and family welfare programmes etc. The training for skill development may include skill upgradation through exposure to latest tools and technology, value addition and diversification of products, entrepreneur development, marketing skills, packaging, labelling etc.

The DRDA will be entitled to meet the expenses, incurred by

the training institution for both Basic Orientation and Skill Development Training from out of the SGSY Fund in the following manner:

(i) The Institutional training cost may be fixed at Rs. 15 per day per trainee only for imparting training, if no boarding and lodging facility is provided to the participants, and at Rs. 35 per day per trainee in case the Institution provides boarding and lodging also with training.

(ii) If the Institution does not provide boarding and lodging then the participants may be paid Rs. 25 per trainee day to meet the cost of boarding and lodging.

(iii) Swarozgaris may be allowed one time to and fro travelling cost from their place of residence to the Training Institute.

Further, DRDAs may incur an expenditure of Rs. 200 per trainee per month for payment of honorarium to master craftsman engaged for imparting skill development training to Swarozgaris identified and selected for economic activity and Rs. 100 per month per trainee, as allowance for raw materials required for the training.

However, the total expenditure on Basic Orientation and skill development training will not exceed Rs. 5,000 per trainee.

Duration of Skill development training will be decided by the State Government depending upon the activities and in order to ensure uniformity of the duration of training for all the Districts.

(VI)
TECHNOLOGY

6.1 The effort under Swarnjayanti Gram Swarozgar Yojana is to ensure the development of sustainable micro enterprises. The self-employment referred under SGSY is moving away from provision of some additional income generation to a well-defined goal in terms of output, incomes and the time within which the assisted family comes above the poverty line. For any successful enterprise, appropriate technology of paramount importance.

The issues involved in technology management are primarily as follows:

(a) What technologies to be identified?
(b) Who will be responsible for technology management, including issues of technology transfer, technology upgradation and most importantly, monitoring of the technology absorption?

6.2 The technology identified for each key activity should be such that it can be managed comfortably by the Swarozgari and at the same time leads to a quality products, either in terms of goods/services. More importantly, it should be something that has been tested on the field. For, it is always possible to have an exhaustive list of technologies fit for rural areas but these may or may not have been proven commercially. Care should be taken to avoid giving unproven technologies to the rural poor, since they do not have the capacity to suffer losses arising out of experimentation. It is not as if technology has to be introduced afresh into each and every activity. Any given activity there is a certain level of technology. It is possible that introduction of certain technology may substantially alter the economics of working, in which case such new technology needs to be introduced. There could be in other cases where the technology can be upgraded to produce better economic results. In any case the technology introduction/upgradation should be such as to suit the needs of rural poor for the given key activity.

6.3 The process of technology identification is closely interlinked with the identification of key activity itself. The technology itself should be such that support services and infrastructure are adequately available. The project profiles of the key activities should clearly state the present status of technology, feasibility and potential for technology upgradation. Technology options may be explored in the area of:

- Processing value addition and packaging.

- Linkages with agricultural and animal husbandry extension services.
- Productive enhancement, efficiency improvement, cost effectiveness, drudgery reduction etc.

6.4 Under SGSY, it is expected that the assisted family would come out of poverty line in three years. It is, therefore, necessary that during this period the swarozgaris be closely monitored. In the earlier self-employment programmes the lack of such nurturing has been acutely felt. Typically in a block about 300-600 people would be assisted in one year. In other words about 900-1800 families need to be nurtured at any point of time. Since SGSY focuses on the group approach, the number of groups would not be far too many. Besides the swarozgaris either individually or in groups would be distributed over the four or five key activities in the block. For each key activity it is necessary to have an institution capable of transmitting technology ensuring skill upgradation and monitoring the performance in terms of the quality of output as well as the recovery. The choice of such agency can vary depending on local situation. The can be the line departments themselves or any of the technical institutions, such as Engineering Colleges, Polytechnics, that is, having competence in the relevant field or an NGO having the necessary competence. This can even be a research institution, a Krishi Vigyan Kendra or even a major private sector unit. All the institutions that are available in a block/district should be considered and the best available option exercised. In this regard, there are a number of community polytechnics (442) in the country with the avowed objective of promoting employment in the rural areas. Each of these community polytechnics has five extension centres. Similarly, there are 14 technology resource centres established by CAPART. The National Research & Development Corporation (NRDC) also has 52 rural technology demonstration-cum-training centres. In addition under TRYSEM itself a number of exclusive training centres have been established. Besides, the KVIC has also a number of training as well as research institutions. In the field of agriculture, a large number of Krishi Vigyan Kendras, Farmers Training Centres and regional centres of Agriculture Universities are available. Thus, a considerable knowledge already exists in the districts. The DRDAs must, therefore, strive to gather the existing knowledge and channelise this only into identification of key activities but also into immediate transfer of technical knowledge to entrepreneurs, so long as its commercial viability is not in question.

6.5 the manner of communicating the technology, either in terms of introduction or upgradation would be important and this should be done in such a manner that the swarozgaris could fully understand the same. Since skill upgradation is already provided for the costs incurred in respect of technology management can be incurred from the SGSY training fund. Any assistance to be provided to an institution identified for transfer of technology should only be nominal and should not be such that it supports the institution as such. The expenditure is meant essentially for swarozgaris.

(VII) MARKETING SUPPORT

7.1 For any goods or services that are produced, existence of a suitable market is essential. Traditionally, the self-employment programmes concentrated on the inputs rather than the outputs and their marketing. It was not uncommon to find production strategies in place overlooking the market aspects. One often finds that the recommendation of an activity is not preceded by the much needed market survey. There is a false notion that market surveys are not required in case of the self-employment opportunities for the rural poor. In fact, it is as critical, if not more, for the poor. For, he/she cannot sustain the loss arising out of a lack of market even for short period. It is, therefore, necessary that the project profile of every key activity identify the market availability. The forecast of the incomes to be earned by the Swarozgari must take into account this factor and forecast the incomes only on the basis of an assured market. This would be a critical factor in the choice of the key activity itself.

7.2 It is possible that this might appear to be formidable proposition and that the field functionaries might feel that they are unequal to the task. Happily, this is not so. While to most of us, market mechanism may appear unintelligible and a complex task, in reality it means checking out what sells and what does not. Goods and services are traded everyday in all parts of the country. What is needed is to see what sells in the local markets. A study conducted some years ago for the Ministry of Rural Development indicated that the rural Haats (Markets) play a significant role. An analysis of these markets therefore reveals the opportunities. Secondly, an analysis of the daily requirements, either for personal use or in agriculture and exploring ways of meeting the demand locally; can lead to some useful results. At times, the product concerned might require some promotional activity in order to raise demand.

7.3 A study of the local markets might reveal that what the villagers purchase can as well be produced locally. The opportunities must be fully explored. At the same time, it must be remembered that it is neither feasible nor desirable to produce all goods in all places. The choice of activity therefore must be governed by the possibilities that exist on account of the resources of an area, the available skills and the market. It is always possible to develop the skills or even the markets but this must be weighed against the fact that it would require time and effort.

7.4 Next in the importance are the markets in urban areas. There is an increasing trend towards urbanization in the country along with a change of consumer tastes and demands. The goods in demand could be in the primary sector or otherwise. An analysis of these urban markets would reveal the consumer preferences and the potential for the rural entrepreneurs. There can be a good potential for value added items, such as cleaned and packaged food items, such as cleaned and packaged food items, processed fruit and vegetables etc. The emerging urban markets can be a good area for developing clientele for the rural products. Provision of marketing infrastructure in these areas can go a long way in enabling the rural poor to market their goods and at the same time building an identity for the products. The Self Help Groups can be encouraged to try out these markets on their own so that they slowly develop marketing skills. They can also start marketing the goods of the individual Swarozgaris. Infrastructure fund can be use for strengthening marketing infrastructure and related activities.

7.5 The marketing of goods outside the districts requires an intermediary agency. This can be in the governmental, non-governmental or private sector. The one aspect that requires to be taken care of is the stability of the agency, their own competence and their capacity to ensure that the rural producer is getting his/her fair share of the profits. Care should be taken to see that only such agencies that do not exploit the rural producers and are well established in the business are chosen for the purpose. These agencies may market the products in the national or international markets.

7.6 Some State Governments have established District Supply and Marketing Societies (DSMS) to provide non-credit inputs like procurement or purchase of raw-material and also for sale of products. Wherever these societies are doing good work, they can be suitably strengthened. Similarly, in States such as Orissa and Kerala, there are marketing societies at the State level. Their capacity and product range can be suitably expanded. However, it is not always necessary to establish new agencies. It should be a felt need after a careful analysis of the existing infrastructure, and should be part of a strategy for promotion of marketing support to products under SGSY.

7.7 Organizations like Handicrafts Boards and Handloom Corporations and also KVIC/KVIB can play a prominent role in promotion of SGSY. The marketing outlets of KVIC/KVIB must be made use of for SGSY products. Keeping the market trends in view, linkages with apex bodies can ensure a stable market at remunerative prices. Such a link will also result in quality improvements while reducing the market risks to the poor. Bankers can also encourage such initiates that liberal credit delivery since the loan recovery can be built into the project. There are several NGO and other independent institutions to market products from rural artisans/craftsmen across the country. DRDAs should strive to develop linkages with such groups.

7.8 A few States have organized Melas to give publicity to the range of products produced by the Swarozgaris. Such efforts need further encouragement so those SGSY Swarozgaris will be integrated with the regional markets. Organizing of Exhibitions periodically in urban centres will offer better price to the goods of SGSY Swarozgaris. This also serves as forum for sensitizing the SGSY group to the demand patterns of the market. The State level organizations and boards have to develop an organic link professional bodies can guide the poor in supply of designs and in quality assurance. Attempts to establish State emporia for display and sales of SGSY Products in major urban cities need to be given a fair trial.

7.9 Quality of products is vital not only for the development of entrepreneurs but also for the nation as a whole. It must be the responsibility of the marketing agencies to ensure that the Swarnjayanti are trained in quality control. The goods marketed must conform to a minimum and uniform quality so as to be able to develop a brand image. This is important even in respect of the goods that are produced for local consumption. The DRDAs must organize periodic meets of the Swarozgaris and ensure that they are given the necessary guidance in quality control. There must also be a system of the experts in the relevant fields visiting the work places and guiding the Swarozgaris.

(VIII) IMPLEMENTATION

8.1 A close involvement of different agencies is essential for the success of Swarnjayanti Gram Swarozgar Yojana (SGSY). SGSY is implemented by District Rural Development Agencies (DRDAs) through the Panchayati Samithis and, with the active involvement of other Panchayati Raj Institutions, the banks, the line departments and the NGOs.

8.2 The DRDAs are expected to co-ordinate the implementation of the programme. In particular their role will be critical in organization of the Self Help Groups and their capacity building as well as in terms of co-ordination with the technical institutions for technology and training, the banks for planning and credit mobilization, the line departments for infrastructure and technical follow up as well as in co-ordinating the marketing activities.

8.3 The Gram Panchayats will play a crucial role in SGSY. The Gram Sabha will first approve the list of BPL families. Besides, at the beginning of each year, the potential Swarozgaris for taking up the designated key activities would be identified in each habitation by a 3-member committee including the Sarpanch. The list of Swarozgaris who are sanctioned the loan by the banks would be placed before the Gram Sabha. The Gram Panchayat would also take steps to provide from its funds under JGSY or any other programme, the common infrastructure necessary for the key activities. The Gram Panchayat would actively monitor the performance of the Swarozgaris and in particular whether they are repaying the loan regularly.

8.4 The Panchayat Samiti (Block Level) will approve the key activities that are identified for the blocks before the list is sent to the BDO through the District Level Technical Group. The Panchayat Samiti would review every month the reports sent by Block SGSY Committee. In particular, the Panchayat Samiti would review the recovery performance. The Zilla Parishad will be reviewing the performance under the SGSY in its general meetings.

8.5 The Bankers play a very critical role in the implementation of Swarnjayanti Gram Swarozgar Yojana. SGSY is a credit-cum-subsidy programme. Credit is the key component and subsidy is only a minor and enabling component. SGSY envisages the close association of bankers at all stages of the programme implementation, right from the identification of key activities, clusters, self help groups, identification of individual Swarozgaris as well as planning for all the elements of the key activities. The bank has the final say in the selection of Swarozgaris. An elaborate mechanism has been put in place to ensure post-credit monitoring as well as for loan recovery.

8.6 The line departments have an important role to play in the entire exercise, for they will be responsible for implementation and monitoring of respective sectoral activities. SGSY would need a very close collaboration between the implementing agencies and the line departments. This collaboration starts with the identification of key activities and preparation of project reports.

The line departments will be responsible for planning and creation of the infrastructure required to make the key activity successful. In addition, once the bank has sanctioned the loan, the line departments must ensure that all facilities including technical guidance are provided to the Swarozgaris. The line departments may also verify whether the Swarozgaris have the necessary skill requirement and take steps to train them. The line departments should also satisfy themselves about the quality of training that is being imparted. They should assist the DRDAs in ensuring that the Swarozgaris are able to derive the expected levels of income. The line departments will treat promotion of self-employment in their sector as much their responsibility as that of DRDA/Panchayati Raj Institutions/Banks and it should be an integral part of their day-to-day functioning.

8.7 The NGOs have also an important role to play. They can be used in the formation and nurturing of the SHGs as well as in the monitoring of the progress of the Swarozgaris. Where feasible, their services can also be utilized for provision of technology support, quality control of the products. What the NGOs can do would depend on the nature of the NGO and its competence. Care must therefore be taken to ensure that only those NGOs are utilized in the programme as are capable of supporting the programme. At the same time, every effort must be made to ensure that all resources available in the district are made use of.

8.8 Similarly, care must be taken to ensure the participation of the technical resource available in the district, in the form of technical institutions. These technical institutions may not always have ready solutions to the problems but if they are properly oriented, they can come up with solutions to different problems. If they are made part of an ongoing process, their own capacity ;will be built up, with long-term benefits. The District SGSY Committee must pay particular attention to this aspect.

Co-ordination Mechanism

8.9 A close coordination between different agencies responsible for implementation of SGSY is critical for the success of the programme. The programme should be treated as a joint programme with all agencies being conscious of their respective roles. In order to ensure the coordination the following committees are constituted under SGSY.

Block Level SGSY Committee

8.10 There shall be a Block Level SGSY Committee in each block. Its composition will be as follows:

1. Project Director – DRDA	:	Chairman
2. Project Officer (Self-employment)	:	Member
3. Branch Managers of all implementing bank branches in Block	:	Members
4. Block Level/Sub-Division Level officers of the concerned line departments	:	Members
5. NGO representative (one)	:	Member
6. Block Development Officer	:	Convenor

The meetings of this Committee shall be convened by the BDO. The Lead Bank Officer, DDM, NABARD and the Lead District Officer, RBI may attend the meetings as special invitees. They may attend as many meetings as possible in each block, so that they are familiar with the ground level problems and can help in sorting them out.

The main functions of Block Level SGSY Committee are:

(a) Selection of key activities at the beginning of the programme;
(b) Selection of villages and number of Swarozgaris to be covered each year;
(c) Distribution of the work among the bank branches;
(d) Monitoring of the performance by different agencies;
(e) Co-ordination issues in respect of infrastructure, credit, technology and marketing;
(f) Review of incomes being earned by Swarozgaris;
(g) Review of the recovery performance; fixing dates for recovery camps etc.
(h) Conduct of sample checks for verification of assets;

(i) Drawing up of the monthly report (the monthly report may be drawn by BDO based on information furnished by the banks. A review of the report in the monthly meeting will help the block level committee in identifying different problems. It is, however, not necessary to hold up the preparation of the report in the absence of this monthly meeting);

(j) Review of progress of Swarozgaris in crossing the poverty line.

The block level committee shall meet between 5th and 10th of every month. It must be ensured that meetings are held regularly. Branch Manager of financing institutions should report in a pre-determined format about the SGSY financing in the Block and the same should be compiled by BDO. The proceedings of the Block Level SGSY Committee shall be sent to Panchayat Samiti for information and necessary action, if any. A copy should also be sent to the PD, DRDA and to the Lead Bank Officer.

District Level

8.11 At the District Level, there shall be a District SGSY Committee under the Chairmanship of the District Collector/ Chief Executive Officer. This Committee meets every month to review the progress of SGSY and suggest corrective action wherever necessary. The composition of District Level SGSY Committee will be as under:

1.	District Collector/Chief Executive Officer	: Chairman
2.	DDM of NABARD	: Member
3.	LDO of RBI	: Member
4.	District level Co-ordinators of the implementing banks	: Members
5.	Concerned Heads of district level line departments	: Members
6.	General Manager, DIC	: Member
7.	District KVIB Officer	: Member

8. Project Director, DRDA : Member
9. 2-3 NGO representatives : Members
10. Lead Bank Officer : Convenor

The functions of the District SGSY Committee include:

(i) Review of SGSY Plan,
(ii) Monitoring and review of the overall progress in physical and financial terms,
(iii) Sorting out inter-agency differences and to prepare items for consideration of State Level Committee,
(iv) Assessing training needs of Swarozgaris and also to review the arrangements for training including identification of appropriate institutions and also,
(v) Monitor the recovery position bank-wise and block-wise so as to initiate corrective measures where necessary.

State Level

8.12 The Department of Rural Development or any other Department to which the subject of Rural Development has been allocated should be responsible for planning, implementation, monitoring and evaluation of the programme at the State Level. A State level SGSY Committee has been provided to oversee the functioning and the performance under SGSY. Its composition is as under:

1. Chief Secretary/Development Commissioner : Chairman
2. Secretary, D/o Institutional Finance : Member
3. Secretary, D/o Planning : Member
4. Secretary, In-charge of Women's Development : Member
5. Concerned Heads of the Line Developments as and when required : Member
6. Secretary In-charge of Welfare of SC/STs : Member
7. Representative of NABARD (local Head of Regional Office) : Member
8. Representative of RBI : Member

9.	Representatives of concerned implementing Banks at State Headquarters	: Members
10.	A representative of the Government of India, not below the rank of Deputy Secretary	: Member
11.	Director, SIRD	: Member
12.	Convenor, SLBC	: Member
13.	Secretary, In-charge of Rural Development	: Member

Secretary

Functions of the State Level SGSY Committee are as under:

(i) To provide leadership and guidance in the planning, implementation and monitoring of the programme.
(ii) To review the district-wise progress under SGSY and suggest remedial actions.
(iii) To monitor and evaluate the implementation of the programme with reference to the objectives of the programme.
(iv) To review the involvement of reputed NGOs in the SGSY and provide directions if necessary.
(v) To provide a forum for a meaningful dialogue between the policy makers at the State level and the implementers at the field as well as the bankers.
(vi) To discuss any other issue relating to SGSY.

Central Level

8.13 The Department of Rural Development in the Ministry of Rural Development, Government of India, New Delhi has the overall responsibility of policy formulation, monitoring and evaluation of the programme and for release of central share of funds. A Central Level Co-ordination Committee (CLCC) has been constituted as under to assist the Department. The CLCC will meet once in six months.

1.	Secretary, Ministry of Rural Development	: Chairman
2.	Deputy Governor, Reserve Bank of India	: Member
3.	Secretary, Department of Agriculture & Cooperation	: Member
4.	Secretary, Department of Expenditure	: Member
5.	Special Secretary, Banking Division, Ministry of Finance	: Member
6.	Secretary, Department of Women and Child Development	: Member
7.	Secretary, Department of Small Scale & Agro-related Industries	: Member
8.	Secretary, Department of Science & Technology	: Member
9.	Secretary, Ministry of Welfare	: Member
10.	Managing Director, NABARD	: Member
11.	Adviser (Rural Development), Planning Commission	: Member
12.	Additional Secretary & FA, Ministry of Rural Development	: Member
13.	State Secretaries of Rural Development	: Member
14.	Chairman-cum-Managing Director of all commercial sector banks	: Member
15.	Director General CAPART	: Member
16.	Director General, NIRD	: Member
17.	Chairman, Indian Banks Association	: Member
18.	Joint Secretary (SGSY) – Department of Rural Development	: Member Secretary

Other officials/non-officials may be invited to the meetings of this Committee if their presence is felt necessary.

The functions of CLCC are as under:

(i) To review and ensure effective implementation of the programmes.

(ii) To review linkages for support services for SGSY.

(iii) To review progress of these programmes in physical, financial and qualitative terms including credit assistance.

(iv) To consider concurrent evaluation reports.

(v) To provide a forum for a continuous dialogue with the State Governments and Bankers.

(vi) To review the credit arrangements and recommend changes and improvements as and when necessary.

Setting Up of SGSY Cells in Banks

8.14 For the purpose of effective monitoring of the implementation of SGSY, the banks may set up SGSY cells in their controlling offices such as Zonal/Regional Offices. These cells should make periodical review of the flow of credit to SGSY Swarozgaris, ensure the implementation of the guidelines issued by Reserve Bank of India and the Government of India, collect data from the branches and make available consolidated data to the Head Office of the Bank.

(IX)
FUNDING PATTERN AND FINANCIAL PROCEDURE

Criteria for Allocation of Funds to the States

9.1 Swarnjayanti Gram Swarozgar Yojana is a Centrally Sponsored Scheme and the financing of the programme will be shared between the Centre and the States in the ratio of 75:25. The Central allocation earmarked for the States will be distributed in relation to the incidence of poverty in the States. However, additional parameters like absorption capacity (based on past trend in utilization of SGSY funds) and special requirement will also be taken into consideration during the course of the year. Devolution of funds to the districts will be indicated by the States and approved by the Government of India. Government of India will release the funds directly to the DRDAs. Devolution to the Blocks may be decided by the Governing Body of the DRDA based on level of poverty and other local factors. Re-allocation may be made by the DRDA within a district. This can be made during January for the remained of the financial year.

Eligible Items of Expenditure

9.2 Each DRDA may incur expenditure on the following items from the funds provided under the SGSY:

(i) Training
(ii) Infrastructure
(iii) Revolving Fund to SHGs
(iv) Subsidy for economic activities

The SGSY is a process oriented scheme, therefore, formation of the Self Help Group (SHG) passes through different stages and the timeframe for each stage may vary from District to District and State to State depending on spatial distribution and capacity of facilitators, literacy awareness and socio-economic status of the people being organized etc. The States/UTs may be in different stages of the implementation of the Scheme. Therefore, the fund required for training and capacity building including basic orientation, skill development, entrepreneurship development, revolving fund to SHGs and subsidy for economic activity may vary from State to State. Therefore, DRDAs may prioritize the expenditure on different components, i.e. training and capacity building, revolving fund and subsidy for economic activity, based on the local requirements and different stages of group formation.

The DRDAs may, however, ensure that there is a balance between the expenditure proposed for different items. The prioritization may be done at the commencement of the year and the expenditure monitored on this basis. However, the expenditure on infrastructure will not exceed 20 per cent of the total annual allocation (25% in case of NE States). Asset creation for the Swarozgaris is one of the core objective of the SGSY. The prioritization of expenditure on the various items should therefore be done in such a manner that the amounts earmarked towards subsidy for asset creation are sufficient to meet the requirements not only of the SHGs which are ready for economic activities but also of the individual swarozgaris for whom viable projects are to be identified.

An amount up to Rs.5 lakhs annually may be spent from the funds available under the scheme on management of professional input related to marketing research, value addition or product diversification or any other input which would facilitate marketing of the produce ultimately resulting in additional income to the Swarozgaris.

Release of Funds

9.3 The Centre releases funds in two instalments. In the case of cold snow bound District, viz. Lahaul and Spiti, Leh and Kargil where the working period is limited to a few months, the entire Central share of assistance can be released in one instalment. These releases should be immediately followed with the releases by the States.

Release Procedure for Central Share of SGSY Funds

(A) Normal Areas

(i) Release of First Instalment

The release of first instalment of SGSY subsidy amount can be made without any formal request if the second instalment in the previous year had been released without any condition. If this instalment was not released at all or was released with some conditions, formal requests for release of first instalment are required from the DRDAs after the conditions have been fulfilled/ reasons for non-release of the second instalment have been met.

The release of the first instalment should ordinarily be completed by the end of the second month of the financial year.

(ii) Release of Second Instalment

The second instalment of Central funds is released on the request of the DRDAs in the prescribed proforma on fulfilment of the following conditions:

1. Budget provision for the current year may be indicated

by the State Governments. The Central release will not exceed it proportionately.

2. The State Government should have released its contribution during the previous year. Deficiency in release of its share will be deducted from the second instalment.
3. The opening balance of the DRDAs should not exceed 15 per cent (20% for the year 1999-2000) of the allocation of the year in which funds are being released. In case, the opening balance exceeds this limit, the Central share of the amount by which it exceeds this limit will be deducted at the time of release of second instalment.
4. Available funds including carry forward funds should have been utilized at least to 60 per cent.
5. Audit reports, utilization certificates for the previous year should be furnished.
6. Annual Plan should have been approved by the Governing Body of the DRDA.
7. Any other terms and conditions imposed at the time of the last release should have been met.
8. The States should ideally get the release of second instalment latest by the end of December. The quantum of second instalment releases while seeking the second instalment will be made dependent on the time of reporting of utilization. Depending on the receipt of complete proposal for second instalment, the quantum will be governed as follows:

Proposals Received

by the end of December	:	50 per cent of allocated funds
by the end of January	:	40 per cent of allocated funds
by the end of February	:	30 per cent of allocated funds
In March	:	20 per cent of allocated funds

(B) Cold Desert Districts

Funds will be released in one instalment but the following conditions should be satisfied before next release:

(a) Conditions laid down at the time of release of funds during the previous year should have been satisfied.
(b) Budget provisions for the current year should have been indicated and Central releases should not exceed it.
(c) State Government should have released its share during the previous year. Deficiency in the release of the State contribution would be deducted from the current year's release.
(d) Carry forward balances should not exceed 15 per cent (20% for the year 1999-2000) of the last year's allocation. Excess carry forward would be deducted from the current year's release.
(e) 75 per cent utilization of available funds including carry forward funds.
(f) Annual Plan should have been approved by the Governing Body of the DRDA.
(g) Audit Report, Utilization Certificate and Bank Reconciliation Certificate for the previous year should have been received.

(X)
MONITORING

10.1 For ensuring the Swarozgari crosses the poverty line, it is not sufficient to provide him assets through subsidy and loan. The progress of management of his assets for generation of incremental income has to be continuously followed up, monitored and evaluated.

10.2 The follow-up on the projects given to the Swarozgari should be done by the DRDA/Block officials, and bankers to see that the Swarozgari is properly managing his assets and is able to generate the projected income. All efforts should be made to remove any difficulties that the Swarozgari may be facing. Every Swarozgari should be given Vikas Patrika. Two copies of this document should be prepared of which one copy should be given to the Swarozgari and the other should be kept at the Block Headquarters. Both the copies should be kept continuously updated regarding the health of the project.

10.3 An annual physical verification of assets may also be undertaken on a drive basis at the end of every year. The results of such verification should be incorporated in the Annual Plan for the next year.

10.4 Follow-up and monitoring will also be done at the different levels and agencies like DRDA, BDO, Panchayats, Bank Branches etc.

10.5 The performance of the implementation of SGSY is to be monitored continuously at all levels. At the Block and District levels this is done through reports and physical verification of the assets. At the Central Government level, the programme will be continuously monitored on the basis of monthly progress report. The States will send district-wise information received from the DRDA to the Centre as under:

(a) Monthly Progress Report

Monthly Progress Report should be sent so as to reach the Centre by the 20th of every succeeding month. The proforma for submission of above monthly progress report will be communicated to the States.

(b) Annual Progress Report

The Monthly Progress Report for the last month of the financial year, i.e. March will be treated as the final Annual Progress Report for that year.

This annual progress report should be sent along with an analytical note on the implementation of the SGSY in the State particularly, on the following points:

(i) The physical and financial progress during the year.

(ii) The linkages provided and availed of for various activities.

(iii) General comments on the implementation of the programme including suggestions, if any.

Qualitative Monitoring of SGSY at Block/DRDA Level

10.6 For effective implementation of the programme, physical monitoring through field inspections is important. Officers dealing with SGSY at the State headquarters shall visit districts regularly and ascertain through field visits that the programme is being implemented satisfactory and is in accordance with the prescribed procedures and specifications. Likewise, officers at the district, sub-division and block levels must closely monitor all aspects of the programme through visits in the interior areas.

10.7 In order to develop a consistent system of monitoring the implementation of SGSY at Block/DRDA level through field visits and physical verification of assets as well as progress of the Swarozgari towards income generation the following schedule of inspection of families by the various levels of officers is suggested:

(i)	District Magistrate/Chairman DRDA	:	10 per month
(ii)	Project Director, DRDA	:	20 per month
(iii)	Project Officer & Project Economist	:	40 per month
(iv)	SDMs	:	20 per month
(v)	BDOs	:	20 per month
(vi)	ADOs	:	20 per month

10.8 District Collector/Chairman DRDA should prescribe suitable number of field visits for the officers of the line departments and obtain their inspection reports. On the basis of these inspection reports the Monitoring Wing at DRDAs will prepare a consolidated report. These reports should be discussed in the meetings of the Governing Bodies of DRDAs. Necessary corrective action should be taken wherever necessary. DRDAs will also send consolidated report on quarterly basis to States along with summary of comments on salient observations and follow up action taken on these issues.

10.9 The State Level SGSY Committee, should review quarterly the findings emerging out of qualitative monitoring of the programme as a standing agenda. Selected Chairmen/Project Directors should be invited to such meetings.

Evaluation Studies

10.10 The States/UTs should conduct periodical evaluation studies on the implementation of the programme.

10.11 Evaluation studies may be given to the reputed institutions and organizations, on issues thrown up by the concurrent evaluation meriting detailed studies. These studies may be given by the Centre as well as the States/UTs. Copies of the evaluation studies conducted by the State should be furnished to the Central Government.

10.12 Remedial action shall be taken by the States/UTs on the basis of the observations made in these evaluation studies and also in the Concurrent Evaluation conducted by the Government of India.

(XI) SPECIAL PROJECTS

Introduction

11.1 Under SGSY, funds are released to the DRDAs and are utilized as per the decisions taken at the local level. Sometimes, the poverty reduction efforts requires co-ordinated action by different departments and it may call for planning and co-ordination which may extend beyond the individual districts. There may also be occasions when the different departments or DRDAs or State Governments might want to try out new initiatives which are in the nature of pioneer projects, capable of triggering much needed growth impulses. Such projects, capable of triggering much needed growth impulses. Such projects would be indicators of possible alternative strategies. In order to take up such projects, 15 per cent of the funds under SGSY will be set apart by the Ministry for such initiatives in conjunction with other departments, semi-government organizations such as, the Khadi & Village Industries Commission, Development Commissioner, Handicrafts, Commodity Boards, etc., or international organizations. This would include initiatives to be taken in the individual districts or across the districts. If during the course of the year, such funds cannot be fully utilized, the balance funds will be distributed among the States along with the programme funds whose redistribution during the year will keep in view the absorption capacity of different States.

Objective

11.2 The objective of each special project would be to ensure a time-bound programme for bringing a specific number of BPL families above the poverty line through self-employment programmes. As per the programme guidelines, every assisted family must be brought above the poverty line in three years. The projects may involve different strategies to provide long term sustainable self-employment opportunities either in terms of organization of the rural poor, provision of support infrastructure, technology, marketing, training, etc., or a combination of these.

Approval of Special Projects

11.3 the State Governments or semi-government organizations at the National level or International Organizations may pose projects under this component. To consider the proposals received, there shall be a two-tier committee system.

(a) Project Screening Committee
(b) Project Approval Committee

(a) Project Screening Committee

The Projects submitted would be examined and considered by the Screening Committee before they are submitted to the

Approval Committee with its recommendation. The composition of the Projects Screening Committee would be as under:

Joint Secretary (IRD), D/o Rural Development	: Chairman
Director/Dy. Adviser(RD), Planning Commission	: Chairman
Deputy Secretary (IFD), D/o Rural Development	: Member
Director/Deputy Secretary/Joint Director dealing with the subject	: Member Convenor

The Screening Committee would also be responsible for periodical review and monitoring of the projects sanctioned under the scheme.

The composition of the Projects Approval Committee would be as under:

Secretary, M/o Rural Development	: Chairman
AS&FA, M/o Rural Development	: Member
Adviser (RD), Planning Commission	: Member
Joint Secretary (IRD)	: Member-Convenor

A project being forwarded to Government of India under special projects of SGSY should *inter alia* include the following details:

(i) Likely beneficiaries/families of beneficiaries and year-wise details of long term and short term benefits (financial and in the nature of assets created and self-employment) expected to flow to the beneficiaries.

(ii) An analysis of the activities proposed to be undertaken and the possibility of its replicability elsewhere.

(iii) The approach proposed to be adopted for achieving the objective and the activities selected under the project proposal in relating to the available resources.

(iv) Details of integration with other on-going rural

development programmes in the area and arrangements for dovetailing funds from non-SGSY resources.

Period of Implementation of Project

11.4 The period of implementation should not normally exceed three years.

Releases Under the Special Projects

11.5 Releases under the projects shall be made as per schedule of releases approved for each programme. Recurring expenditure such as creation of posts or vehicles or maintenance expenditure shall not be admissible in the projects.

11.6 The reports and returns will be submitted to the Central Government by the implementing agencies as prescribed generally or for specific projects.

The Ministry of Rural Development *vide* its D.O. letter No. V-24015/4/2000-IRD-V dated 3rd May, 2002 has communicated all the States/UTs regarding the revised guidelines for Special Projects under Swarnjayanti Gram Swarozgar Yojana (SGSY).

The revised guidelines are as follows:

(i) The maximum investment, inclusive of credit and State share, under each Special Project should not exceed Rs. 15.00 crores and the minimum project cost shall not be below Rs. 1.00 crore.

(ii) Special Projects should be formulated/posed particularly with focus on backward districts having high incidence of poverty.

(iii) Ordinarily one project shall be approved for one district at a time. In exceptional cases, Project Approval Committee (PAC) may approve a second project for the district. However, under no circumstances there shall be more than two on-going projects in a district.

(iv) No project will be approved for a State unless the State indicates its commitment to provide 25 per cent of the project cost as its matching share.

(v) There should be prior commitment from the banks for funding the projects.

(vi) Credit component of projects may be arranged from the banks or other institutions such as SC/ST/Women Corporation etc.

(vii) The release of funds to the Implementing Agency should be normally in three installments in the ratio of 40:40:20. However, if a release schedule is indicated in the proposal and approved, funds will be released according to the schedule.

(viii) Attempt should be made to cover maximum BPL families under the Project. At least 80 per cent of the beneficiaries under the Project shall be from BPL families. The number of BPL families to be covered should be specifically indicated in the Project Proposal.

(ix) The district specific Projects will be formulated by the DRDAs in consultation with the Line Departments so as to ensure desired linkage with the BPL families and technical support being provided by the line Department.

(x) Special Project Proposals of Line Departments, which may cater to more than one district, shall also be considered. However, in such cases, the proposals would have to be routed through the Rural Development/ Panchayati Raj Department, which is in charge of implementation of the SGSY in the State. This would ensure convergence of activities and their focus on BPL families.

A list of points, which may be kept in mind, while formulating the proposals for special projects under the SGSY, is at Annexure I.

Annexure I

MAJOR POINTS WHICH MAY BE KEPT IN MIND WHILE FORMULATING A SPECIAL PROJECT UNDER SGSY

1. Name of the Project
2. **Conceptual Background ot the Project** and features which make it special for sanction under Special Projects of SGSY and not under normal SGSY. Possibility of replicability of the project.
3. Project Objective
4. Strategy
5. **Project Period and Action Plan** (year-wise) for implementation of the Project.
6. **Area of the Project and Area Profile** (how the key activity suitable for the area and the people).
7. Key activities to be taken in the Project
8. **Beneficiaries' details:** in terms of numbers/categories and their linkage with the activities taken in the Project.
9. **Implementing Agency:** DRDA or a body of the SHGs, or if it is a Project which involves more than one DRDA than the name of the DRDA to whom the funds would be released for implementation.
10. Role of Line Departments/NGOs/PRIs
11. **Bench Mark Survey** for indicators on which the Success of the project would be monitored and evaluated
12. **Integration With Other On-Going Rural Development Programmes** in the area and arrangements for dove-tailing funds from non-SGSY resources.
13. Raw Material Supply
14. **Technical Know-How**, if any. What arrangements have been made for flow of technical know-how like Memorandum of understanding (MoU) signed etc.
15. **Training** component Existing skill, training institutes identified, funds arrangements, duration of training etc.

16. **Marketing arrangement of the Produce:** existing markets, strategy for expanding the markets in future, details of forward and backward linkages
17. **Infrastructure Development:** Infrastructural facility, if to be built, then mention how it is linked with direct benefit of Swarozgaris. How the provision for staff, running cost etc. would be met.
18. **Benefits/Impact of the Project:** in terms of increase in income, year-wise income growth identified parameters etc.
19. **Risk Factors** affecting the Project objectives of increase in income etc.
20. Modalities to Minimize Risks
21. **Criteria for monitoring and evaluation of Project:** mention various parmeters on which the project is to be monitored and evaluated. How it will be monitored after the completion of the Project?
22. **State's Commitment to Match the Share** of the project cost
23. **Bank's Commitment for Credit.** The amount of Bank Credit should clearly be indicated vis-à-vis the number of Swarojgaris.
24. **Technical Scrutiny and Technical Feasibility** of the Project (Please indicate whether the concerned technical department of the State Government has vetted the Project, if yeas, the comments thereof)
25. **Economic Appraisal of the Project** (the Project may be got appraised and results of the appraisal indicated appropriately in the Proposal) i.e. viability of the project.
26. **Estimated Cost** (Please indicates the Central and State share and the Credit component, if applicable, including contribution by the Swarozgaris). The estimated cost should indicate the total cost and activity-wise/ beneficiary-wise costs also.
27. Repayment Schedule
28. Whether the Project or part thereof has been submitted to any other agency? If yes, the results thereof. If the project or its part had been rejected the reasons.

Annexure II

STATE SPECIFIC POVERTY LINE (1999-2000)

(Rupees Per Capita Per Month)

Sl. No.	State	Rural	Urban
1.	Andhra Pradesh	262.94	457.40
2.	Assam	365.43	343.99
3.	Bihar	333.07	379.78
4.	Gujarat	318.94	474.41
5.	Haryana	362.81	420.20
6.	Himachal Pradesh	367.45	420.20
7.	Karnataka	309.59	511.44
8.	Kerala	374.79	477.06
9.	Madhya Pradesh	311.34	481.65
10.	Maharashtra	318.63	539.71
11.	Orissa	323.92	473.12
12.	Punjab	362.68	388.15
13.	Rajasthan	344.03	465.92
14.	Tamil Nadu	307.64	475.60
15.	Uttar Pradesh	336.88	416.29
16.	West Bengal	350.17	409.22
17.	Delhi	362.68	505.45
	All India	327.56	454.11

The poverty line (implicit) at all-India level is worked out from the expenditure class-wise distribution of persons and the poverty ratio at all-India level. The poverty ratio at all India level is obtained as the weighted average of the state-wise poverty ratio.

Annexure-II D

CENTRAL RURAL SANITATION PROGRAMME (TOTAL SANITATION CAMPAIGN)

Department of Drinking Water Supply
Ministry of Rural Development
Government of India
(December 2007)

CENTRAL RURAL SANITATION PROGRAMME: TOTAL SANITATION CAMPAIGN BACKGROUND

1. Individual Health and hygiene is largely dependent on adequate availability of drinking water and proper sanitation. There is, therefore, a direct relationship between water, sanitation and health. Consumption of unsafe drinking water, improper disposal of human excreta, improper environmental sanitation and lack of personal and food hygiene have been major causes of many diseases in developing countries. India is no exception to this. Prevailing High Infant Mortality Rate is also largely attributed to poor sanitation. It was in this context that the Central Rural Sanitation Programme (CRSP) was launched in 1986 primarily with the objective of improving the quality of life of the rural people and also to provide privacy and dignity to women.

2. The concept of sanitation was earlier limited to disposal of human excreta by cesspools, open ditches, pit latrines, bucket system etc. Today it connotes a comprehensive concept, which includes liquid and solid waste disposal, food hygiene, and personal, domestic as well as environmental hygiene. Proper sanitation is important not only from the general health point of view but it has a vital role to play in our individual and social life too. Sanitation is one of the basic determinants of quality of life and human development index. Good sanitary practices prevent contamination of water and soil and thereby prevent diseases. The concept of sanitation was, therefore, expanded to include personal hygiene, home sanitation, safe water, garbage disposal, excreta disposal and waste water disposal.

3. A comprehensive Baseline Survey on Knowledge, Attitudes and Practices in rural water supply and sanitation was conducted during 1996-97 under the aegis of the Indian Institute of Mass Communication, which showed that 55 per cent of those with private latrines were self-motivated. Only 2 per cent of the respondents claimed the existence of subsidy as the major motivating factor, while 54 per cent claimed to have gone in for sanitary latrines due to convenience and privacy. The study also showed that 51 per cent of the respondents were willing to spend up to Rs.1000 to acquire sanitary toilets.

4. Keeping in view the above facts, the CRSP was improved. In the new format, CRSP moves towards a "demand driven" approach. The revised approach in the Programme titled "Total Sanitation Campaign (TSC)" emphasizes more on Information, Education and Communication (IEC), Human Resource Development, Capacity Development activities to increase awareness among the rural people and generation of demand for sanitary facilities. This will also enhance people's capacity to choose appropriate options through alternate delivery mechanisms as per their economic condition. The Programme is being implemented with focus on community-led and people centered initiatives. Children play an effective role in absorbing and popularizing new ideas and concepts. This Programme, therefore, intends to tap their potential as the most persuasive advocates of good sanitation practices in their own house holds and in schools. The aim is also to provide separate urinals/toilets for boys and girls in all the schools/Anganwadis in rural areas in the country.

OBJECTIVES

5. The main objectives of the TSC are as under:

(a) Bring about an improvement in the general quality of life in the rural areas.
(b) Accelerate sanitation coverage in rural areas to access to toilets to all by 2012.
(c) Motivate communities and Panchayati Raj Institutions

promoting sustainable sanitation facilities through awareness creation and health education.

(d) In rural areas, cover schools by March 2008 and Anganwadis by March 2009, with sanitation facilities and promote hygiene education and sanitary habits among students.

(e) Encourage cost effective and appropriate technologies for ecologically safe and sustainable sanitation.

(f) Develop community managed environmental sanitation systems focusing on solid and liquid waste management.

STRATEGY

6. The strategy is to make the Programme 'community led' and 'people centred'. A "demand driven approach" is to be adopted with increased emphasis on awareness creation and demand generation for sanitary facilities in houses, schools and for cleaner environment. Alternate delivery mechanisms would be adopted to meet the community needs. Subsidy for individual household latrine units has been replaced by incentive to the poorest of the poor households. Rural School Sanitation is a major component and an entry point for wider acceptance of sanitation by the rural people. Technology improvisations to meet the customer preferences and location specific intensive IEC Campaign involving Panchayati Raj Institutions, Co-operatives, Women Groups, Self Help Groups, NGOs etc. are also important components of the Strategy. The strategy addresses all sections of rural population to bring about the relevant behavioural changes for improved sanitation and hygiene practices and meet their sanitary hardware requirements in an affordable and accessible manner by offering a wide range of technological choices.

IMPLEMENTATION

7. Implementation of TSC is proposed on a project mode. A project proposal emanates from a district, is scrutinized by the State Government and transmitted to the Government of India

(Department of Drinking Water Supply, Ministry of Rural Development). TSC is implemented in phases with start-up activities. Funds are made available for preliminary IEC work. The physical implementation gets oriented towards satisfying the felt-needs, wherein individual households choose from a menu of options for their household latrines. The built-in flexibility in the menu of options gives the poor and the disadvantaged families opportunity for subsequent upgradation depending upon their requirements and financial position. In the "campaign approach", while a synergistic interaction between the Government agencies and other stakeholders, intensive IEC and advocacy, with participation of NGOs/Panchayati Raj Institutions/resource organizations, take place to bring about the desired behavioural changes for relevant sanitation practices, provision of alternate delivery system, proper technical specifications, designs and quality of installations are also provided to effectively fulfil the generated demand for sanitary hardware.

8. The TSC is being implemented with a district as unit. The States/UTs are expected to prepare TSC Projects for all the districts and submit before the Government of India for sanction. The TSC Project cycle in the Project Districts is expected to take about 4 years or less for implementation.

COMPONENTS

9. The Programme components and activities for TSC implementation are as follows:

(a) Start-Up Activities

The start-up activities include conducting of preliminary survey to assess the status of sanitation and hygiene practices, people's attitude and demand for improved sanitation, etc. with the aim to prepare the District TSC project proposals for seeking Government of India assistance. The start-up activities will also include conducting a Baseline Survey (BLS), preparation of Project Implementation Plan (PIP), initial orientation and training of key programme managers at the district level. The cost of

Start-up activities will be met fully by the Government of India assistance and, should not exceed 5 per cent of the total project.

(b) IEC Activities

Information, Education and Communication (IEC) are important components of the Programme. These intend to create demand for sanitary facilities in the rural areas for households, schools, Anganwadis, Balwadis and Community Sanitary Complexes. The activities carried out under this component should be area specific and should also involve all sections of the rural population, in a manner, where willingness of the people to construct latrines is generated. IEC is not a one-time activity. IEC strategy and plan have to be implemented not just to create demand but also for use, maintenance and upgradation, so that sanitation and hygiene become an integral part of rural life and thereby sustainable. Community and culture specific plans may be necessary to achieve 100 per cent sanitation coverage.

A national communication strategy and plan has been developed by Government of India giving emphasis on inter personal communication at the grassroots level. The details of the communication strategy and the tools are hosted on the website www.ddws.gov.in. As part of this strategy motivators can be engaged at the village level for demand creation and taking up behaviour change communication. The motivator can be given suitable incentive from the funds earmarked for IEC. The incentive will be performance based, i.e. in terms of motivating the number of households and schools/Anganwadis to construct latrines and soakage pits and also use the same subsequently. The IEC should also focus on health and hygiene practices and environmental sanitation aspects.

Under IEC, mass media campaign should be taken up only at the national and state level and not at the district level. At district level, focus should be on inter-personal communication, use of folk media and also outdoor media like wall painting, hoarding etc.—IEC funding will be in the ratio of 80:20 between GOI and the State Governments and the total IEC cost including start up grant will be limited to 15 per cent of the total project cost.

Each project district should prepare a detailed IEC Annual Action Plan by February of the preceding financial year, with defined strategies to reach all sections of the community. The aim of such a communication plan is to motivate rural people to adopt hygiene behaviour as a way of life and thereby develop and maintain all facilities created under the programme. The Annual IEC Action Plan should be duly approved by the District Panchayat (or the DWSM where such bodies are not in existence. The Communication and Capacity Development Units (CCDUs) set up at the state level must support the districts in developing a good IEC plan and also in implementing it.

For effective dissemination of the IEC material, funds may also be provided under this component to blocks and gram panchayats for execution of works. They may take up such activities like engaging local NGOs for interpersonal communication; selecting motivators; executing works like wall paintings, street plays etc. The development of such material executed by the panchayats may be standardized by the district or the CCDU.

Funds available under IEC may be used for imparting hygiene education to the rural communities, general public, as well as children in schools. The IEC plan should include a component for raising awareness among school going children, teachers and PTAs. It can also include training programmes for masons, Self Help Groups etc., for activities related to sanitation, such as production of sanitary pan, sanitary napkins, etc.

(c) Rural Sanitary Marts and Production Centres

The Rural Sanitary Mart is an outlet dealing with the materials, hardware and designs required for the construction of not only sanitary latrines but also other sanitary facilities, such as soakage and compost pits, vermi-composting, washing platforms, certified domestic water filters and other sanitation and hygiene accessories required for individuals, families and the environment in the rural areas. RSM should necessarily have those items, which are required as a part of the sanitation package. It is a commercial venture with a social objective. The main aim of having a RSM is to provide materials, services and guidance needed for constructing different types of latrines and other sanitary facilities, which are technologically and financially suitable to the area. Production Centres are the means to improve production of cost effective affordable sanitary materials. The Production Centres/Rural Sanitary Marts could be opened and operated by NGOs/SHGs/women Organizations/Panchayats etc. Support of private entrepreneurs may also be taken for ensuring an effective supply chain.

Sufficient RSMs may be established with Production Centers or otherwise. Depending upon its function, the DWSC will decide the amount of revolving fund up to a maximum of Rs. 3.5 lakhs. RSMs who decide not to run production centres may procure good quality pans with rural specification from suppliers through competitive bidding. They should ensure that a variety of pans (ceramic, mosaic, HDP, fibreglass) are available for choice. To meet the needs of remote and difficult areas, mini-RSMs are permissible, run by CBOs/women SHGs/co-operatives.

For this purpose, less than 5 per cent (subject to a maximum of Rs. 35.00 lakhs) of the total Government outlay has been earmarked. Funding for this component will be in the ratio of 80:20 between the GOI and the State Government. Further, under the TSC project, maximum amount of Rs. 3.5 lakhs per Rural Sanitary Mart/Production Centre can be provided. The fund may be provided to the NGOs/Panchayats/other agencies for setting up of RSMs/PCs. The fund can be provided for construction of shed, training of masons and also as a revolving fund. After RSM/PC attain a level of sustainability, the revolving fund should be refunded to the District Implementing Agency. The District Implementing agency should identify key training institutions/Resource persons to train the Mart/Production Centre Managers, after ascertaining their training needs. They should also have a Memorandum of Understanding with the RSMs/PCs and, a system of joint monitoring evolved to ensure that the RSMs & PCs are on track with production plans and production targets, are able to respond to local requirements, have a method of quality certification of its products and a band of trained masons and motivators. They should demonstrate success as an enterprise and, function in accordance with the objectives of the Programme.

(d) Provision of Revolving Fund in the District

Based on the successful initiative taken by Self Help Groups and Dairy Cooperative Societies in arranging low/zero interest finance to their members for toilet construction in many parts of the country, a sum of upto Rs. 50 lakhs, subject to the restriction of 5 per cent earmarked for alternate delivery mechanism (which includes the cost for setting up RSMs and PCs) may be given to each TSC project as revolving fund. This revolving fund may be further given by the Project Implementing Agency to Co-operative Societies or Self Help Groups whose creditworthiness is established, for providing cheap finance to their members. Loan from this fund should be recovered in 12-18 installments. District TSC projects will have the flexibility to decide the other terms and conditions for sanction of the revolving fund. This revolving fund can be accessed by APL households also. Loan can also be given to the owner of the household where ICDS center is located for construction of baby friendly toilet for ICDS provided the ICDS authorities agree to refund the loan from the rent paid to the house owner.

(e) Construction of Individual Household Latrines

A duly completed household sanitary latrine shall comprise of a Basic Low Cost Unit with a super structure. All existing bucket latrines in rural areas should be converted to sanitary latrines. The programme is aimed to cover all the rural families. Incentive as provided under the scheme may be extended to Below Poverty Line (BPL) families, if the same is considered necessary for full involvement of the community. The construction of household toilets should be undertaken by the BPL household itself and on completion and use of the toilet by the BPL household, the cash incentive can be given to the BPL household in recognition of its achievement. The financing pattern including the incentive for

BPL household for construction of Individual house hold latrines is as follows:

Table 1: Incentive Pattern for IHHL

Basic Low Cost Unit Cost	Contribution Percentage					
	GoI		*State*		*Household*	
	BPL	*APL*	*BPL*	*APL*	*BPL*	*APL*
Model 1: Upto Rs. 1500 (including superstructure)	60	Nil	20	Nil	20	100
Model 2: Between Rs. 1500/- and Rs. 2000/-	30	Nil	30	Nil	40	100
Above Rs.2000/-	Nil	Nil	Nil	Nil	100	100

The incentive given by the Central Government will continue to be admissible with reference to the cost of the basic low cost unit as given in the above Table and in no case will the overall quantum of Central incentive exceed the admissible amount. As per the above table the maximum incentive per toilet available to a BPL household will be Rs. 1200.00 (Centre + State), irrespective of the model chosen by it. State Government may provide for more incentive for household toilet than the amounts prescribed above from its own funds. The BPL household may also contribute to value addition to the basic unit at its own expense. All houses constructed for BPL families under Indira Awaas Yojana shall invariably be provided with a toilet under this programme.

It is assumed that APL families, through motivation, will take up construction of the household latrines on their own. The IEC activities, will, however, cover all the families in the district, without exceptions. APL families facing cash crunch may access the revolving fund as outlined in the previous paragraph.

Construction of bucket latrines is not permitted in the rural areas. The existing bucket latrines, if any, should be converted to sanitary latrines and the unit cost and sharing pattern shall be identical to that of construction of individual house hold latrines.

(f) Community Sanitary Complex

Community Sanitary Complex is an important component of the TSC. These Complexes, comprising an appropriate number of toilet seats, bathing cubicles, washing platforms, wash basins etc., can be set up in a place in the village acceptable to women/men/landless families and accessible to them. The maintenance of such complexes is very essential for which Gram Panchayat should own the ultimate responsibility or make alternative arrangements at the village level. User families may be asked to contribute a reasonable monthly user charge for cleaning and maintenance. Maximum unit cost prescribed for a community complex is up to Rs. 2 lakhs. However, it will be approved by the National Scheme Sanctioning Committee based on the detailed design and estimates. Sharing pattern amongst Central Government, State Government and the community is in the ratio of 60:20:20. The community contribution, however, can be made by the Panchayat out of its own resources, from grants of the Twelfth Finanace Commission or from any other fund of the State duly permitted by it. However, total expenditure proposed on Community Sanitary Complex and Individual Household Toilets should be within the ceiling of 60 per cent of the total Project outlay. Ordinarily such complexes should be constructed only when there is lack of space in the village for construction of household toilets and the community owns up the responsibility of their operation and maintenance. The ultimate aim is to ensure construction of maximum IHHLs and construction of community complexes will be restricted to only when IHHLs cannot be constructed, for whatever reason, and also teach the community of "Hygiene practices". Such complexes can also be made at public places, markets, etc. where large scale congregation of people takes place.

(g) Institutional Toilets

Children are more receptive to new ideas and schools/Anganwadis are appropriate institutions for changing the behaviour, mindset and habits of children from open defecation to the use of lavatory through motivation and education. The experience gained by children through use of toilets in school and sanitation education imparted by teachers would reach home and would also influence parents to adopt good sanitary habits. School Sanitation, therefore, forms an integral part of every TSC Project.

School Toilets

Toilets in all types of Government Schools, i.e. Primary, Upper Primary, Secondary and Higher Secondary and Anganwadis should be constructed. Emphasis should be given on toilets for Girls in Schools. Funding for School Sanitation in a TSC Project is provided by the Central and State Government, in the ratio of 70:30. The Central assistance per unit will be restricted to Rs.14,000 for a unit cost of Rs.20,000. Separate toilets for girls and boys should be provided in all co-educational schools, which are to be treated as two separate units and each unit is entitled to Central assistance up to Rs.14,000. State/UT Governments, Parent-Teachers Association and Panchayats are free to contribute from their own resources over and above the prescribed amount.

School toilet designs should be developed reviewed and standardized to address quality and cost concerns and more importantly to comply with benchmarks set for "child friendliness", "gender responsiveness" and to provide access opportunities to children with special needs (children with disabilities). In addition to creation of hardware in the schools, it is essential that hygiene education is imparted to the children on all aspects of hygiene. For this purpose, at least one teacher in each school must be trained in hygiene education who in turn should train the children through interesting activities and community projects that emphasize hygiene behaviour. The expenditure for this purpose can be met from the IEC fund earmarked for the project. The district and panchayat implementing agencies should ensure good co-ordination with Department of Education and Health and other partners in order to fulfil the objective of SSHE, i.e. to provide a safe, healthy learning environment to all children.

Anganwadi Toilets

In order to change the behaviour of the children from very early stage in life, it is essential that Anganwadis are used as a platform of behaviour change of the children as well as the mothers attending the Anganwadis. For this purpose each anganwadi should be provided with a baby friendly toilet. One toilet of unit cost up to Rs. 5,000 can be constructed for each Anganwadi or Balwadi in the rural areas where incentive to be given by Government of India will be restricted to Rs. 3,000. Additional expenses can be met by the State Government, Panchayats or funds from Twelfth Finance Commission, MPLADS, MLALADS etc. Since there are a large number of Anganwadis operating from private houses, following strategy may be adopted: (a) In all the Anganwadis, which are in Government buildings, baby friendly toilets should be constructed from out of the TSC funds to the extent laid down. (b) Those Anganwadis, which are in private buildings, the owner must be asked to construct the toilet as per design, and, he/she may be allowed to charge enhanced rent for the building to recover the cost of construction. Alternatively, the toilet may be constructed from revolving fund component under the TSC and, suitable deductions made from the monthly rental paid to the owner to recover the cost over a period of time. (c) For new buildings, which are going to be hired for Anganwadis, buildings having baby friendly toilet facility only should be hired.

(h) Solid and Liquid Waste Management

One of the objectives of TSC is bringing about an improvement in the general quality of life in rural areas. This objective cannot be met if the general cleanliness of villages is not maintained properly. Panchayati Raj Institutions (PRIs) are required to put in place mechanisms for garbage collection and disposal and for preventing water logging. Up to 10 per cent of the project cost can be utilized for meeting capital costs incurred under this component. The fund sharing pattern between the Centre, State and Panchayat/Community would be in the ratio of 60:20:20. Under this component activities like common compost pits, low cost drainage, soakage channels/pits, reuse of waste water, system for collection, segregation and disposal of household garbage etc. may be taken up. Successful models may be further replicated dovetailing funds from other Rural Development programmes. NGO co-operation may be sought to develop/test/document/ replicate such models.

(i) Administrative Charges

The Administrative Charges include money spent on training, salary of temporary staff deployed during project period, support services, fuel charges, vehicle hire charges, stationery, monitoring and evaluation of TSC project. However, in any case no additional posts shall be created nor separate vehicle purchased for the implementation of the TSC project. But in order to implement the projects professionally, specialist consultants from the fields of Communication, Human Resource Development, School Sanitation and Hygiene Education and Monitoring may be hired for the project period. The fees of the consultants may be paid from the administrative charges. Purchase of one computer with accessories is permissible per district.

The following items of expenses are specifically prohibited under "administrative expenses":

(a) Purchase of vehicles
(b) Purchase of land and buildings
(c) Construction of official buildings and rest houses (this excludes toilet units needed for TSC projects)
(d) Purchase of office equipments
(e) Expenses for any political party and religious organisations
(f) Expenses for gifts and donations
(g) Purchase of cell phones
(h) Transfer of funds to the State level institutions for meeting administrative expenses.

NATIONAL SCHEME SANCTIONING COMMITTEE

10. National Scheme Sanctioning Committee (NSSC) was constituted to approve the project proposals for the select districts, as received from the State/UT Government. There will

be seven members in the NSSC. The constitution of the NSSC shall be as follows:

1. Secretary, Department of Drinking Water Supply, Ministry of Rural Development—Chairperson and Financial of Rural Development.
2. Additional Secretary Adviser, Ministry of Development—Member
3. Four non-official experts in the field of rural sanitation—Members
4. Secretary in-charge of rural sanitation of the State whose proposal is to be considered—Member
5. Joint Secretary, Department of Drinking Water Supply, Ministry of Rural Development—Member Secretary

IMPLEMENTING AGENCIES

11. Implementation of the Total Sanitation Campaign requires large scale social mobilization so its implementation at the District level should be done by the Zilla Panchayat. However, in case Zilla Panchayat is not in existence, District Water and Sanitation Mission should implement the project. The line departments will play the catalytic role in implementation.

12. At the state level, State Government should set up a Communication & Capacity Development Units (CCDUs) for taking up state level HRD & IEC activities as well as monitoring of TSC projects. In states where Water Supply and Sanitation are handled by two different departments, a separate CCDU may be set up, subject to the condition that officials handling water supply should be actively associated with this CCDU. Specialist consultants from the fields of Communication, Human Resource Development, and Monitoring and School Sanitation and Hygiene Education may be engaged by the CCDU. The expenses towards engaging these consultants will be borne by the GoI and the States as per CCDU guidelines separately issued by the Department of Drinking Water Supply.

ROLE OF PANCHAYATI RAJ INSTITUTIONS

13. As per the Constitution 73rd Amendment Act, 1992, Sanitation is included in the 11th Schedule. Accordingly, Gram Panchayats have a pivotal role in the implementation of Total Sanitation Campaign. The TSC will be implemented by the Panchayati Raj Institutions at all levels. They will carry out the social mobilization for the construction of toilets and also maintain the clean environment by way of safe disposal of wastes. PRIs may engage suitable NGOs for interpersonal IEC and training. Community Complexes constructed under the TSC will be maintained by the Panchayats/Voluntary Organizations/ Charitable Trusts. Panchayats can also contribute from their own resources for School Sanitation over and above the prescribed amount. They will act as the custodian of the assets such as the Community Complexes, environmental components, drainage etc. constructed under the TSC. Panchayats can also open and operate the Production Centres/Rural Sanitary Marts.

Panchayats can play a key role in promoting regular use, maintenance and upgradation of toilets and inter-personal communication for hygiene education. Panchayats and NGOs who are in the frontline of implementation have a key role in ensuring that safety standards are being met with all components of TSC—e.g. the distance between water source and a latrine—adhering to the minimum distance for IHHL, school and AW toilets and community sanitary complexes; regulating pit-depth, pit lining to prevent pollution, collapse of pit etc. The same will apply to key hygiene behaviour such as keeping the environment around hand pumps/water sources clear and tidy and free of human and animal excreta.

Panchayats must also play a role in the monitoring of the TSC programme. Both Block level and District level PRIs must regularly monitor the implementation along with the concerned officials.

ROLE OF NON-GOVERNMENTAL ORGANISATIONS

14. NGOs have an important role in the implementation of TSC in the rural areas. They have to be actively involved in IEC (software) activities as well as in hardware activities. Their services

are required to be utilized not only for bringing about awareness among the rural people for the need of rural sanitation but also ensuring that they actually make use of the sanitary latrines. NGOs can also open and operate Production Centres and Rural Sanitary Marts. NGOs may also be engaged to conduct basc line surveys and PRAs specifically to determine key behaviours and perceptions regarding sanitation, hygiene, water use, O&M, etc. Selection of NGOs should be done following a transparent criterion.

PROJECT FUNDING

15. The Table below gives the percentage share of the allocation (i.e. the total approved TSC project cost) for different components of a TSC Project, the GOI/State share and the beneficiary contribution towards each component. In the case of Union Territories, the State share under the TSC will be borne by the Government of India.

Table 2: TSC Component-wise earmarking and funding pattern

Sl. No.	*Component*	*Amount earmarked as per cent of the TSC project outlay*	*Contribution per cent*		
			GoI	*State*	*Beneficiary Household/ Community*
(a)	IEC and Start Up Activity, Including Motivational Awareness and Educative Campaigns, Advocacy etc.	Up to 15%	80	20	00
(b)	Alternate Delivery Mechanism (PCs/RSMs)	Up to 5% (Subject to a maximum of Rs. 35 lakh per district for PC/RSMs and additional Rs.50 lakhs as revolving fund for group lending activity)	80	20	00
(c)	(i) Individual Latrines for BPL/disabled house-holds (ii) Community Sanitary Complexes	Actual amount required for full coverage	60	20	20

(*Contd.*)

(*Contd.*)

Sl. No.	*Component*	*Amount earmarked as per cent of the TSC project outlay*	*Contribution per cent*		
			GoI	*State*	*Beneficiary Household/ Community*
(d)	Individual household latrines for APL	Nil	00	00	100
(e)	Institutional Toilets including School and Anganwadi Sanitation (Hardware and Support Services)	Actual amount required for full coverage	70	30	00
(f)	Administrative charges, including training, staff, support services, Monitoring & Evaluation etc.	Less than 5%	80	20	00
(g)	Solid/Liquid Waste Management (Capital Cost)	Up to 10%	60	20	20

18. In case the amount sought for/utilized for under any component of the TSC is less than the earmarked percentage, the balance per cent will be adjusted for construction of individual household latrines. In no case the per cent earmarked for components relating to start-up activities and administrative charges should exceed 5 per cent of the project outlay.

RELEASE OF FUNDS

16. The Central assistance shall be released to the Implementing Agency in four installments (30, 30, 30, and 10). The first installment will be released immediately after approval of the project proposal by the National Scheme Sanctioning Committee subject to receipt of details of the Implementing Agency at District level and name of the bank, IFSC Code and A/c. No. etc. All bank accounts shall be Saving Accounts. The release of further installments will be subject to the following conditions:

I. **Release of State share:** The State share must be released to the concerned project district at least in the same proportion as central share has been released within a fortnight of release of the central share.

II. *Household/Community Contribution*: For all the hardware activities executed, the corresponding household/community contribution, including APL households must be taken and reflected appropriately in the progress report.

III. *Expenditure and Utilization Certificate:* At least 60 per cent of the total available funds under Central share as well as State share, including interest must have been properly utilized. There should be more than 60 per cent utilization under Central and State share separately. Separate utilization certificate for the Central fund and the State fund should be submitted. The Utilization certificate should be furnished for each financial year since the year in which the project was sanctioned and fund released. All utilization certificates should be countersigned by Chairman DWSM/DRDA/District Collector or CEO of District Panchayat as the case may be. (Annexure-VIII)

IV. *Audit Certificate*: The accounts of the TSC project should be audited annually by a Chartered Accountant. At the time of submission of the proposal for release of further installments, the audited statement of the preceding financial year should be submitted. It should be duly countersigned by the Chairman DWSM/DRDA/District Collector or CEO, District Panchayat as the case may be. In case two installments of funds are claimed in the same financial year, the accounts should be audited for the part of the financial year (up to the period for which utilization certificate is submitted). The audit report of the Chartered accountant should cover the issues as given in Annexure-II and should be submitted in the format annexed (Annexures-III to VII).

V. A Certificate regarding not purchasing any inadmissible items: A certificate must be given by the Chairman of the DWSM/DRDA/District Collector or CEO, Zilla Parishad as the case may be, certifying that no expenditure on any inadmissible item as mentioned in these Guidelines has been made.

VI. The proposal for release of second or subsequent installment should be sent by the District Implementing Agency through the concerned administrative Department in the State Government dealing with Rural Sanitation.

VII. The last installment will be released only if the expenditure is at least 80 per cent of the available funds (separately for Centre and State) and on submission of the Utilization Certificate and AG Certificate/Chartered Accountant Certificate of previous year.

VIII. Other conditions that may be prescribed from time to time.

17. The implementing Agency shall be required to transfer the funds for the works to the Gram Panchayat (VWSC in States where GPs do not exist) with 15 days of receipt of funds.

INTEREST EARNED ON PROJECT FUNDS

18. The TSC funds (Central and State) should be kept in a bank account. The household/beneficiary contribution need not be deposited in this account. The interest accrued on TSC funds shall be treated as part of the TSC resources. The District Implementing Agency has to submit utilization of interest accrued on TSC funds along with claim/s for subsequent installments and it should be reflected in the Utilization Certificates.

MAINTENANCE

19. It is essential to train the community, particularly all the members of the family in the proper upkeep and maintenance of the sanitation facilities created. The IEC activities should include awareness of the community on how to maintain the sanitation facilities. The maintenance expenses of individual household sanitary latrines should be met by the households. The maintenance cost of community sanitary complexes may be met by the panchayats/voluntary organizations/charitable trusts/Self Help Groups. Institutions/Organizations operating and

maintaining the Sanitary complexes may charge suitable user charges to meet the operation and maintenance cost fully. The concerned departments should provide adequate funds for maintenance of school/Anganwadi toilets. Funds are also available under the Grants made by the Twelfth Finance Commission, which recommended that priority should be given to expenditure on the O&M costs of water supply and sanitation, along with recovery of at least 50 per cent of recurrent costs as user charges.

INSPECTIONS

20. Monitoring through regular field inspections by officers from the State level and the district levels is essential for the effective implementation of the Programme. The inspection should be to check and ensure that construction work has been done in accordance with the norms, the community has been involved in construction, the latrines are not polluting the water sources and also to check whether there has been correct selection of beneficiaries and proper use of latrines after construction. Such inspection should ensure that the sanitary latrines are not used for any other purpose. Inspection should be done to check whether TSC information of a Gram Panchayat has been displayed transparently in Gram Panchayat (by wall painting or special hoarding). Project authorities should constitute a team of experts in the district who should review the implementation in different blocks frequently. Such review should be held at least once a quarter. Similarly the State Government should conduct review of projects in each district once a quarter and for this purpose they should constitute a panel of experts available in the state. In addition, Government of India will send its review missions to the states periodically to assess the quality of implementation.

REVISION IN PROJECT

21. It is expected that after conducting the Baseline survey, the exact requirement for different category of hardware may undergo change which will necessitate revision in the project. In

addition, revision will be required due to change in the funding norms. Each district requiring revision in TSC project should submit a proposal in the prescribed template along with a revised PIP to the Department of Drinking Water Supply. Such revision in the project will be allowed after proper scrutiny and the project recast suitably by the Department of Drinking Water Supply. The matter will be placed before the NSSC for ratification.

REPORTS

22. The Department of Drinking Water Supply has developed an online monitoring system for TSC. All TSC project districts are to submit the physical and financial progress reports through this on line software for which user-id and password have been generated and communicated by DDWS-NIC cell. Progress reports in hard copy are discouraged. An Annual Performance Report only is to be submitted, as given in Annexure I.

Monitoring of the TSC project should be carried out at all levels. Block PRI and Block level officials must review progress in each Gram Panchayat. The CEO of the District Panchayat/ Secretary of the DWSC must review the progress of the project with Block Officials on a monthly basis. Similarly, Secretary in-charge of rural sanitation in the State must review progress with the District Officials on a quarterly basis.

EVALUATION

23. The States/UTs should conduct periodical Evaluation Studies on the implementation of the TSC. Evaluation studies may be got conducted by the reputed Institutions and Organizations. Copies of the reports of these evaluation studies conducted by the States/UTs should be furnished to the Government of India. Remedial action should be taken by the States/UTs on the basis of the observations made in these evaluation studies and also in the Concurrent Evaluation conducted by or on behalf of the Government of India. The cost of such studies can be charged to the HRD component of the TSC.

24. For a group of TSC Projects in State(s), implementation

progress review may be organized by the Government of India as required. A multi-agency team of officers/professionals will be constituted as the time to undertake the review.

RESEARCH

25. Research Institutes, organizations and NGOs with proven track record in the areas of Sanitation and National/State level institutions involved in the research related to the issue of Health, Hygiene, Water Supply and Sanitation should be involved to study the present technology of human excreta and waste disposal systems in the rural areas. The research outcome should enable improvement of technology, making it more affordable and environmentally safe to suit the requirements of different geo-hydrological conditions. This will encourage and promote ecologically sustainable long term solution for disposal of wastes. Research on latrine design, appropriate technology to suit varying soil conditions, high water table situations, floods, water scarcity conditions, coastal areas will be a priority. Ecological sanitation/ on-site waste management will be encouraged to prevent high costs of waste transportation and pollution of water bodies through discharge of untreated waste. On submission of a self contained proposal by the State Government, the NSSC may sanction the Research projects and the fund will be provided by the Government of India from the R & D fund specifically earmarked for the purpose.

ANNUAL AUDIT

26. The District Implementing Agency should get the accounts audited annually by a Chartered Accountant and submit the report to the State Government and Government of India. Further, District Implementing Agency should furnish audited accounts while filing claims for the second and subsequent installments.

PROJECT COMPLETION

27. When a Project gets completed fully in a District, the

Implementing Agency at the District level shall submit a completion Report along with Audit Certificate and Utilization Certificate through the State Government to the Department of Drinking Water Supply, Ministry of Rural Development, Government of India. Acceptance or otherwise of the Completion Report will be informed to the State Government and the District Implementing Agency by the Government of India. The TSC Project cycle in the Project Districts is expected to take about 4-5 years. Some districts may take lesser time and a few others may take more, however, all out efforts should be made to complete the projects by the end of 11th Five Year Plan. Post Project evaluations, at random, will be taken up by the Government of India. The states may also take initiative for conducting such evaluations, and seek GOI assistance, for the purpose.

Annexure I

CENTRAL RURAL SANITATION PROGRAMME TOAL SANITATION CAMPAIGN ANNUAL PERFORMANCE REPORT

Report ending 31st March 20___
Project District: ____________________ State/UT:

A. Physical Performance

Components	*Project Aim*	*Cumulative Performance*	*Percentage Achievement*
Individual Household Latrines—BPL			
Individual Household Latrines—APL			
Sanitary complex			
Toilets for schools			
Toilets for Balwadi/Anganwadi			
Rural Sanitary Mart			
Production Centres			

B. Special Provisions:

Category	*Project Aim*	*Cumulative Performance*	*Percentage Achievement*
Household latrines for SCs			
Household Latrines for STs			
Household Latrines for Physically Handicapped			

C. Financial Performance

Item	*Amount (Lakh Rupees)*
1. *Receipts*	
(a) Opening Balance as on first day of the year	
(b) Central Releases during the year	
(c) State Releases during the year	
(d) Household/Panchayat contribution during the year	
(e) Interest accrued during the year	
(f) Total availability of funds (a + b + c + d + e)	
2. *Expenditure*	
(a) From Central Share	
(b) From State Share	
(c) From Interest / Household / Panchayat contribution	
(d) Total Expenditure (a + b + c + d)	
(e) Per cent of expenditure to total availability of funds	

Office seal **Signature with date:**

Name: Designation:

Annexure II

ISSUES TO BE COVERED IN CHARTERED ACCOUNTANT'S AUDIT REPORT

- Number of Bank Accounts being maintained by the Implementing Agency (A separate single Savings Bank Account should be maintained for the scheme)

- Funds held in fixed Deposits, if any (the programme funds are not allowed to be kept in fixed deposits and should be kept only in Savings Account).
- Whether interest accrued in Savings Account has been credited into the Account, taken as receipt and utilised for the scheme.
- Delay, if any, in crediting the Accounts of the Implementing Agency by the receiving Bank. If so, the period of delay.
- Whether Bank reconciliation in respect of Cash Book Balance and Pass Book Balance is being done fortnightly. The Bank reconciliation should also cover interest accruals. The Bank reconciliation statement as on 31st March should be attached to the Audit Report.
- Proper maintenance of Cash Book by the Implementing Agency.
- Cheques issued but not encashed as on 31st March as per the Bank reconciliation (this should be taken as a part of the opening balance).
- Actual expenditure village-wise out of advances to all the VWSCs and closing balance with VWSCs. Attach statement to the Audit Report.
- Inadmissible items of expenditure, if any.
- Diversion of funds, if any.

Annexure III

FORMAT A

District Water and Sanitation Mission/D.W.S.C./Core Group/ VWSC

Receipt and Payment Accounts for the period 1.4. to 31.3.
Name of Scheme

Receipt	Amount	Payment	Amount
1. Opening Balance DWSM/DWSC/Core Group/VWSC (as the case may be)		1. Advances given to: (a) VWSC (b) SO (c) Service Agencies (d) Any other implementing Agencies	
2. Receipt of Grants (a) Central Government (b) State Government (c) Other Agencies		2. Audit Fees	
3. Interest received from Banks DWSM/DWSC/Core Group		3. Expenses on Administration (if allowed under the schemes) (a) Salary and Allowances (b) Travelling Expenses (c) Rent, Rates and Taxes (d) Printing and Stationery (e) Publicity and Advertising (f) Postage (g) Telephone (h) Leave Salary and Pension Contribution (i) Motor Vehicles maintenance and repairs (j) Office Contingencies (k) Any other item	
4. Refund of Advance/ Loan/Grant From (a) VWSC (b) SO (c) Service Agencies Any Other Implementing Agency		4. Advances to Staff if any (if allowed under the scheme)	
5. Refund of Advances from Staff		5. Bank Charges if any	
6. Miscellaneous		6. Payment made for creation of Capital asset for DWSC	
		7. Miscellaneous	
		8. Closing Balance DWSM/DWSC/ Core Group	

FORMAT B

District Water and Sanitation Mission/D.W.S.C./Core Group/ VWSC

Income and Expenditure Account for the period 1.4 ______ to 31.3.

	Expenditure	*Amount*		*Income*	*Amount*
1.	Schemes Expenditure (a) VWSC (b) SO (c) Service Agencies (Based on UCs received)		1.	Grants in Aid received during the year from (a) Central Government. (b) State Government (c) Other Agencies *Add*: Grants in Aid receivable during the year* *Less*: Grants in Aid related to previous year	
2.	Audit Fees		2.	Interest received during the Year from the Bank Accounts Received during the year Add: Accrued during the year Less: related to previous year	
3.	Expenses on Administration *I. Agency Office* (a) Salary and Allowances (b) Travelling Expenses (c) Rent, Rates and Taxes (d) Printing and Stationery (e) Publicity and Propaganda (f) Postage (g) Telephone (h) Leave Salary and Pension Contribution		3.	Refund of unutilized grants by the Implementing Agencies	

(*Contd.*)

(*Contd.*)

	Expenditure	Amount		Income	Amount
	(i) Motor vehicles maintenance and repairs (j) Other contingencies (k) Other items				
4.	Miscellaneous Expenses		4.	Miscellaneous Receipts	
5.	Excess of Income over Expenditure carried over to the Balance Sheet.		5.	Excess Expenditure carried over to Balance sheet.	

This item would include amount of Grants in Aid sanctioned during the year but not received during the current year.

Annexure V

FORMAT C

Balance Sheet as at 31st of March

Name of the District Water and Sanitation Mission/VWSC

Capital Fund and Liabilities	*Current Year*	*Previous Year*
Accumulated Fund Opening Balance Add/Deduct Balance Transferred From Income & Expenditure Account +/- Closing Balance Current Liabilities Outstanding Expenses/Payables Any other Liability		
Total		

(*Contd.*)

(*Contd.*)

Capital Fund and Liabilities	*Current Year*	*Previous Year*
Assets Fixed Assets Vehicles Furniture & Fixtures Office Equipment Computers and Peripherals Library Books Others Current Assets & Advances Stock Closing Balance Cash in Hand (DWSM) Cash at Bank (DWSM) Account receivables and Advances recoverable VWSC SO Service Agencies Staff		
Grants in aid receivable during the year but not actually received. *		
Total		

Certified that assets amounting to Rs. ________ were created during the year as per schedule attached.

* This item would include amount of Grants in Aid sanctioned during the year but not received during the current year.

Annexure VI

FORMAT D

Format of V.W.S.C.-wise Payment Register for Blocks

Name of the Scheme
{Chapter No. IV}

Sl. No.	Date	Particulars (Details of Project)	Cheque No.	Amount released	Utilisation Certificate Details	
					Date	Amount
Total						

Annexure VII

FORMAT E

Format of Payment Register for

V.W.S.C. Name of the Scheme

Sl. No.	Date	Particulars (Detail of Project)	Cheque No.	Amount Released
Total				

Annexure VIII

FORMAT F

Form GRF 19-A

Form of Utilization Certificate

Sl. No.	*Letter No. and date.*	*Amount*
	Total	

2. Certified that I have satisfied myself that the conditions on which the grants-in-aid was sanctioned have been duly fulfilled/are being fulfilled and that I have exercised the following checks to see that the money was actually utilized for the purpose for which it was sanctioned. Certified that out of Rs. .... of grants-in-aid sanctioned during the year .... in favour of .... Under this Ministry/Department Letter No. given in the margin and Rs............ on account of unspent balance of the previous year, a sum of Rs. .... has been utilized for the purpose of .... For which it was sanctioned and that the balance of Rs........ remaining unitilized at the end of the year has been surrendered to Government (*vide* No..............., dated ....)/will be adjusted towards the grants-in-aid payable during the next year ....

Kinds of checks exercised

1.
2.
3.

Physical Output for the above utilized funds

Components	*Performance*
Individual Household Latrines - BPL	
Sanitary complex	
Toilets for schools	
Toilets for Balwadi/Anganwadi	
Rural Sanitary Mart	
Production Centers	

Signature ....

Designation ....

Date ....

Annexure-IIE

FAMILY TYPE BIOGAS PLANTS PROGRAMME

National Biogas and Manure Management Programme (NBMMP)

PROMOTION OF BIOMASS BASED IMPROVED CHULHAS RELEASE OF FUNDS

1.1 Introduction

Biogas is a clean and efficient fuel. It contains about 65 per cent methane, about 34 per cent carbon dioxide and traces of other gases, such as hydrogen sulphide and ammonia. Biogas is produced when organic materials, such as cattle dung, are digested in the absence of air, in 'Biogas Plant'.

The Central Sector Scheme on National Biogas Programme, which mainly caters to setting up of family type biogas plants, has been under implementation since 1981-82. National Biogas and Manure Management Programme provides for Central subsidy in fixed amounts, turn-key job fee linked with three years' free maintenance warranty; financial support for repair of old-non-functional plants; training of users, masons, entrepreneurs, etc.; publicity and extension; service charges or staff support; State level Biogas Development and Training Centres (BDTC); (fixed amount of CFA to institutional biogas plants); financial support for institutions for cattle dung based power generation plants, etc.

1.2. Objectives

The objectives of programme are as follows:

(i) To provide fuel for cooking purposes and organic manure to rural households through family type biogas plants;

(ii) To mitigate drudgery of rural women, reduce pressure on forests and accentuate social benefits;

(iii) To improve sanitation in villages by linking sanitary toilets with biogas plants.

2. POTENTIAL AND ACHIEVEMENT

A cumulative total of 3.93 million family type biogas plants have been set up in the country against estimated potential of 12 million plants. State-wise information on achievement *vis-à-vis* potential is given in **Annexure I.**

3. TECHNOLOGY

Approved Designs of Family Type Biogas Plants

(i) Following models of biogas plants are approved for promotion:

(a)	KVIC Floating Drum Type Biogas Plants having digester made of bricks or stones.	1 to 10 cubic metre
(b)	KVIC Type Biogas Plants with Ferro cement digester	1 to 10 cubic metre
(c)	KVIC Type Biogas Plants with Fibre Glass Reinforced Plastic (FRP) Gas holder	1 to 10 cubic metre
(d)	Deenbandhu Model (i) Brick masonry (ii) In ferrocement with *in-situ* technique	1 to 6 cubic metre
(e)	Pre-fabricated RCC fixed dome model	2 & 3 cubic metre
(f)	'Flxi' model Bag digester type plant made of rubberised nylon fabric manufactured by Swastik Rubber Products Ltd., Pune.	1 to 6 cubic metre

(ii) Size of plants, requirement of cattle dung and estimated cost

Size of plant	*Quantity of cattle dung required daily*	*No. of cattle heads required*	*Estimated cost**
1 cubic metres	25 kg	2-3	Rs. 7,000
2 cubic metres	50 kg	4-6	Rs. 9,000
3 cubic metres	75 kg	7-9	Rs. 10,500
4 cubic metres	100 kg	10-12	Rs. 12,500

* The cost is higher by 30 per cent and 50 per cent in hilly areas and North Eastern Region States, respectively.

(iii) Applications

Cooking: Biogas can be used in a specially designed burner for cooking. A biogas plant of 2 cu.m. capacity is sufficient for providing cooking fuel to a family.

Lighting: Gas lamps can be fuelled by biogas. The requirement of gas for powering a 100 candle lamp (60 W) is 0.13 cu.m. per hour.

Power Generation: Biogas can be used to operate a dual fuel engine and can replace upto 80 per cent of diesel.

4. IMPLEMENTING AGENCIES

The programme is implemented by State Nodal Departments / Agencies and Khadi and Village Industries Commission (KVIC), Mumbai.

5 Patterns of Central Financial Assistance for 2007-08.

(i) *Central Subsidy*:

Category	*Amount (Rs.) for different capacity plant*	
	Capacity	
	1 cubic meter (fixed dome)	*2-6 cubic meter*
North Eastern Region States and Sikkim (except plain areas of Assam).	Rs.11,700/-	Rs.11,700/-
Plain areas of Assam.	Rs.9,000/-	Rs.9,000/-
Jammu & Kashmir, Himachal Pradesh, Uttaranchal (excluding terai region), Nilgiris of Tamil Nadu; Sadar Kursoong and Kalimkpong sub-divisions of the Darjeeling district (WB), Sunderbans, Andaman and Nicobar Islands.	Rs.4,500/-	Rs.3,500/-
Scheduled Caste, Scheduled Tribe, desert districts, small and marginal farmers, landless labourers, terai region of Uttarankhand, Western Ghats and other notified hilly areas.	Rs.3,500/-	Rs.2,800/-
All Others	Rs.2,700/-	Rs.2,100/-

(ii) *Turn-Key Job Fee:* The amount of turn-key job fee is Rs. 800 per plant for North-Eastern Region States (excluding the plain areas of Assam), Sikkim, Jammu and Kashmir, Himachal Pradesh, other notified hilly areas and Andaman and Nicobar Islands. For other areas the rate is Rs. 700 per plant.

(iii) *Household toilet linked plants*: An additional Central Subsidy of Rs. 500 per plant is given for linking the cattle dung based plant with a sanitary toilet, wherever feasible.

(iv) *Repair charges for old non-functional plants*: Financial support is given up to a maximum of 50 per cent of the rate of Central subsidy as applicable for a given category of beneficiary and area for repair of plants, which have been used for a period of at least five years and have developed structural defects.

(v) *Service charges and staff support*: The rates of service charges are linked with a given target range allocated to States and agencies, except North Eastern Region States, Sikkim and Jammu and Kashmir, where full financial support is given for the staff sanctioned for the State Headquarters and selected districts. The rates of service charges applicable for 2002-03 are mentioned below :

Target Range (No. of plants)	*Amount of Service Charges*
100-3000	Rs.0.50 lakh + Rs.300 per plant in excess of 200 plants
3001-7000	Rs.8.90 lakh + Rs.150 per plant in excess of 3000 plants
Above 7001	Rs.14.90 lakh + Rs.100 per plant in excess of 7000 plants subject to a maximum of Rs.30.00 lakhs

(vi) *State Level Biogas Development and Training Centres*: State Level Biogas Development and Training Centres are functioning at: (i) Bangalore (Karanataka), (ii) Coimbatore (Tamil Nadu), (iii) Indore (Madhya Pradesh), (iv) Kharagpur (West Bengal), (v) Lucknow (Uttar Pradesh), (vi) Ludhiana (Punjab), (vii) Palampur (Himachal Pradesh), (viii) Pantnagar (Uttarakhand) and (ix) Udaipur (Rajasthan) and (x) IIT, Guwahati for providing technical, training and publicity support to State nodal departments and programme implementing agencies.

(vii) *Training courses*: Financial assistance is given for organising different kinds of training courses as mentioned below :

Course	Duration	No. of Trainees per course	Central Financial Assistance per course
Users	One day	50-60	Rs. 1,000/-
Staff	2-3 days	10-15	Rs. 5,000/-
Refresher/Construction-cum-Maintenance	16 days	10	Rs. 19,000/-
Turn-Key Workers	21 days	10	Rs. 38,500/-

(viii) *Communication and publicity*: Assistance is given for communication and publicity work linked with target ranges to State nodal departments and agencies as mentioned below:

Target range (no. of plants)	Support for communication and publicity
Up to 1,000	Rs. 1.00 lakh
1,001 - 10,000	Rs. 2.50 lakh
More than 10,000	Rs. 5.00 lakh

6. PROGRAMME DURING TENTH PLAN

Promotion of biogas plants continued during the Tenth Plan. A target of setting up of 10.00 lakh family type biogas plants has been fixed with a plan outlay of Rs.350.00 crore. Year-wise achievements vis-à-vis targets and budget expenditure during 2002-03 to 2006-07 is given below:

Year	(No. of Plants)		(Rupees in Crore)	
	Target	Achievement	BE/RE	Expenditure
2002-03	1,50,000	1,53,000	59.50/44.70	44.78
2003-04	1,70,000	1,41,000	54.00/42.03	37.23
2004-05	1,00,000	1,09,000	40.15/40.15	21.91
2005-06	66,000	62,528	14.00/28.00	28.10
2006-07	1,01,860	97,165	41.00/53.00	51.50

7. PROGRAMME FOR 2007-08

Physical Target	:	1,01,860 plants
Achievement	:	9,815 plants (April-August 2007)
BE/RE	:	Rs.36 crore
Actual Expenditure (April to September, 2007)	:	Rs. 14.64 crore

8. MONITORING

A three-tier monitoring system exists, which consists of self-reporting by State Governments and agencies involving 100 per cent physical verification of biogas plants at the block level and random basis verification by State nodal departments and implementing agencies. The second-tier involves filed inspection on random basis by the Regional Offices of the Ministry.

9. EVALUATION STUDIES

At the instance of the Ministry, a diagnostic survey study on National Project on Biogas Development has been conducted in 2001-02 by the Programme Evaluation Organisation (PEO), Planning Commission. The study covered a sample of 615 plants set up during the years 1995-96 to 1999-2000 in 19 States, namely Andhra Pradesh, Arunachal Pradesh, Assam, Bihar, Gujarat, Haryana, Himachal Pradesh, Karnataka, Kerala, Madhya Pradesh, Maharashtra, Meghalaya, Orissa, Punjab, Rajasthan, Sikkim, Tamil Nadu, Uttar Pradesh and West Bengal. The report received in May 2002, indicated that about 81 per cent plants were commissioned, 6 per cent plants were lying un-commissioned, 4 per cent plants were incomplete and 9 per cent plants were dismantled. Out of the commissioned plants, only 66 per cent plants were found in use.

The Indian Institute of Technology, Delhi was assigned a study entitled, "Determining the extent of installation and impact assessment study of MNES supported programmes relating to improved chulhas, family type biogas plants and community, institutional and night soil based biogas plants in four selected

States, namely Andhra Pradesh, Karnataka, Madhya Pradesh and Uttar Pradesh" in January 2002. The primary survey was based on structured questionnaire for two respondent categories, i.e. State nodal department/nodal agencies and beneficiaries. It covered a sample of 3755 biogas plants set up during 1996-97 to 2000-01 in 367 villages selected from 28 districts of the four States. Report on the first part of the study on determining the extent of installation received in August 2002 indicated that on an overall average basis 77 per cent of plants were functional, 19 per cent plants were non-functional, 4 per cent were not installed and dismantled. State-wise status of biogas plants found in the study is given below:

State	Sample		Status of plants			
	No. of district	No. of plants	Installed and Functional	Installed and non-Functional	Not-Installed	Dis-mantled
Uttar Pradesh	9	653	402	138	41	72
Madhya Pradesh	8	846	723	118	1	4
Andhra Pradesh	5	1353	1052	261	5	36
Karnataka	6	903	703	194	0	6
Total	**28**	**3755**	**2880 (77%)**	**710 (9%)**	**47 (1%)**	**118 (3%)**

Annexure I

NATIONAL BIOGAS AND MANURE MANAGEMENT PROGRAMME (NBMMP)

State-wise achievement for family type biogas plants from 1981-82 to 2006-07

State/ Union Territories	Cumulative achievement as on 31.03.2007 (Number of plants)
Andhra Pradesh	419884
Arunachal Pradesh	2345
Assam	59942

(*Contd.*)

(*Contd.*)

State/ Union Territories	Cumulative achievement as on 31.03.2007 (Number of plants)
Bihar	125306
Goa	3807
Gujarat	387251
Haryana	50266
Himachal Pradesh	45046
Jammu & Kashmir	2212
Karnataka	396681
Kerala	114183
Madhya Pradesh	258747
Maharashtra	735196
Manipur	2128
Meghalaya	4586
Mizoram	3570
Nagaland	2892
Orissa	228295
Punjab	83771
Rajasthan	66990
Sikkim	5959
Tamil Nadu	211242
Tripura	2549
Uttar Pradesh	413052
West Bengal	273287
A&N Islands	137
Chandigarh	97
Dadra & Nagar Haveli	169
Delhi	677
Pondicherry	573
Chhattisgarh	23399
Jharkhand	2543
Uttarakhand	7354
Total	**3934136**

Bibliography

Agarwal, Amba, *Fiscal Decentralisation: Financing of Panchayati Raj Institutions in India,* New Delhi: Serial Publications, 2005.

Bardhan, P. and Mookerjee, D. (eds.), *Decentralisation and Local Governance in Developing Countries: A Comparative Perspective,* New Delhi: Oxford University Press, 2007.

Commission on Centre-State Relations, *Local Self-Governments and Decentralized Governance*, Volume IV, New Delhi: Government of India, 2010.

Gopal Jayal Niraja, Amit Prakash and Pradeep K. Sharma (eds.) *Local Governance in India: Decentralization and Beyond,* New Delhi: Oxford University Press, 2006.

Government of India, *Local Governance: An Inspiring Journey into Future,* New Delhi: Second Administrative Reforms Commission, 2007.

Government of India, *Second Administrative Reforms Commission Sixth Report: Local Governance: An Inspiring Journey into Future*, New Delhi: Government of India, 2007.

Institute of Rural Management, *The Status of Panchayats: 2007-08*, Vols. I, II and III, New Delhi: Ministry of Panchayati Raj, Government of India, 2008.

Konrad Adenauer Foundation, *Local Government Finance in India,* New Delhi: Manohar, 1998.

Krishnan Sivarama, K.C., *Power to the People*? New Delhi: Konark Publishers Private Limited, 2000.

Manor, James, "Local Governance" in *Oxford Companion to Politics in India* (eds.) Gopal Jayal Niraja and Bhanu Mehta Pratap, New Delhi: Oxford University Press, 2010.

Ministry of Panchayati Raj, *Devolution of Functions in Tamil Nadu to Panchayats—A Status Report,* New Delhi: N-1011/82005 policy II.

Mikesell, John L. "Fiscal Administration in Local Government: An overview" in *Local Budgeting* (ed.) Anwar Shah Washington DC: The World Bank, 2007.

Mohanty, Ranjita and Tandon, Rajesh (eds.) *Participatory Citizenship: Identity, Exclusion, Inclusion*, New Delhi: Sage Publications, 2006.

Ommen, M.A., "Rural Fiscal Decentralisation in India: A Brief Survey of Literature" in L.C. Jain (ed.), *Decentralisation and Local Governance,* Hyderabad: Orient Longman Private Limited, 2008.

Palanithurai, G., "Local Governance as a Factor in Centre-State Relations in India", *The ICFAI University Journal of Public Administration*, Vol. 5: No 2 April, 2009.

Prud'homme, Remy, "The Dangers of Decentralization", *The World Bank Research Observer*, Vol. 10, No. 2, 1995.

Rajaraman, Indira, *A Fiscal Domain for Panchayats*, New Delhi: Oxford University Press, 2003.

Roy Bahl, *The Rules of Fiscal Decentralisation*, Georgia: Georgia State University, 1999.

Shah, Anwar (ed.), *Local Governance in Developing Countries,* Washington D.C.: The World Bank, 2006.

Shah, Anwar (ed.), *Local Governance in Industrial Countries,* Washington D.C.: The World Bank, 2006.

Shah, Anwar, "Fiscal Decentralisation in Developing Countries and Transitive Economies: An Overview" in L.C. Jain (eds.) *Decentralisation and Local Governance,* Hyderabad: Orient Longman Private Limited, 2008.

Singh, S.K., *Panchayati Raj Finances in Madhya Pradesh,* New Delhi: Concept Publishing Company Pvt. Ltd., 2004.

World Bank, *Fiscal Decentralisation to Rural Governments in India,* New Delhi: Oxford University Press, 2004.

Index

113-MAN